PRAISE FOR
BELONGING WITHOUT BARRIERS

'*Belonging without Barriers* is a deeply insightful and practical resource that speaks to the heart of Christian community. It combines rich theology with compassionate, real-world application, challenging churches to move beyond mere inclusion towards true belonging for every individual. Triona Brading, Lois Bunyan, and Claire Wood write with clarity, warmth, and conviction, offering both biblical foundations and actionable steps for accessibility. It is a timely and essential guide for anyone committed to building communities where every person is valued, honoured, and enabled to flourish.'
Mark Arnold, Additional Needs Ministry Director, Urban Saints

'This is a book that I would have found invaluable when I began ministry with adults with learning disabilities 25 years ago. The content is not only biblically based but also biblically shaped, ensuring that themes of God's image and the value he places on all people are reiterated throughout the book. *Belonging without Barriers* is not a quick read, nor is it so lengthy and complicated that its audience is likely to be limited to professionals and theologians. There is something here for everyone, with plenty of information and advice. I wholeheartedly commend this book to anyone looking to understand and support individuals and families affected by disability.'
Pete Winmill, Founder, Count Everyone In

'Every church needs spiritual and practical help on how to serve those with disabilities in their congregations – and this book is the answer! Every leadership team should appoint someone to read and absorb this excellent and thoughtful resource. The theology is rich, the advice practical, the tone gracious, and the content encyclopaedic. I cannot recommend it highly enough.'
Andy Mason, Mission Director, Co-Mission

'This beautifully written book invites everyone to reflect on what it truly means to belong in church. As an adoptive and birth parent of two neurodivergent children, for whom church has often been a struggle, I was grateful to find a book that gently weaves biblical principles with real-life stories, helping us to consider and understand what it looks like to create church communities where no barriers exist.'
Louise MacDiarmid, Therapeutic Parenting Coach

'I wish I had read this book 50 years ago. It is life-changing. It is a handbook for church leaders and those organising any kind of Christian activity – enhancing your understanding of how to include people with all kinds of visible or invisible additional needs (that's one in three people). This has the potential to hugely increase the scale and fruit of your ministry. In fact, it is a book for every Christian who wants to get inside the head of those in their circle who have any kind of physical, mental, or emotional special need and reach into their heart with the good news.'
Max Sinclair, author of *Halfway to Heaven* and a member of the first Through the Roof Council of Reference

'When a book contains so much helpful, practical information there is a temptation to skip straight to those chapters. Resist the temptation! The first four chapters challenge our theology and perspective around difference and inclusion, and offer an imperative to be sacrificial in removing the barriers some people encounter as they see to belong within the church.'
Mary Hawes, Former National Children's Advisor, Archbishops' Council

'*Belonging without Barriers* offers churches a clear and compelling vision of what costly, Christ-shaped belonging looks like when it is taken seriously across the whole congregation. Refusing to reduce disability to a niche concern of children's or seniors' ministry, the authors address the full spectrum of needs present in a genuinely multigenerational church community. Grounded in scripture and shaped by the pattern of the cross, the book shows that accessibility is not an act of charity but a faithful response to the gospel itself.'
Graham Miller, CEO, London City Mission

'*Belonging without Barriers* is a comprehensive and practical guide that will help churches reflect more deeply on what it means to be a truly inclusive Christian community. Rooted in scripture and shaped by real pastoral experience, the authors challenge us to move beyond access and attendance towards genuine belonging, where every person is meaningfully welcomed into the family of faith without barrier. The book's theological clarity and practical wisdom make it invaluable not only for church leaders, but also for anyone involved in ministry.'
Paul Cable, Lecturer in Youth and Community Work, Moorlands College

'This book is a goldmine for any church leader or Christian wanting to take the inclusion of *all* of God's people seriously. As a vicar in the Church of England, I haven't thought these issues through nearly as thoroughly as I should have. I have felt both challenged, but more importantly equipped, by this wonderful and compassionate book, full of testimonies and tips that can take any church community forward, even from a standing start. Perhaps the most important takeaway for me was realising that helping people belong is about more than just being good people, it's about being gospel people.'
Pat Allerton, Vicar of St Peter's Notting Hill, author of *A Pocketful of Hope***, @theportablepriest on Instagram**

'What a carefully, beautifully written book! Open this book expecting gentleness and care. No question feels too basic. The authors allow us to know how it feels to be in the family who would welcome your love.'
Ed Drew, Director, Faith in Kids

'As a youth pastor and a mother of a young adult with quadriplegic cerebral palsy who also faces physical and learning challenges, I found this book to be both informative and inspiring. My daughter and I have been on a 23-year journey of discovery, exploring how we can use our gifts and abilities to serve God more effectively. The book offers clear insights that combine theological understanding with practical application, emphasising the importance of celebrating and supporting all members of our diverse church communities with unconditional love and encouragement. The message conveyed throughout the book is essential for us as the body of Christ.'
Trish Hahn, Messy Church SEND Co-ordinator

 Ministries

15 The Chambers, Vineyard
Abingdon OX14 3FE
+44(0)1865 319700 | brf.org.uk

Bible Reading Fellowship (BRF) is a charity (233280)
and company limited by guarantee (301324),
registered in England and Wales.

EU Authorised Representative: Easy Access System Europe – Mustamäe tee 50,
10621 Tallinn, Estonia, gpsr.requests@easproject.com

ISBN 978 1 80039 420 9
First published 2026
10 9 8 7 6 5 4 3 2 1 0

All rights reserved
Text © Triona Brading, Lois Bunyan, and Claire Wood 2026
This edition © Bible Reading Fellowship 2026
Cover by Ben Bloxham using illustrations by mast3r/stock.adobe.com

The authors assert the moral right to be identified as the authors of this work.

Unless otherwise stated, scripture quotations are taken from The Holy Bible, New International Version® Anglicized, NIV® Copyright © 1979, 1984, 2011 by Biblica, Inc.® Used by permission. All rights reserved worldwide.

Scripture quotations marked 'NIRV' are taken from the Holy Bible, New International Reader's Version®. Copyright © 1995, 1996, 1998, 2014 Biblica. All rights reserved throughout the world. Used by permission of Biblica.

'Welcome to Holland' is copyright ©1987 by Emily Perl Kingsley. All rights reserved. Reprinted by permission of the author.

Every effort has been made to trace and contact copyright owners for material used in this resource. We apologise for any inadvertent omissions or errors, and would ask those concerned to contact us so that full acknowledgement can be made in the future.

A catalogue record for this book is available from the British Library.

Printed and bound by CPI Group (UK) Ltd, Croydon CR0 4YY.

Triona Brading, Lois Bunyan, and Claire Wood

BELONGING WITHOUT BARRIERS

BUILDING ACCESSIBLE CHRISTIAN COMMUNITY

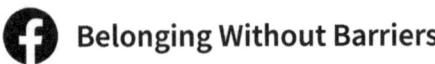 Belonging Without Barriers

@belonging_without_barriers

Photocopying for churches

Please report to CLA Church Licence any photocopy you make from this publication. Your church administrator or secretary will know who manages your CLA Church Licence.

The information you need to provide to your CLA Church Licence administrator is as follows:

Title, Author, Publisher, and ISBN

If your church doesn't hold a CLA Church Licence, information about obtaining one can be found at uk.ccli.com

Some names and other details have been changed throughout to protect people's identities.

Contents

Foreword 11

Acknowledgements 15

Introduction 17

PART I THEOLOGY

1 The basis for love: image-bearing 22

2 The community of God's people: inclusion 36

3 It seems too hard: sacrifice 47

4 The future of disability: the new creation 57

PART II ACCESSIBILITY IN PRACTICE

Introduction to part II 70

5 Physical disabilities 74

6 Age-related disabilities and impairments 98

7 Learning disabilities 109

8 Specific learning difficulties 133

9 Autism 147

10 Sensory processing disorder 172

11 Attention deficit hyperactivity disorder (ADHD) 180

12 Social, emotional, and mental health (SEMH) in children 199

Conclusion 219

APPENDICES

1. Glossary 223
2. Accessibility audits 226
3. Other organisations offering help in this area 227

   Bibliography 229
   Notes 241
   About the authors 247

Foreword

This is a book we have been waiting for! A book the UK church needs, to reduce the fear around talking about disability and help people catch the vision for disability inclusion.

There are as many different understandings and experiences of disability as there are people in the church, so you may find that your experience and views differ from those in the book. Yet we hope this book will open up conversations and inspire action in the church to progress disability inclusion.

In recent years, conversations about inclusion and accessibility are moving from the margins to the mainstream. Wider cultural shifts have opened doors for greater understanding of neurodivergence – including autism, ADHD, and sensory processing differences – and the lived realities of those with physical or learning disabilities. Mental health and social well-being are now recognised as integral to human flourishing. Equality, diversity, inclusion, and belonging (EDIB) is now high on the agenda in many areas of society, and our ageing UK population means that nearly a quarter of people identify as disabled. These changes present the church with both a challenge and an opportunity: to embody the radical hospitality of Christ in ways that are practical, thoughtful, and rooted in scripture. This book equips us to do that.

Belonging without Barriers is not just another resource on inclusion. It is a call to action. It combines deep theological reflection with practical strategies, making it invaluable for leaders, trustees, children and youth workers, and anyone involved in ministry wanting to love others and create communities where everyone truly belongs. The authors remind us that accessibility is not an optional extra – it is a gospel imperative. When we remove barriers, we reflect the heart of God, who welcomes all people into his family.

At Through the Roof, the Christian disability charity, we have been advocating for disability inclusion in the UK church for over 25 years. Change has come slowly, but it feels like God is really moving in our times! We have just marked a milestone in our 1,000th Roofbreaker disability champion, volunteering to journey alongside disabled people in their local church. We pray that this movement will grow, so every church will actively welcome disabled people and experience the blessings of knowing their presence.

As I write this (in 2026), the number of UK young people under 18 is about the same as the number of disabled people in the UK. If we think about how much time, resource, and energy goes into children and youth ministry and compare that to disability ministry – there's a huge difference! That's why we're so committed to work together to enable every member of God's family to experience the true belonging which is theirs in Christ.

The book addresses two essential themes: theology and accessibility in practice.

At its core, accessibility is a theological issue. The church is the body of Christ and every member is an indispensable part of it (1 Corinthians 12). Part I explores what scripture teaches about inclusion, dignity, and (one of Through the Roof's core values) interdependence. In a world that often prioritises independence and perfection, the gospel offers a different vision: interdependence and grace. Interdependence recognises that we are dependent on God and interdependent upon one another. Arguably it is modelled by God: Father, Son, and Holy Spirit.

The authors question assumptions we might make in our churches and show how the Bible gives a mandate to include disabled people: 'Go out quickly into the streets and lanes of the town. Bring in those… who can't see or walk… I want my house to be full' (Luke 14:21, 23, NIRV). It challenges us to see accessibility not as charity, but justice. Accessibility is not about doing something 'extra' for a few; it is about reshaping our communities so that everyone can participate fully. When we do this, we discover that inclusion enriches the whole body. We learn new ways of worshipping, serving, and loving – expressions of God's kingdom breaking into the world.

Theology must lead to action, and Part II will help you take practical steps towards becoming a disability-inclusive church. You will find practical tools: a checklist of questions for physical access, multisensory ideas and activities, and strategies for supporting neurodivergent individuals.

One of the strengths of *Belonging without Barriers* is the use of personal stories to ground the writing in real life. Throughout the book, individuals share first-hand experiences – both the joys of inclusion and the pain of exclusion. These testimonies remind us that accessibility is not abstract; it is about real people longing to encounter God and God's people without unnecessary obstacles. Their voices call us to listen, learn, and act.

Also included is a helpful glossary of common terms, signposts to access audits, and an appendix of helpful organisations.

Small groups in churches will find the book a good choice for a study text (with discussion questions at the end of every chapter), yet it is also lively and engaging to read for individuals, as well as a practical reference book for pastoral teams to find guidance and insight into a wide range of disabilities.

We may feel burdened by the size of the challenge or lack of resources, but small changes can make a huge difference. Whether you serve in a large urban church or a small rural fellowship, you will find ideas and suggestions which are realistic and adaptable that can be implemented without breaking your budget.

At Through the Roof, we see the infinite value and the immense potential of every disabled person. A church without disabled people is an incomplete church – missing potential parts of the body of Christ. We talk about disability inclusion in terms of a journey: from access to belonging to commission (ABC) – working with disabled people to build God's kingdom and ensuring everyone is encouraged to use their giftings, actively.

As you read, I encourage you to approach this book with an open heart and a willingness to act. Change may require effort, but the reward is immeasurable: a church that reflects the inclusive love of Christ and offers a foretaste of heaven, where everyone will worship together as equals.

May this book inspire you so that, together, we can build communities without barriers – places of belonging where all God's people can flourish.

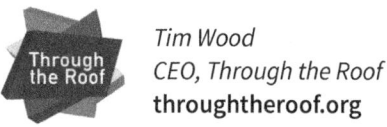

Tim Wood
CEO, Through the Roof
throughtheroof.org

Acknowledgements

Where better to begin a page of thanks than to borrow from Paul's thanks for the church in Rome:

> To all… who are loved by God and called to be his holy people: Grace and peace to you from God our Father and from the Lord Jesus Christ. First, I thank my God through Jesus Christ for all of you.
> ROMANS 1:7–8

We are enormously grateful to God for all the supporters he has blessed us with as we have written this book. There are so many people who have supported us with encouragement, with advice, and with direct contributions to this book – so many that we cannot name everyone! We give thanks that he has put us in a church family at St Michael's, who have loved and cared for each of us and have encouraged this project right from the beginning.

First, we want to thank our editor at BRF Ministries, Rachel: we are so grateful to you for taking a chance on three unknown writers with a controversial topic. Our thanks also go to the wider team at BRF Ministries: to Daniele, Felicity, Karen, Tracey, Eley, Josh, and Simon, for their support in getting this book into people's hands.

Next, we want to thank the team at Through the Roof. Your willingness to partner with BRF Ministries in backing this book gave us both confidence and practical support. Through the Roof's support goes back even further than the idea for this book – the Roofbreaker project supported and encouraged us with a vision that extended beyond our church and circumstances.

We would also like to thank Co-Mission, whose early support and encouragement was very significant in our early experiences of disability ministry in churches. We are grateful for your support in enabling us to develop the SEND ministry at Revive, which started us thinking beyond our own church and context.

There are also a huge number of people who have contributed their own stories to this book, without which it would be far less valuable (and readable). Many have been anonymised in the text, but in alphabetical order we would like to thank Alyssa, Ann, Annabelle, Arthur, Bethanie, Carolyn Thomas, Celeste, Chich, Claire, Corrin, DB, Debbie, Dorothy, Graham, Ian, Isla, James, James, Jo, Joe, Lauren, Lis, Louise, Maureen, Merryn, Mike, Miriam, Nat, Paul, Peter, Reuben, Sam, Rod, Rosie, Sarah, Steven, and Wendy.

Very early in writing the book, we knew we wanted to include 'Welcome to Holland'. As a piece of writing, it spoke to us powerfully about both the initial sorrows and subsequent beauty of parenting a child with a disability. We are very grateful to Emily Perl Kingsley for allowing us to use it in our book.

We would like to thank all those who supplied advice, encouragement, and their experience to our early drafts: Ann, Annette, Ed, Elizabeth, Emily, Georgia, Jonny, Louise, Simon, Tim, Travis, and Verity. You each brought your own valuable skills to our early drafts. Thank you for the time, energy, and wit you put into your marginal comments.

We would like to thank our families and housemates, who put up with our endless meetings and late nights as we wrote the book, cheered us on, gave up precious family time at weekends to allow us to go to conferences, and offered sounding boards for our ideas when we were still formulating the exact nuances of what we wanted to say.

Finally, we want to thank you, the reader. Thank you for taking the time to listen to the voices of Christians with different additional needs. Thank you for your desire to love your church family more and grow in understanding about how you can do this. We pray that God would use you for his glory in your church families and communities.

Introduction

We have the privilege of knowing a wonderful family. Their daughter, Sara, is autistic and has ADHD, and she struggles with any kind of 'demand' placed on her. When we met them, they were attending an annual Bible festival at which we were supporting children with special educational needs and disabilities (SEND). Sara wouldn't even leave her room: the noise, the large group, and her fears of instructions, rules, and demands made it impossible for her to attend the children's activities. There will be many Saras in our local areas: children, or adults, who we may never see at church services, children who won't attend our midweek groups or holiday clubs. They find the whole thing too hard, too overwhelming, too difficult, or their physical needs mean that they can't actually get to our church buildings, can't get through the doors, can't use our toilets. How can we show love to someone who can't even access what we're running? In Sara's case, her family helped us to get to know her. By the end of the weekend, she was willing to stay with us in the coffee tent while her parents went to one adults' session.

The next year, the family returned to the Bible festival, and we continued to build a relationship with Sara. Eventually, she was happy to sit with a volunteer leader, acting as one-to-one support for her. This allowed both her parents to attend all the main sessions. By the third year, she was excited about using the sensory tent and one-to-one support. We might call this inclusion: she was now part of the children's stream at the festival. We may think of others whose immediate needs have been met, allowing them to get through the doors of the building – maybe we have already put in a disabled ramp or provided a large-print service sheet to allow people to feel included, despite additional needs. This is a wonderful start, but the metaphors for God's people in the Bible call for more. We see images of a body, a family, and a household. Our goal is more than attendance and participation. The Bible paints a picture of a body where every member matters, every member serves, every member loves the others. No one is a consumer, just along for the ride.

Sara's story didn't end there. Towards the end of that third weekend, we were surprised to see her being a bit secretive and wanting to spend time alone at the art table. At the end of the session, she excitedly produced a piece of art she had created for us during that time. It had the words 'Jesus loves you', surrounded by abstract watercolours, which she explained represented the storms of life. As we received this picture, we were reminded afresh of God's love for us, of the firm foundation he offers through the storm. We were teaching and supporting her, addressing her needs, and removing barriers. She was then able to teach us as much as we taught her. She is now begging her parents to sign up for the festival the next time it happens! When any individual is given the opportunity to serve and participate fully, they will not just be included – they will belong.

WHO IS THIS BOOK FOR?

This book is for church leaders and trustees, who can make policy decisions or spend money on their buildings – but not only for them. Nor is it only for youth and children's workers trying to include children with additional needs. This book is for everyone trusting in God, wanting to love God's people sacrificially, generously – the way Jesus loves the church. The 2014 Church of England diversity audit found that 'every congregation includes someone with at least one illness, impairment or disability'.[1] This means that on a Sunday morning, there is likely to be someone already at your church with additional needs. Christian life goes beyond Sunday gatherings: we see Christians coming together for prayer groups at work, activity holidays, Christian Unions at school or university, midweek clubs, and much more. There are likely to be settings with much higher numbers of disabled people, like services run in residential homes. The needs of the people in our groups are changing all the time: disability is dynamic, meaning that many 'able-bodied' individuals will one day be disabled. Not every need is visible from the outside – we may discover that an individual is experiencing challenges only after we have known them for some time.

In the UK, 13% of young people are diagnosed with special educational needs (SEN).[2] Almost a quarter (24%) of the UK's total population have a disability.[3] Nearly a third (32%) of households in the UK have at least one disabled family member.[4] In addition to those declaring themselves disabled in the UK census, there will be many others who experience difficulties due to neuro-cognitive differences but who may not consider themselves disabled. In a world where, wonderfully, medical care is advancing rapidly and life expectancy is improving, we should expect these statistics to rise. This means that we cannot and should not leave caring for those with additional needs to a small committee of people.

We hope this book will lift your eyes to God's vision for his covenant community, the church, today. We hope this book will increase people's understanding of others' needs, and help us all become more loving. We have certainly found this to be the case ourselves as we have researched some of the areas we were less familiar with.

We have tried throughout to use language which conveys our love and respect for every individual. If anything we have said causes offence, we hope that it will be read in the spirit in which it is intended. There is a wide range of preferred language within the disabled community, which we have tried to reflect in the book. Where there is particular disagreement, we have explained the reasons for our linguistic choices in the practical section of the book.

PART I

THEOLOGY

①
The basis for love: image-bearing

Many additional needs arise out of differences. Why should we go out of our way for people who are not like us? The Bible tells us that we have more in common than we think. We share an identity far more significant than we might guess. We are all made in God's image. When we look at another human being, whether they are in a wheelchair or using augmented or alternative communication, whether they are partially sighted or struggle with chronic pain, we see God's image reflected in them. This identity is fundamental to the value of every human being.

A BRIEF HISTORY

The Greek and Roman world of the early church was one which considered any deviation from physical or intellectual 'norm' to be a sign of divine curse, and one where unwanted babies were routinely exposed at birth to die. People were valued according to their contribution to society, their wealth, and their skills, and therefore babies and children were considered almost worthless. There were no hospitals to care for the sick.

Christians applying the teachings of Jesus on how we should treat others created free healthcare, campaigned against infanticide, and built communities which cared for those with additional needs. Of course, Christians have never got these things perfectly 'right', and one could easily focus on the mistakes made by past Christians. However, a core Christian teaching has always been clear that every human being is worthy of dignity, a dignity founded on bearing God's image. This fundamental understanding of humanity has shaped the way the western world has approached care for those with additional needs.

Over the past couple of centuries, developments in scientific understanding have subtly changed the way many see their fellow human beings. Evolutionary theory sees *Homo sapiens* as a supremely well-adapted ape. This 'survival of the fittest' model has been used by some to provide a rationale underpinning our natural tendency to value output, income, and skills more than God's image in our fellow humans. Although in many ways our culture still values caring for the weak, people with impairments can sometimes be viewed negatively, to be hidden, removed, and, if possible, prevented from occurring through gene selection or abortion. While society has never clamoured louder for the inclusion of those with differences, much of the discussion is around valuing competency and productivity: for example, 'dyslexic thinking' being listed as a skillset one can select on LinkedIn, telling autistic children their neurotype is a 'superpower', or a focus on the sporting prowess of some physically disabled individuals.

There is much in this to celebrate, but as Christians, we can go much further and deeper and address some of the uncomfortable topics left unsaid by the modern discourse in this area. To do this, we need to drill down deeper into what it means to be made in the image of God, and what the Bible has to say about humanity.

THE IMAGE FORMED: GENESIS 1

> Then God said, 'Let us make mankind in our image, in our likeness, so that they may rule over the fish in the sea and the birds in the sky, over the livestock and all the wild animals, and over all the creatures that move along the ground.'
>
> > So God created mankind in his own image,
> > in the image of God he created them;
> > male and female he created them.
>
> God blessed them and said to them, 'Be fruitful and increase in number; fill the earth and subdue it. Rule over the fish in the sea and the birds in the sky and over every living creature that moves on the ground.'
> Then God said, 'I give you every seed-bearing plant on the face of the whole earth and every tree that has fruit with seed in it. They will be yours for food. And to all the beasts of the earth and all the birds in the sky and all the creatures that move along the ground – everything

that has the breath of life in it – I give every green plant for food.' And it was so.

God saw all that he had made, and it was very good. And there was evening, and there was morning – the sixth day.

GENESIS 1:26–31

The very first chapter of the Bible lays the foundations of how we should see humanity. In it we see identity, purpose, and blessing for humanity, all culminating in God's appreciation of all that he has made as 'very good': the pinnacle of creation. These all fit together to shape our understanding of what it means to be human, which in turn can inform how, why, and whether we relate to those who have disabilities or additional needs.

IDENTITY

Our society is obsessed with creating our own identity: self-expression is one of the gods of our age. We see it in the groups we make for ourselves: seven-year-old Claire starting the 'August birthdays club' at school with a couple of friends, or the caricatured cliques in the canteen in *High School Musical*. For people with additional needs, there can be great value in getting a formal diagnosis and recognising what this adds to our identity. But beneath these identities is an unchanging foundation – the identity God has already given to us, better than anything we could promote on social media or copy from our favourite celebrity.

God says, 'Let us make mankind in our image, in our likeness' (Genesis 1:26). God, as Trinity, uses a different formula from that used up to this point in creation. No longer does he say, 'Let there be', or, 'Let the land produce', but, 'Let us make'. In this act of creating humanity, God expresses his intimate involvement, his divine intervention into the natural order. If all of creation is made by God, brought into being by his words alone, humanity is somehow an even more personal act of creation. We see the plural forms used: 'Let *us* make… in *our* image', expressing something of the intimacy of the Trinity itself, Father, Son, and Holy Spirit, in the creation of humanity.

Adam and Eve are made to reflect God to the world around them, to bear his likeness, as nothing else in creation does. We get a hint of this from the fact that God describes creation as 'good' until he makes humanity, after which it is 'very good'.

In verse 28, all the creatures are explicitly placed under humanity's rule. In Genesis 2, we see Adam naming the animals, but unable to find a suitable helper among them. Yet again, we see humanity as set apart and distinct from other living beings, the only beings made in God's image. Our dignity, our value, our worth as human beings is not something we have to create for ourselves. It is not something which can be increased by our ability to make choices for ourselves or decreased by becoming physically incapacitated. Our value comes from outside ourselves, from the God in whose image we are made.

Part of this identity as image-bearers, it would seem, involves diversity. Just as God is Father, Son, and Spirit, humanity is 'male and female' (Genesis 1:27). From the very beginning, before the divine image is marred by human sin and God's curse on creation, equality and difference are enshrined within God's chosen image-bearers. However, the focus is not so much on difference as on equality: our identity as humans should be found first and foremost in what we share – God's image.

This is a wonderful, and yet hard-to-remember, truth. Every single human being, whether disabled or not, is made to reflect God to his world. They are the pinnacle of God's creation. They are of great worth in God's eyes, and therefore should be in ours as well.

PURPOSE

Unlike Claire's founding membership of the 'August birthdays club', this identity comes with a purpose: 'so that they may rule' (Genesis 1:26). God directly instructs them: 'Be fruitful and increase in number; fill the earth and subdue it' (v. 28). God makes humanity in his image so that they can act, under him, as rulers of the world he has made. They are uniquely fitted to do so by being made in his image, bearing his likeness.

What does this tell us about the nature of God's image in humanity? We can get some hints from what we've already been told about God. God's character in creation has been emphasised by the way the narrative has been told: he creates order out of chaos, forms spaces and fills them. One way God's image is reflected in humanity is through the work he has given us. As humans create order, as they are creative and inventive, they reflect God's nature. We share this responsibility collectively. Even if someone is not able, because of physical or cognitive impairments, to exercise creativity, bring order out of chaos, or exercise responsibility for creation, they are still 'in the image of God, in his likeness'. This passage does not set out particular capabilities as being markers of God's image in humanity, but rather a shared purpose and responsibility. We can also see many of these capabilities in the most unlikely places, when we take the time to look. The wonderful dancing of the adult with learning disabilities shows great creativity, even if it doesn't conform to any sets of rules we might want to apply!

BLESSING

Finally, God gives the man and woman all seed-bearing plants to eat. We see God's generosity in providing enjoyable and bountiful food. While Adam and Eve do work in the garden, there is (at this point) no barrier to their full enjoyment of everything God has made. The repetition inherent in '*every* seed-bearing plant on the face of the *whole* earth and *every* tree that has fruit with seed in it' (v. 29, emphasis added) points to the generosity of God. We are told in Genesis 2 that these trees 'were pleasing to the eye and good for food' (v. 9). It is clear that God made the world perfect, without any of the hardship we associate with disability and additional needs.

RELATIONSHIPS

We also see humanity created with a series of special relationships. Adam and Eve rule over the earth, working in the garden and taking responsibility for everything in it. They walk with God, and they live under his rule as they follow his commands and live within the limits he has placed on them. Eve is a 'helper' for Adam, the only being suitable to join Adam in his work. Community and companionship are assumed from the outset: 'It is not good for the man to be alone' (Genesis 2:18). They are able to be naked without feeling shame, illustrating their unbroken relationship with one another (v. 25). From the beginning, we see that humanity is created for mutual service – to help one another do the work God has given them. When we come later to consider what it means for someone to 'belong' in the church, we will see that true belonging includes the opportunity to serve – sometimes in unexpected ways.

It is good to take some time to see God's image the way it was originally intended – humanity living perfectly under God's rule, relating perfectly to one another, and lovingly ruling God's world as God's representatives. We see in creation the first instance of God's people, in God's place, with God's presence, which we see worked out imperfectly again and again through the rest of the Bible. Humanity experiences true belonging and inclusion within God's perfect world, and nothing hinders their access to God or their ability to live in community together. For those living with disabilities and for those of us experiencing the challenges and struggles associated with others' disabilities, it is important to spend some time dwelling on God's 'very good' creation. The challenges we will encounter later in this book can certainly be used by God, and we will explore his sovereignty over them, but this suffering was not part of the world God created.

THE IMAGE MARRED: GENESIS 3

Yet these blessings have a counterpart in God's curses on humanity following Adam and Eve's rebellion, as we read in Genesis 3:

So the Lord God said to the serpent, 'Because you have done this,

'Cursed are you above all livestock
   and all wild animals!
You will crawl on your belly
   and you will eat dust
   all the days of your life.
And I will put enmity
   between you and the woman,
   and between your offspring and hers;
he will crush your head,
   and you will strike his heel.'

To the woman he said,

'I will make your pains in childbearing very severe;
   with painful labour you will give birth to children.
Your desire will be for your husband,
   and he will rule over you.'

To Adam he said, 'Because you listened to your wife and ate fruit from the tree about which I commanded you, "You must not eat from it,"

> 'Cursed is the ground because of you;
>   through painful toil you will eat food from it
>   all the days of your life.
> It will produce thorns and thistles for you,
>   and you will eat the plants of the field.
> By the sweat of your brow
>   you will eat your food
> until you return to the ground,
>   since from it you were taken;
> for dust you are
>   and to dust you will return.'
> GENESIS 3:14–19

Adam and Eve's role in ruling over the animals is spoiled, with 'enmity' between them and the serpent (v. 15). Their role in filling the earth is marred by 'pains in childbearing'. The relationship between the man and his wife is spoiled, with each vying for supremacy (v. 16). The plentiful fruit will now only be produced by 'painful toil' (v. 17). Finally, death and decay become part of their existence (v. 19). Yet at no point does God rescind their identity as image-bearers. Despite their sin, despite their decaying bodies, despite their marred relationships with the world and their creator, their identity remains.

This is underlined in Genesis 9:6, when God says: 'Whoever sheds human blood, by humans shall their blood be shed; for in the image of God has God made mankind.' Here, an explicit link is drawn between humanity's ongoing image-bearing and its inherent dignity and worth, rooted in God's own nature. This means every person, whatever their physical or neurological differences, is in God's image, valuable and precious to him.

This passage provides an important foundation for understanding the origins of disability. While this book is not intended to be a book on suffering (there are some excellent ones listed at the end of the book), we must pause for a moment on this. God did not create a world with suffering and frailty. That came as a direct result of humanity's choice to disobey God. In their disobedience, humanity sought to be 'like God' (Genesis 3:5, 22), rejecting the created order and choosing to rule for themselves. This attitude of rebellion is what we call 'sin', symptoms of which we see in thousands of individual choices every day. God does not allow Adam and Eve to reinvent themselves as gods, but instead emphasises their physical, created existence: 'Dust you are, and to dust you will return' (v. 19). Their choice shuts them off from the source of life, and so their physical bodies begin to decay. In Romans 8:21, Paul describes the result of this choice – all creation being in bondage to decay. Disability and disease are part of the physical degeneration of our bodies; errors in cell division leading to chromosomal abnormalities and the suffering experienced by individuals and their loved ones are all the result of the fall – humanity's choice to mar the beautiful, perfect image of God in their disobedience and selfishness.

Disability often makes our world feel uncomfortable, because it reminds us of what we'd rather forget: we are fragile beings, and one day we will die. The brokenness of our bodies or minds is a result of the fall, but disabled people are not uniquely or specially fallen. Each of us shares fully in this weakness and frailty, regardless of whether it is yet visible on the outside. It is hard to be reminded that we are weak, that humanity cannot be its own saviour. But deep down we know it to be true of ourselves, whether we are disabled or not. Our bodies are dust, and to dust they will return.

PHYSICAL AND SOCIAL EFFECTS OF SIN AND THE CURSE

We must pause and weep with those who weep here. The Bible is full of laments for suffering – God did not originally create it to be this way. However, he is not without rule or authority over suffering. Even over horrific acts of evil by humanity, where we can directly see the spiralling effects of sin on many people's lives, God is sovereign. Even over random accidents with devastating consequences, God is sovereign.

This is a hard truth, as from our perspective, it is impossible to comprehend fully why God allows such suffering to continue. However, the alternative, a God without power or authority, is surely worse. And the cross gives us a clear example of how human responsibility for evil and God's divine sovereignty can go gloriously hand in hand.

The Bible is also full of God's compassion for those who are weak and suffering. Isaiah 40, after many chapters explaining God's judgement on both his people and the nations, offers comfort to God's people. They have been suffering the consequences of their sin in exile, and can be seen as a picture of all humanity, exiled from God as a result of their sin. The passage opens:

> Comfort, comfort my people,
>   says your God.
> Speak tenderly to Jerusalem.
>
> ISAIAH 40:1

The same chapter explores God's power and sovereignty, and the relative inability of humanity to comprehend God's actions. It closes with a crescendo of wonderful promises, which give great hope to all who trust God, and can feel especially powerful for those feeling the disabling effects of disease, disability, or cognitive impairment.

> Why do you complain, Jacob?
>   Why do you say, Israel,
> 'My way is hidden from the Lord;
>   my cause is disregarded by my God'?
> Do you not know?
>   Have you not heard?
> The Lord is the everlasting God,
>   the Creator of the ends of the earth.
> He will not grow tired or weary,
>   and his understanding no one can fathom.
> He gives strength to the weary
>   and increases the power of the weak.
> Even youths grow tired and weary,
>   and young men stumble and fall;
> but those who hope in the Lord
>   will renew their strength.
> They will soar on wings like eagles;
>   they will run and not grow weary,
>   they will walk and not be faint.
>
> ISAIAH 40:27–31

For all those feeling their weakness or grappling with the challenges of a loved one suffering as a result of disability, we are called to contemplate the creator God, who 'will not grow tired or weary'. For those struggling, feeling that no one understands the way they think or behave, who fight for accommodations to be made for them or those they love, we know we have a God 'whose understanding no one can fathom'. Our way is not hidden from him; our cause is not disregarded.

In relating human disability and suffering to sin, we must also be clear here that the Bible does not say that disability is the result of an individual's sin. While it is possible for sickness to be a means of discipline pointing to a particular sin which needs to be addressed (1 Corinthians 11:30), the vast majority of disability in the Bible is related to the effects of the curse on all of creation generally, not a specific punishment for an individual's sin. Jesus makes this very clear in John 9, to which we will return later in the book.

However, it is clear in the Bible that sinful, selfish hearts have a real impact on how disabling a particular condition can be. When we are talking about 'disability', there are two important facets: an individual's physical reality – whether that is a broken bone, an extra chromosome, or a brain with different prevailing neural pathways – and their environmental reality. The extent to which they will feel the disabling effects of their physical reality will depend hugely on their environment. For example, someone with a hearing impairment in the developed world in the 21st century will be hugely less 'disabled' – that is, made 'less able' – as a result of cochlear implants or hearing-aid technology available to them.[1]

For this reason, many people talking about disability distinguish between 'medical' and 'social' models of disability. One model (medical) sees the individual primarily in terms of their medical diagnosis and tends to focus on impairments. The other (social) focuses heavily on environment and the impact of other people's choices on how an individual experiences their physical or neurological differences.

The Bible does not privilege either of these models. As we have seen, the physical effects of the fall are made abundantly clear from Genesis 3 onwards. Creation is cursed, in bondage to decay, not as it should be. We cannot describe every physical impairment as 'difference' and deny that reality. However, the Bible is also clear that, following the fall, the perfect relationships experienced by Adam and Eve in the Bible are spoiled. Humans act selfishly, both wilfully and thoughtlessly. The choice in the garden set humanity on a pathway towards evil thoughts and actions. We look at those who are different from us – cognitively, physically, or in some other way – and our human pride naturally seeks our own superiority. We oppress those who are 'weak', either deliberately or by not using our strengths to serve others. Ensuring that everyone's needs are met is the result of hard, painful toil, which we are more willing to exert on our own behalf or for our close friends and family members, than for those who we don't know so well.

The results of human rebellion are seen as much in our treatment of those who are different, as in disability and difference itself. There are many aspects of disability which make life harder for the individual, but many of these are not so much the result of their own physical or cognitive difference as of the unwillingness of society to bend or adapt to their needs. When a wheelchair user struggles to access all aspects of the service because we haven't thought about how to allow them to come up for Communion, when we roll our eyes because an autistic child is having a noisy meltdown during the service, when we choose not to engage the person with Down syndrome in conversation because we'd rather speak to our friends, we see the fall at work. We see it not only in the limitations of the disabled individual, but also in our own sinful tendency to think of ourselves first. When we know the good we ought to do and fail to do it, we sin (James 4:17). Of course, there is complexity and often conflicting needs at work, and sometimes we are genuinely doing our best with what we have. However, we can acknowledge that our own tendency to be 'bent in on ourselves'[2] leads us to make choices which hurt others.

James, in his letter to Jewish Christians, picks up on behaviour stemming from the same selfish motives:

> My brothers and sisters, believers in our glorious Lord Jesus Christ must not show favouritism. Suppose a man comes into your meeting wearing a gold ring and fine clothes, and a poor man in filthy old clothes also comes in. If you show special attention to the man wearing fine clothes and say, 'Here's a good seat for you,' but say to the poor man, 'You stand there' or 'Sit on the floor by my feet,' have you not discriminated among yourselves and become judges with evil thoughts? Listen, my dear brothers and sisters: Has not God chosen those who are poor in the eyes of the world to be rich in faith and to inherit the kingdom he promised those who love him?
> JAMES 2:1–5

Although James is speaking of material wealth in these verses, the same root lies at the heart of much of the suffering experienced by those who are physically or cognitively different from us. We naturally want to discriminate, to judge, to look for those who can do us a favour. We fail to remember that the kingdom of God is an upside-down kingdom, where those who are 'last' will be 'first' (e.g. Matthew 20:16).

We do not want to deny or diminish the suffering that results simply from the curse on creation – it is clear that we should expect physical pain and suffering, not only as a result of sinful decisions by other people, but also from the fall (e.g. Romans 8:22). This should not excuse us from examining our own hearts and identifying our own sin as part of the cause of others' suffering. We do not need to see all aspects of difference as something broken and in need of fixing. More nuance and thought will lead us to see beauty and diversity within the (inevitably marred) image of God in humanity.

As we come to practical suggestions for our churches and other Christian groups in the second half of this book, it will be important to hold all these truths together: that *all* people are made in God's image and derive worth and dignity from that identity, not from their capabilities or lack thereof; that the suffering that comes from the disabling effects of difference is real and should be seen as part of the curse resulting from humanity's sin; and that human selfishness has an important role to play in the experience of disability alongside physical conditions. Wonderfully, we have a good and glorious God who can redeem and bring beauty out of the tragedy and sorrow, and use the very differences which caused us pain to build his church. If we need evidence of this, we need only look to Jesus.

THE PERFECT IMAGE OF GOD: THE EXAMPLE OF JESUS

As we rightly mourn the effects of the fall both in our broken world and in humanity's broken hearts, we can be driven in two directions – to hopelessness and despair or to energetic campaigning. The Bible calls us to start somewhere else: with the true and perfect image of God.

The language of 'God's image' doesn't crop up a lot in the rest of the Old Testament, but it is picked up again in the New Testament. If the image of God in all humanity is a reason to treat all humanity with dignity, we also see a means and a hope in Christ. In Jesus we see a 'new Adam'. He is the perfect image of God: 'The Son is the image of the invisible God, the firstborn over all creation' (Colossians 1:15). Because of his life, death, and resurrection, death no longer reigns: 'If the many died by the trespass of the one man, how much more did God's grace and the gift that came by the grace of the one man, Jesus Christ, overflow to the many!' (Romans 5:15). This offers hope both for the physical, broken creation and for our own sinful hearts.

Paul continues: 'Just as sin reigned in death, so also grace might reign through righteousness to bring eternal life through Jesus Christ our Lord' (Romans 5:21). We will return to this aspect of Jesus as the perfect image of God in chapter 4. We also see hope right now for our sinful hearts: that 'those God foreknew he also predestined to be conformed to the image of his Son' (Romans 8:29) and that those in Christ 'have put on the new self, which is being renewed in knowledge in the image of its Creator' (Colossians 3:10). The language of being in God's image is used again, focused particularly on Christians. We *are* being sanctified, made more like Jesus and therefore renewed in the image of God.

Jesus, the perfect image of God, offers us a radically different vision of love and other-centredness. Humanity was dead in sins (Ephesians 2:1), objects of wrath, without hope and without God. We weren't just spiritually blind; we were utterly incapacitated by sin. Jesus didn't just pity from afar or settle for a half-hearted solution. He was willing to incapacitate himself, becoming fully man (Philippians 2:6–8) and limiting himself in ways we cannot comprehend. In this, we are not claiming that Jesus at any point set aside his divine nature to become man, but that he chose to take on a human nature in addition to his divine nature, meaning that he entered into our experience of human frailty (for example, we see the God who created food experiencing hunger in the wilderness). Not only this, but he suffered further pain and degradation at the cross. Jesus experienced spiritual torment, and his resurrection body still bears physical scars (John 20:27).

Jesus becoming a man sets us the ultimate example of what it looks like to love those who are different, those who are in need. He does not consider it too much effort or unworthy of his time to act on behalf of humanity. His sacrificial service, his willingness to become lower than the lowest, weaker than the weakest, is an example of how the church must be ready to exert itself on behalf of those who do not look impressive, but who deeply need our love and care. Throughout Jesus' earthly ministry, we see him pouring himself out for the needs of others, paying particular attention to those rejected and on the edges of society, as we will see in the next chapter.

Jesus also offers us a glimpse of beauty to be found within pain, sorrow, and weakness:

> [Jesus] did not consider equality with God something to be used to his own advantage; rather, he made himself nothing, by taking the very nature of a servant, being made in human likeness… he humbled himself by becoming obedient to death – even death on a cross!
> PHILIPPIANS 2:6-8

In weakness, God's strength is most clearly seen. In the same way, in weakness and disability, even in death, God's love and power is made manifest. When the risen Jesus appears to his disciples and tells Thomas to place his hands on his wounds, Jesus' resurrection scars are glorious, as they point to his love and self-sacrifice. If physical brokenness and self-limitation were possible for the full and perfect image of God, then we certainly should not see them as barriers to seeing God's image in our fellow humans.

DISCUSSION QUESTIONS

1. How does knowing they are made in God's image affect the way we see people with additional needs?

2. What are the problems with putting abilities and competence at the centre of how we see other people?

3. Where do you experience frailty and brokenness in your own life?

4. How do you see sinful choices affecting the lives of people around you?

5. How does Jesus offer us hope?

②
The community of God's people: inclusion

At the end of chapter 1, we began to see how Jesus, as the perfect image of God, offers hope to broken image-bearers. Wonderfully, he chooses to do this through community, through drawing together a people united in him. From the beginning of the Bible, we see God shaping his covenant community and placing a priority on love for the outsider.

> He defends the cause of the fatherless and the widow, and loves the foreigner residing among you, giving them food and clothing. And you are to love those who are foreigners, for you yourselves were foreigners in Egypt.
> DEUTERONOMY 10:18–19

God insists that his people care for those with obvious needs, not for the sake of return or because of some intrinsic benefit they may bring to the community, but for two reasons. First, that it is in God's nature to care for these people: *he* defends their cause and loves them. God is shaping his covenant community into his likeness, and this love for the weak is a key part of his character. Second, God's people are to love foreigners because they have experienced similar need. This was true for God's people in the Old Testament, who had experienced the hardship of slavery and exclusion from society in Egypt. It is also true, and even more so, for the church community today. We have experienced the ultimate act of inclusion and integration – while we were still sinners, Christ died for us (Romans 5:8). The non-Jewish Christians in Ephesus were called to:

> Remember that formerly you who are Gentiles by birth and called 'uncircumcised' by those who call themselves 'the circumcision' (which is done in the body by human hands) – remember that at that time

you were separate from Christ, excluded from citizenship in Israel and foreigners to the covenants of the promise, without hope and without God in the world. But now in Christ Jesus you who once were far away have been brought near by the blood of Christ.
EPHESIANS 2:11–13

God's people could look back on their former slavery as a motivation to include those who were not necessarily easy to include, and care for their needs. We have been set free, too – not from physical slavery, but from slavery to sin. We also have gone from being excluded, foreigners, and without hope, to being brought near and included in God's family. This process of bringing-in was not cheap, tick-box inclusion, but bought with the death of Jesus.

As we look at those in our community who have additional needs – the adult with learning disabilities which mean that she will never be able to hold an in-depth conversation about the latest book you have read, the child who shouts out in the middle of the prayers in church, or the adopted child diagnosed with foetal alcohol syndrome with complex emotional and physical needs – it can feel like a lot of work: unrewarding, unexciting, unfair. Yet this is exactly the work to which God calls his people – the work of becoming more like him, of reflecting in practice the spiritual reality of unity.

RUTH AND BOAZ

Perhaps one of the most striking examples of generous inclusion can be found in the Old Testament in the book of Ruth. In this story we see a wonderful model of this love for the 'foreigner residing among you' in the character of Boaz.

Ruth is a foreigner, a Moabitess, who has married a local boy while his family were living abroad during a famine. Remarkably, she has chosen to return with her mother-in-law to Israel after her husband, brother-in-law, and father-in-law have all died. She consigns herself to a future as a foreigner, living in poverty and reliant on a strange people for charity. She has no expectation of getting married, having children, or even making friends in this society, yet in spite of all this she chooses to align herself with her mother-in-law, Naomi. Boaz is a distant relative of Naomi's husband, in whose field Ruth goes to work, accepting food welfare in the form of grain dropped round the edges of a field at harvest time.

It is an intriguing narrative, full of twists and turns, that culminates with Ruth and Boaz – an unlikely couple – getting married. In that beautiful union, Boaz (described in the book as Ruth's 'guardian-redeemer') takes Ruth as his wife, restoring her reputation and status and giving her love and security. Boaz in this story, while he is still very much a fallen human being, points us to our ultimate guardian-redeemer, Jesus, and our own glorious union with Christ. While this book is about inclusion of those who are ethnically 'foreign', the wider biblical narrative, as we have already seen, supports its application in the area of inclusivity towards those made different by disability.

A deep dive into Boaz's character and how he treats Ruth in Ruth 2 gives us some principles for what thoughtful provision for need can look like in our Christian communities. It is immediately clear that Boaz knows the workers in his field. He greets them all, 'The Lord be with you!', and immediately recognises a strange woman gleaning behind the harvesters (vv. 3–5).

The first step towards inclusion is *awareness*. We all recognise the need for churches to be places of deep relationships. We might excuse our lack of care for individuals through ignorance. 'I didn't know!', we say. The authors of this book include ourselves in this – it is easy to be preoccupied with our own needs or those of our immediate circle of friends. Boaz gives us an example of someone who clearly has a deep connection with his own people, yet is quick to spot the outsider and want to find out more about them and their needs.

Boaz next shows a remarkable degree of *perceptiveness in meeting Ruth's needs*. He makes sure she knows she's welcome there, and invites her to join the women working for him:

> 'My daughter, listen to me. Don't go and glean in another field and don't go away from here. Stay here with the women who work for me. Watch the field where the men are harvesting, and follow along after the women.'
> RUTH 2:8

He *anticipates her insecurity*, not only making explicit arrangements for safeguarding her, but letting her know that he has done so: 'I have told the men not to lay a hand on you' (v. 9).

Finally, he *provides for her physical needs*, inviting her to share his own men's water supplies, and later offering her bread and wine vinegar at lunchtime:

'And whenever you are thirsty, go and get a drink from the water jars the men have filled' (v. 9).

He sees his own opportunity to provide in the context of God's provision and protection, rather than taking pride in his own position of strength.

> 'May the Lord repay you for what you have done. May you be richly rewarded by the Lord, the God of Israel, under whose wings you have come to take refuge.'
> RUTH 2:12

We immediately see the effect of this thoughtful provision – Ruth says he has 'put [her] at ease by speaking kindly to [her]' (v. 13).

This welcoming invitation, safeguarding, and provision for need can give us a framework for how we take care of those on the outside. Boaz was probably very busy – it was the height of harvest, he was a landowner with his own workforce to take care of – and no doubt many of us could relate to the pressures of work in the busy season. Yet he notices and acts immediately to protect and care for Ruth, reflecting God's refuge as he does so.

What also stands out is the dignity Boaz offers Ruth. If he had wanted to, he could have given her some of his own grain, as he clearly doesn't mind the financial loss, yet he allows her the opportunity to work for herself.

> 'Let her gather among the sheaves and don't reprimand her. Even pull out some stalks for her from the bundles and leave them for her to pick up, and don't rebuke her.'
> RUTH 2:15–16

While offering her this opportunity for meaningful self-provision, he also makes arrangements to ensure a maximum level of success. Part of involving those with additional needs in meaningful service may involve adaptations to allow the work to be carried out more successfully. Ruth is a remarkable character in the Old Testament, as she seems to have everything against her – a woman in a strange country with no close male relatives or income – and yet God chooses to show her redeeming love in the Christ-like character of Boaz, and includes her in the family line of Jesus as the great-grandmother of King David. Here we see a beautiful picture of how radical inclusion and integration reflects God's heart and glorifies him.

JESUS AND A HURTING WOMAN

As we move into the New Testament, we see this same pattern of inclusion and dignity in many of Jesus' encounters. One that stands out is his treatment of the woman who has been bleeding for twelve years in Luke 8. Again, we have a woman who is at the margins of society – ceremonially unclean because of her bleeding, which would have rendered her an outcast among her people, in constant pain and discomfort, having spent all her money on unsuccessful treatments. Today, we might describe her as having a hidden disability or a chronic condition. She is desperate to get to Jesus, her last hope of healing.

But Jesus is busy. He's got a crowd around him, who've all been waiting for his return. He's got a local big-wig, a synagogue leader, asking for help to heal his daughter – and it seems like this one is pretty urgent. Jesus could be forgiven for focusing on what seem like the urgent needs at the time; isn't Jairus' willingness to come forward an excellent opportunity to get some of the religious establishment on side? The woman also knew she wasn't allowed to touch anyone, as doing so would make them ceremonially unclean under Jewish law. She is barred by her physical needs from approaching the one she knows she needs.

So she decides to go in secret. In the crush of the crowd, she risks reaching out and touching the edge of Jesus' cloak. Miraculously, she is healed of her bleeding. This could have been the whole story – but Jesus wants to offer so much more than physical healing. As we see time and time again in the gospels, outward physical healing, which Jesus can and does give, is only a sign of the far greater inward, spiritual healing he offers.

> 'Who touched me?' Jesus asked.
> LUKE 8:45

We can feel the tension in the air – there's a crowd 'pressing against' Jesus, 'almost crush[ing] him', he's got an urgent appointment at Jairus' house, and yet he's holding everyone up to find out who touched him? What is Jesus trying to do here?

Just like Boaz, we first see that he *notices* the woman. 'Then the woman, seeing that she could not go unnoticed, came trembling and fell at his feet' (v. 47). She is seen, even in the middle of all the other needs and urgent matters vying for attention in Jesus' mind.

We might wonder why he forces her to be so public when she had sought secrecy – but here we see him protecting her and *meeting her social needs*. He has already met her physical need in healing her, but she also has a social need – to be welcomed back into community and no longer treated as unclean. As Jesus calls on her to tell her story 'in the presence of all the people', he ensures that everyone will know that this woman is now to be reinstated as a member of the local community, no longer unclean.

Finally, he offers her *dignity* in calling her 'daughter', in offering her agency in her act of faith: 'Then he said to her, "Daughter, your faith has healed you. Go in peace"' (v. 48).

We will return to a discussion of healing and disability in chapter 4. For now, we want to draw your attention to Jesus' remarkable willingness to take time for individuals, to identify and anticipate their needs. He offers a model for us, when it all seems too much. There are so many needs in a church, all competing for priority. We are always short-staffed, struggling to fill rotas and ensure that everything keeps running smoothly. Taking time for a needy individual, who we know will take more effort from us, and who may not have obvious contributions to make to church life, just seems like too much. We are not Jesus – and yet as the body of Christ, we are called to follow the example of Christ, not as a burden, but as a joyful act of love.

THE BODY OF CHRIST

The Corinthians were a church who struggled to get this right – they were placing extra value on those who seemed able to contribute more to the church, those who were skilled speakers, or wealthy members of society. Paul speaks into this situation (which I think we can all relate to in some way!) with the analogy of the body.

> Just as a body, though one, has many parts, but all its many parts form one body, so it is with Christ. For we were all baptised by one Spirit so as to form one body – whether Jews or Gentiles, slave or free – and we were all given the one Spirit to drink. And so the body is not made up of one part but of many.
> Now if the foot should say, 'Because I am not a hand, I do not belong to the body,' it would not for that reason stop being part of the body. And if the ear should say, 'Because I am not an eye, I do not belong to

the body,' it would not for that reason stop being part of the body. If the whole body were an eye, where would the sense of hearing be? If the whole body were an ear, where would the sense of smell be? But in fact God has placed the parts in the body, every one of them, just as he wanted them to be. If they were all one part, where would the body be? As it is, there are many parts, but one body.

The eye cannot say to the hand, 'I don't need you!' And the head cannot say to the feet, 'I don't need you!' On the contrary, those parts of the body that seem to be weaker are indispensable, and the parts that we think are less honourable we treat with special honour. And the parts that are unpresentable are treated with special modesty, while our presentable parts need no special treatment. But God has put the body together, giving greater honour to the parts that lacked it, so that there should be no division in the body, but that its parts should have equal concern for each other. If one part suffers, every part suffers with it; if one part is honoured, every part rejoices with it.
1 CORINTHIANS 12:12–26

We see the same principle of including those on the margins extended to the New Testament covenant community, the body of the church. Paul points out that the body is one, but has many parts. Some of them might feel like they don't belong, because they're not the same as the others – their needs or outward appearance, their ability to serve, might all contribute to this sense of not belonging. This is likely to be particularly the case for those in our communities who suffer from physical or cognitive disabilities or who are not 'neurotypical' – their neurotype may already make them more prone to anxiety, and their feeling of insecurity is likely to be increased by feeling that they have no valid contribution to make. For some, they may have enthusiastically offered to serve in the past and been met with patronising preconceptions that it would not be possible or a negative response. For those with physical disabilities, they may feel like they are more of a burden than a benefit to the community. It can be hard for people in this situation to feel as though they truly 'belong' in the body.

Yet Paul says: 'The eye cannot say to the hand, "I don't need you!"' (v. 21) – we cannot say to any part of the body of Christ that they are not needed. 'On the contrary, those parts of the body that seem to be weaker are indispensable' (v. 22). Note that Paul says 'seem to be weaker': our human ideas of weakness and strength so often do not match up with God's idea about who he can use to bring him glory. Throughout the Bible, we see him choosing to use the weak, the outsiders, those without significant skills or social standing, to do his work.

Similarly, there might be members of our church who we don't think can contribute much – they struggle to read aloud or they are non-verbal. Their behaviour is embarrassing. They interrupt the sermon. They, or indeed we, may feel like they are in the way, causing trouble, giving everyone extra work. And yet, 'God has put the body together, giving greater honour to the parts that lacked it, so that there should be no division in the body, but that its parts should have equal concern for each other' (vv. 24–25). The same idea is expressed negatively and positively for emphasis – no division, despite our outward differences, and equal concern for each other. This means actively looking out for each other's needs, understanding those whose needs are utterly different from ours, and rejoicing that we are more perfectly reflecting unity in Christ as we do so.

Not only this, but God says that the parts that seem weaker are indispensable. Just get your head around that: the child with ADHD who cannot sit still at the back of church is indispensable to your church. The stroke victim with a brain injury who can no longer speak – they are indispensable. Those with Down syndrome, cerebral palsy, autism, Rett syndrome – God says they are indispensable. God says we need them as we grow together in Christ.

And not only do we need them, but in verse 23 we see that they are to be treated with special honour and dignity. This instruction answers the question, 'But we don't treat anybody else that way; why should we go out of our way to make these provisions for this individual?', and fears that it will be seen as unfair for others. While our value as humans all made in the image of God is equal, regardless of ability or disability, Paul makes it clear 'our presentable parts need no special treatment'. In thinking through the ways we can best make our gatherings, groups, and services accessible, we will not be giving everyone the same treatment. We will be thinking how we can best give everyone what they need to be a valued, loved, cared for, and indispensable part of the body of Christ. Paul paints an image of the church being a place that not only is inclusive to people with additional needs, but showers people who have additional needs with dignity and respect.

We have seen the reality of these truths in our own church experience. Eight years ago, a family arrived at our church who had a son with additional needs. After a chat with the family, the youth and children's team began to adjust the way we ran our youth and children's provision on Sundays, midweek, and in our all-age services. We knew making these adjustments would take effort and come at a cost, but we considered it worthwhile because we wanted to serve him and his family well. What we hadn't really grasped at that stage was how much we would benefit as a church. God used this time to shape us as a staff team and congregation; we grew in our ability to be flexible, to listen, and love one another. We went back to basics and learnt to communicate the gospel simply and in doing so we were struck afresh by the beauty and power of the gospel. We needed to learn these things to grow together in Christ. This young man proved to be indispensable. In fact, I doubt there would be this book without him. The family have since moved away, but I am confident God will be using them to do a similar thing in their new church community.

WHAT ABOUT THE OLD TESTAMENT LAW?

A quick search through the Bible for passages explicitly talking about disability will throw up a potentially confusing passage in Leviticus 21. Moses is explaining God's rules for right worship of a holy God, which require God's people to be externally and ritually 'clean'. The whole book emphasises again and again that God is a perfect, pure God, who has chosen to live with an impure people. The people's need for ritual purity is an outward, physical representation of the fact that it is impossible for sinful people to live with a perfect, holy God. The priests, who offer sacrifices and serve in the tabernacle/temple, are held to an even higher standard of external 'perfection':

> The Lord said to Moses, 'Say to Aaron: "For the generations to come none of your descendants who has a defect may come near to offer the food of his God. No man who has any defect may come near: no man who is blind or lame, disfigured or deformed; no man with a crippled foot or hand, or who is a hunchback or a dwarf, or who has any eye defect, or who has festering or running sores or damaged testicles."'
> LEVITICUS 21:16-20

Does this contradict everything we have seen in this chapter about God's desire that the disabled should be included, welcomed, and allowed to fully belong in the covenant community of God?

First, it is worth recognising that this restriction applied to the priesthood only: this was not a general rule preventing disabled people from entering the temple. Second, in this passage we see that disabled descendants of Levi could still be priests:

> He may eat the most holy food of his God, as well as the holy food; yet because of his defect, he must not go near the curtain or approach the altar, and so desecrate my sanctuary. I am the Lord, who makes them holy.
> vv. 22–23

These verses show that disabled priests were still considered to belong to the priesthood, set aside or 'holy' to the Lord. Phrases like 'I am the Lord, who makes them holy' are repeated throughout this chapter, making it clear that the priest's worthiness to minister ultimately comes from God.

Third, we should note that the same book makes it clear that God will not tolerate any disrespect for the disabled: 'Do not curse the deaf or put a stumblingblock in front of the blind, but fear your God. I am the Lord' (Leviticus 19:14).

So why does God appear to discriminate in this way within his priesthood? The priests' physical bodies, like the sacrifices they administered, had to be externally 'whole' to point to the need for spiritual purity. Old Testament law uses lots of external features (everything from haircuts to diets) to mark out God's people, and particularly his priests, as special, set apart. This wasn't because cutting your hair in a particular way made you a better person, but because it was an obvious, external sign of the inward reality God wanted. Ultimately, just like the sacrifices, the Old Testament priesthood was never intended to be the end of the story, as their hearts remained sinful. In their role as representatives of the people before God, their sin prevented them from being sufficient mediators. Instead, they point to the need for Jesus, who is both our perfect, sinless sacrificial victim and the perfect high priest (Hebrews 4:15; 9:14).

> For Christ did not enter a sanctuary made with human hands that was only a copy of the true one; he entered heaven itself, now to appear for us in God's presence. Nor did he enter heaven to offer himself again and again, the way the high priest enters the Most Holy Place every year with blood that is not his own. Otherwise Christ would have had to suffer many times since the creation of the world. But he has appeared once for all at the culmination of the ages to do away with sin by the sacrifice of himself.
> HEBREWS 9:24–26

Physical perfection was not what was required to be truly without blemish. Our great high priest Jesus, although his bones were not broken, was surely physically 'blemished' at the cross, and yet is considered both perfect priest and a perfect sacrifice for sin.

This chapter has shown God's desire for his covenant community to be a place of inclusion and respect. This should drive us to worship, to recognise something more of the glory of a God who chooses the weak, who uses those on the edge, who calls his people to reflect him in ensuring that people's needs are met and everyone has free access to meeting him in our churches, Christian Unions, youth groups, activity holidays, or any setting where Christians are gathering to meet with one another and with Jesus.

However, it will also no doubt have raised lots of questions. While we may understand the rationale and the theological framework, we also know the practical reality of ministry in the church. It is often hard work, done by a small number of people and sometimes doesn't feel like it goes anywhere. The next chapter will explore some of these questions, with a particular focus on the value of inclusion and accessibility for our evangelism.

DISCUSSION QUESTIONS

1. How have we experienced being included (both spiritually and practically)?

2. Which of the stories struck you most? Why?

3. How have you seen the reality of the 'body of Christ' metaphor in your experience of church?

4. How do these passages challenge the world's assumptions about disability?

5. What do these passages tell us about God?

③
It seems too hard: sacrifice

When we start to think about inclusion, we can instinctively lean towards the 'easy' end of the spectrum – a few small adjustments, like offering large-print Bibles, to allow us to shrug off any further responsibility. Others might want to see change but be overwhelmed and uncertain about where to start. What happens when the local residential home decides to come en masse to your Sunday service? To what extent is it right for church members to set aside their own needs for an orderly, quiet service, to enable those with additional needs to participate? Is access and welcome only something feasible for those with moderate learning difficulties or physical impairments? How can we reach the small but significant number of people with severe mobility or cognitive disabilities, for whom even leaving their house is a challenge? How can we help the single mum with a non-speaking autistic son, whose daily reality is being bitten, having her hair pulled, or managing meltdowns? Is it even reasonable for us to aim to do anything to meet such complex needs?

In this chapter, we will investigate what the Bible says about God's call on his people to make sacrifices. We will also reflect on God's choice of the weak to show that his strength, and not ours, is what matters. We will look at passages showing God's love for the lost and explore how these truths might call us to reframe the challenges of ministry.

TAKE UP YOUR CROSS

Jesus makes it very clear that we should not expect serving him to be easy. He speaks on this theme many times, telling his disciples to 'take up their cross and follow [him]' (Matthew 16:24) and that 'anyone who loves their life will lose it, while anyone who hates their life in this world will keep it for eternal life' (John 12:25). Jesus isn't telling us to seek out a rubbish life – elsewhere in John he promises 'life… to the full' (John 10:10) – but rather that we need to turn our worldly expectations on their head. Choosing to follow Jesus is choosing a path of sacrifice, but a path which he has travelled ahead of us, showing us the way to go.

There are many reasons why following Jesus is the way of the cross, one of which is his call to servant-hearted service. He sets the example, washing his disciples' feet, a job usually reserved for the lowliest of servants. In Matthew 19—20, he tells his disciples three times – particularly in response to those who want to hold on to worldly ideas of power and wealth – that the last will be first and the first last. He repeatedly reminds them that the pattern of his kingdom is not one of power and seeking promotion, but one of taking on service which seems unglamorous or simply too hard.

> Jesus called them together and said, 'You know that the rulers of the Gentiles lord it over them, and their high officials exercise authority over them. Not so with you. Instead, whoever wants to become great among you must be your servant, and whoever wants to be first must be your slave – just as the Son of Man did not come to be served, but to serve, and to give his life as a ransom for many.'
> MATTHEW 20:25–28

This gives us the first hint of an answer to our questions above. Seeing God's image in all of humanity; loving those relegated to the fringes of our societies; building a covenant community which sees every member as part of the body – these things will be hard. They come at a considerable cost of time and effort. There will always seem to be more that could be done. In those moments of choice – when we are having a coffee after church and looking around for someone to chat to; when we are frustrated by someone with severe learning disabilities disrupting the flow of the service; when the call goes out for a rota for one-to-one support volunteers for the children's groups – in these moments, we have an opportunity to choose the way of the cross.

HE CHOOSES THE WEAK TO SHAME THE STRONG

Sometimes we can look at the effort required to make changes, to meet needs, to accommodate and include differences, and it seems overwhelming. Too much. Too hard. Beyond our power as small, resource-poor, time-poor churches. But that is precisely the attitude which is intended to drive us to God's strength, to stop relying on our own capacity and skills, and to cry out to him for help.

As we read through the Bible, we are constantly presented with situations where help comes from the most unlikely people. The book of Judges is a brilliant example of this. When we think of Judges, we might bring to mind stories of heroic men and women battling to save Israel against invaders and foreign oppression. Yet when we read it more closely, we see God reminding his people time and time again that it is not by their strength or power that they will live peacefully in the land he has given them, but by his power and intervention.

We see Ehud, the unlikely assassin of Eglon, King of Moab, whose left-handedness[1] enables him to smuggle a sword into the king's presence (Judges 3:12–30). We see Deborah and Jael, two women God uses to enable victory against Sisera and the Canaanites. Barak, the commander of the army, is too scared to go into battle without Deborah, the prophetess, superstitiously believing that her presence will guarantee the Lord's favour. Later, Sisera flees battle and takes refuge in Jael's tent, who brutally kills him in his sleep. Again, God uses the unlikely and socially 'weak' to bring about his purposes (Judges 4:1–24).

Gideon's story (Judges 6—8) explicitly returns time and time again to God's use of weakness: Gideon is weak, the youngest son of the weakest tribe, lacking faith (he needs several miraculous reassurances from God that he has indeed been chosen), so fearful of his own family and friends that he will only destroy Baal's altar by night – and yet he is the one God chooses to fight his battles. Unexpectedly, Gideon amasses a large army, but God says: 'You have too many men. I cannot deliver Midian into their hands, or Israel would boast against me, "My own strength has saved me"' (Judges 7:2), and reduces their army to only 300. The battle is won not by their numerical strength, but by God's intervention.

Samson, another judge, might seem like the perfect example of strength – but again he gives us an example of weakness, this time moral weakness (Judges 13—16). He is constantly unfaithful to God's law in marrying Philistine women, yet God uses this as part of his plan to save Israel. After he has been famously tricked by his wife Delilah into betraying his Nazirite vows and having his hair cut, he is captured by the Philistines, who blind him. Samson's greatest act of destruction against the Philistines, pulling down the temple of Dagon, the god of the Philistines, and killing many of their aristocracy in the process, is done when he is chained and blind. In his disability, God is the source of his strength.

This theme extends beyond the book of Judges. Hannah's prayer (1 Samuel 2) and Mary's song (Luke 1) both echo these themes of God's care for the weak, reversals of fortune, and the foolishness of trusting one's own strength. Hannah, having suffered with infertility and resultant bullying, has had a child, and dedicated him to God. She says:

> 'It is not by strength that one prevails;
>   those who oppose the Lord will be broken.
> The Most High will thunder from heaven;
>   the Lord will judge the ends of the earth.'
> 1 SAMUEL 2:9–10

Similarly, Mary, the mother of Jesus, bursts into song on meeting her cousin Elizabeth. Remarkably, she doesn't complain that God has given her a hard job: pregnant, not yet married, at risk of social rejection or worse. Instead, she says:

> 'My soul glorifies the Lord
>   and my spirit rejoices in God my Saviour,
> for he has been mindful
>   of the humble state of his servant.'
> LUKE 1:46–48

She sees her pregnancy as God's blessing on her. God has done 'great things' for her, a powerless woman. Like Hannah, she praises God, who brings down the mighty and arrogant and raises up the weak, poor, and needy. These two women do not see God's work in their life as unusual, but characteristic of the way God acts.

In chapter 2 we looked at an extract from 1 Corinthians, a letter written by the apostle Paul to a church obsessed with strength. They were starting to form factions based on who had baptised them, and they were complaining about how weak and unimpressive their founder Paul was, looking instead to flashier, more impressive teachers. Paul berates them for their attitude, reminding them: 'For Christ did not send me to baptise, but to preach the gospel – not with wisdom and eloquence, lest the cross of Christ be emptied of its power' (1 Corinthians 1:17). Why would wisdom and eloquence rob the cross of Christ of its power? 'For the message of the cross is foolishness to those who are perishing, but to us who are being saved it is the power of God' (1 Corinthians 1:18). A religion based on a crucified man, not just executed but executed by a superpower in the most shameful way possible, doesn't seem like a strong start. However, that is the very point: 'God chose the foolish things of the world to shame the wise; God chose the weak things of the world to shame the strong' (1 Corinthians 1:27).

God's work is often not flashy or impressive. While caring for those with additional needs in our congregation, we will be brought to our knees by a shortage of time, skill, and resources. We will even look at other churches and think, *It's easy for them, they have a full-time children's worker/a larger staff team/a bigger congregation...* Yet God's work has never been about impressive people putting on an impressive show, but the humble and needy coming to God in their weakness, on their knees, crying out for him to do his work.

These examples from the Bible offer us hope in our weakness, but they should also reframe our expectations of how God can use those we see as weak. In the previous chapter, we saw God's heart for the outsider and his desire that the church be a place where those who seem weak are given special dignity. We also began to explore how they might be indispensable for our church communities. As we look at the biblical narrative, we see that this is not a one-off or something new we've invented; it is the heartbeat of God's work in the world.

Many reading this book will be neurotypical, able-bodied people wanting advice on how to support their brothers and sisters with additional needs. We must be careful, in this attitude of love and service, not to think in terms of *our* strength and *our* ability meeting needs, but to see ourselves as equally weak and in need. Throughout the Bible we see God using the most unlikely people to do his work, and as God changes our heart towards our own strength, he will also begin to open our eyes to how he is using even our most severely disabled church family. This isn't because they have some untapped strength or ability – though they may – but because it is the Lord who builds his church, not us. He works through the most unlikely people precisely to ensure that the glory goes to him, that we cannot claim, 'It was my strength. I did it.'

God will often use people with additional needs to teach us something new about his character. They may be wonderful pray-ers or enthusiastic welcomers. They may light up a room with their smile. The practical chapters of this book share many stories of individuals whose needs have been met so that they can serve their churches. It is wonderful to find the gifts God has given to those in whom we may least expect to find gifts, but the language of 'gifts' is often overlaid with our obsession with tying up worth with capabilities. God is the one with all the strength, and wonderfully, he chooses to use those we least expect to demonstrate that, both to his people and to the watching world.

LOVE FOR THE LOST

We all have a calling to embrace weakness and self-sacrifice within the covenant community. What does this mean as we look outside the church, to mission? Disabled people around the world are considered by some to be one of the world's largest unreached people groups.[2] In the UK, there are many reasons why we may be less likely to come into contact with people with disabilities: they are almost twice as likely to be unemployed,[3] so we may not see them in our workplaces; public transport may be harder to use, so they may struggle to get to outreach activities where we would typically bring new people into the church. For many living with disabilities and for their families, life is just a lot more complex – the need for accessible toilets or changing places, the sensory challenge of coming into new environments, the fear of judgement, the exhaustion of caring for a family member with additional needs.

In addition to the moderate forms of disability most people will be familiar with, there is a small but significant proportion of the population dealing with severe needs. Many of us will never come into contact with these people in our everyday lives due to their isolation from wider society and natural tendency to seek friendship within the disability community. As our churches become places of belonging for those already within our communities with additional needs, we will also begin to be ready to look beyond our church to this group of people who desperately need the gospel.

Two episodes in Luke's gospel give us some helpful principles to apply. The first is the story of the paralysed man in Luke 5:

> One day Jesus was teaching, and Pharisees and teachers of the law were sitting there. They had come from every village of Galilee and from Judea and Jerusalem. And the power of the Lord was with Jesus to heal those who were ill. Some men came carrying a paralysed man on a mat and tried to take him into the house to lay him before Jesus. When they could not find a way to do this because of the crowd, they went up on the roof and lowered him on his mat through the tiles into the middle of the crowd, right in front of Jesus.
> LUKE 5:17–19

Jesus is teaching, and word has got about that he is worth hearing. A crowd of people have gathered, some enthusiastic and some sceptical. But most striking is the behaviour of 'some men', who are desperate to bring their friend 'to lay him before Jesus'. He is paralysed, unable to walk, and lying on a mat. He is completely unable to get to Jesus on his own, and the friends' first attempt to make a conventional entry via the door is thwarted by the crowd.

However, they don't give up and say, 'It's too hard, it's not worth the effort,' or, 'Other people need to hear Jesus, too; maybe another day.' Instead, 'they went up on the roof and lowered him on his mat through the tiles' (v. 19). They climb up onto the flat roof with their friend, and break through the remaining barrier standing between their friend and Jesus: the roof. The Christian disability charity 'Through the Roof' has taken this story as the basis for their name, as it so clearly shows us the lengths to which we can and should go to allow everyone to meet with Jesus. We should be looking at the barriers which might stand in the way of others meeting him and be willing to tear them down when needed.

Of course, the needs of one person might be exactly the opposite of another: one person might find loud music a barrier to meeting with Jesus, while another finds it an encouragement and support in their worship. It is really hard! When the whole body of Christ is involved and not just a small team, we can share the responsibility and find solutions and compromises which allow needs to be met, or at least recognised and understood.

However, the second story is also a surprise when considering balancing the needs of different individuals. Jesus tells a series of parables in Luke 15 to demonstrate why he is welcoming sinners and eating with them. All of them illustrate the effort a seeker will go to in order to find something they value that is lost, and the rejoicing caused by finding what was lost. By the final parable, the parable of the lost son, it is clear that the seeker is God, that the 'lost' is the unrepentant sinner, and that those unwilling to rejoice when that sinner repents are the Pharisees, who therefore are themselves left on the outside.

The opening words of the first parable, however, may surprise us when we think again. 'Suppose one of you has a hundred sheep and loses one of them. Doesn't he leave the ninety-nine in the open country and go after the lost sheep until he finds it?' (Luke 15:4). I am no shepherd, but I think I'd be inclined to cut my losses when one sheep ran off, to ensure the safety of the 99. Surely 99% of the sheep are more important, more worth spending time and effort on, than the 1% which has strayed from home? Yet the shepherd goes after that sheep, finds it, and 'joyfully puts it on his shoulders' (v. 5). The shepherd, in other words, is disproportionately invested in the one outside the flock, the one whom he wishes to bring home. Similarly, we should be willing as a whole church body to sacrifice some of our own needs and pleasures for the sake of those on the outside, the 'lost sheep'.

This passage is primarily about evangelism, but as Christians, we continue to point one another to Jesus. Our discipleship can follow the same pattern as our evangelism: one which prioritises the individual over efficiency. What might this look like in our church? Maybe it's setting up an extra service which particularly seeks to enable those with additional needs to meet Jesus in our churches. Maybe it's putting on a midweek ministry to offer respite care for families caring for family members with disabilities. Maybe it's asking newcomers what they need to enable them and their children to access the service. Even if you're not a church leader or not on the welcome team, you can keep your eyes open, ask questions, and change your own behaviour. There is often a small change which could meet a need when we are willing to look beyond our needs and ask humbly what help would make a difference.

This will depend a lot on the resources available to us – and the needs of the community around us. The outworking will look different in different settings, but should look like conspicuous efforts to enable everyone inside *and* outside the church to come and hear about Jesus.

WHO SHOULD HAVE TO MAKE THE SACRIFICES?

As we have been exploring themes of sacrifice, all kinds of questions may occur to us. What if the changes made to accommodate one person are the opposite of what another person needs? When we get into the practical chapters later on, we will see that even within any one particular diagnosis, there will be diametrically opposed sets of needs. One person may be sensory seeking, another sensory avoidant. Someone with Tourette syndrome shouting out in the middle of a service may be distracting for neurotypical people and terrifying for an autistic person who finds unexpected noises painful. Yet their needs matter too, and ostracising them from the gathering for the sake of others doesn't seem right. Suddenly our desire to love the whole body of Christ is transformed into paralysis as we do not know what to do, which choices to make, what changes to prioritise.

It is refreshing to see the way wisdom is consistently described in the Bible. In Job 28, we are reminded that wisdom cannot be mined, bought, or found through scientific endeavour or exploration, despite the riches and variety of the natural world. Instead, we are told 'the fear of the Lord – that is wisdom' (v. 28). When we turn to the book of Proverbs, where we are told the same thing again (Proverbs 1:7), we find that wisdom in its outworking often involves holding things in tension: 'Plans fail for lack of counsel, but with many advisers they succeed', yet 'Many are the plans in a person's heart, but it is the Lord's purpose that prevails' (Proverbs 15:22; 19:21). We are reminded by this that we must return to the heart. There will inevitably be times when it is extremely challenging to put into place arrangements to suit everyone's needs, but in these circumstances, we must examine our heart attitude: first to the Lord, and then to our neighbour. How this is worked out will be unique to your set of circumstances, but the fear of the Lord will be the starting point for making wise choices. We can pray for wisdom (James 1:5), and remember that our generous God is the source of all wisdom.

We may be feeling burdened by the statistics, by the extent of the challenge, by our lack of specific knowledge. We may feel guilty, worried we have excluded someone without realising it. We may worry that time and effort spent in this area will distract us from other priorities. Our experience has been that small changes can make a huge difference. Our heart attitude towards God and towards others should come first. Over time, we will see those who have experienced exclusion elsewhere find a warm welcome among the people of God. Over time, our awareness of others' needs will grow. Everyone will need to make sacrifices, and some needs will not be perfectly met. It is also right that this awareness should make us long more for the new creation, which is the focus of the next chapter.

DISCUSSION QUESTIONS

1. What areas of life do you find it most difficult to make sacrifices in?

2. Can you think of any scenarios where there will be multiple needs to consider? What ideas can you come up with as to how they could be approached considering *everyone's* needs?

3. How does the Bible speak into our feelings of inadequacy, weakness, or guilt that we haven't done enough?

4. How do the story of the paralysed man and the parable of the lost sheep challenge our assumptions about how much effort is 'reasonable' to allow people to meet Jesus?

5. Why do we need wisdom as we consider which sacrifices are the right ones to make?

The future of disability: the new creation

The previous few chapters have worked through some of what the Bible teaches us about the nature of humanity, both in creation and following the curse of the fall; the nature and purpose of the covenant community; and our expectations of following Jesus' call to sacrificial service and weakness. We have looked back, to creation and the fall, and looked around, at our relationship to our church family, our society, and ourselves. Finally, we will look forward.

The Bible has much to say about our expectations for the new creation, but there is also much disagreement about what this will look like, particularly for our friends with disabilities. We will attempt to navigate what we do know and what we can infer from what we are told. We can start with the ministry of Jesus, whose first coming gives us a taste of what to expect of the coming kingdom.

LOOKING FORWARD TO THE IMAGE RESTORED: JESUS' HEALING MINISTRY

Echoing promises throughout the Old Testament, Jesus picks up on this in Matthew 11, in response to John's disciples, who are questioning whether he is God's chosen Messiah:

> Jesus replied, 'Go back and report to John what you hear and see: the blind receive sight, the lame walk, those who have leprosy are cleansed, the deaf hear, the dead are raised, and the good news is proclaimed to the poor. Blessed is anyone who does not stumble on account of me.'
> MATTHEW 11:4–6

Jesus points to the healing of the blind, of those unable to walk, and of those with skin diseases (which also represented their being unclean before God), and even to the raising of the dead. He explicitly highlights these as signs of the coming kingdom, the beginning of the curse being reversed. All the way through his ministry, we see him healing those who come to him with physical and spiritual ailments, and pointing to these healings as signs of a deeper spiritual reality. This has led some to suggest that Jesus is linking sin and disability directly, as many have done in an attempt to 'blame' individuals for their own condition.

Jesus' interaction with disability is far more nuanced than this. In John 9, Jesus encounters a man blind from birth. Jesus' disciples are keen to develop their disability theology and ask whose sin (this man's, or his parents') resulted in this disability. Jesus' answer makes it clear that disability is not linked to an individual's sin, but is part of God's bigger purpose and plan. In this instance, 'so that the works of God might be displayed in him' (John 9:3). We might think that the 'works of God' will be the man's healing, demonstrating Jesus' divinity and ability to heal the man. His act of making mud with his saliva may even deliberately echo God's act of creating humanity out of dust and spirit. However, the ensuing narrative shows that a far greater work of God is taking place in the man's heart.

After being healed, the man engages in several discussions with the Pharisees, who reject Jesus' authority and are therefore very unwilling to accept his healing power. As the conversations develop, the man goes from uncertainty about Jesus – 'Whether he is a sinner or not, I don't know. One thing I do know. I was blind but now I see!' (v. 25) – to a greater level of understanding – 'Now that is remarkable! You don't know where he comes from, yet he opened my eyes. We know that God does not listen to sinners. He listens to the godly person who does his will. Nobody has ever heard of opening the eyes of a man born blind. If this man were not from God, he could do nothing' (vv. 30–33). In contrast, the initially cautious Pharisees become ever ruder to the once-blind man, eventually hurling insults at him and throwing him out.

The climax of the story comes in verse 38, when the man, speaking to Jesus once more, says, 'Lord, I believe,' and worships him. The story reveals that what matters far more than the man's physical sight is his insight into who Jesus is. The true work of God in this man is not so much his physical healing, miraculous though this is, as his spiritual growth towards understanding.

The Pharisees, by contrast, are revealed to be spiritually blind, even if they are able to see with their eyes (vv. 39–40).

While Jesus' healing ministry shows his compassion, his power, and his role in bringing about the kingdom of God, he makes it clear that whatever the physical or cognitive state of the individual, *everyone* needs God's work in their lives to enable them to see and know him. Jesus does not focus on disability as a particular marker of God's curse; he looks at the heart. Some people with disabilities would prefer that we did not pray for their healing. This may be hard to understand, but we must remember that someone's spiritual health is of far greater significance to the Lord and the body of Christ than their physical health.

This is worth remembering when we deal with people with disabilities and differences. There could be a tendency to see them as more prone to sin than others – the adult dealing with chronic pain who is short-tempered, the child with ADHD who has poor impulse control and often says or does the 'wrong' thing, or the autistic adult whose differences in social communication lead to them saying something hurtful to their friend. We can also swing the other way – the more we understand their condition, the more inclined we are to say that these behaviours are merely communicating unmet needs and have no moral significance.

Jesus tells people adopting both these positions to stop looking at the outside and to look at the heart. These behaviours may reveal sinful heart attitudes, such as selfishness or lack of love. A sinful heart may be more visible as a result of a lack of impulse control. However, this behaviour may stem from a lack of knowledge or social awareness. It is also worth remembering that socially acceptable behaviour, such as sitting still and saying the expected thing, does not necessarily indicate a heart inclined towards God either. These things can stem from a selfish desire to be loved by others or from a people-pleasing mentality. It is also important to question whether our definition of sin is rooted more in the motives and choices of the person or in how they are inconveniencing us. Particularly in children, we are prone to label actions 'misbehaviour' purely because we find them annoying or distracting.

A helpful framework used by Biblical Counselling UK (BCUK) describes Christians as sinners, sufferers, and saints.[1] While we wait for the new creation, we will continue to sin – both the able-bodied and the disabled, the neurotypical and the neurodivergent. What this looks like for each individual will be different, but we should not be surprised to find sin at work in Christians. We are also sufferers – we live this side of the new creation, where we suffer the effects of a fallen, cursed world. However, we are also saints – we have been washed clean by Jesus' blood and have his perfect righteousness. This is true both for the non-disabled and for those with disabilities and differences who have put their trust in Jesus. If we see each member of God's family in this light, it will help us understand and love them better.

Jesus' healing ministry isn't just an outward physical sign of an inward spiritual reality. It doesn't just provide a helpful parallel to his offer of spiritual wholeness and sight. It also looks forward to a day when these ailments will no longer afflict humanity, when *all* our bodies and minds will be without suffering. When we think about heaven, we can fall into two traps: we can either expect God to fix everything right now and look for all the benefits of heaven now, or we can have too pessimistic an expectation of what God is able to do in the church now. This is sometimes called 'over-realised' and 'under-realised' eschatology (theology concerned with the end times).

OVER-REALISED ESCHATOLOGY: HEAVEN ON EARTH?

Many of the blessings we are promised in Christ we have already: we are forgiven, we have the Holy Spirit living in us, we are members of Christ's body, the church. However, our attitude to disabilities can reveal that we're expecting all of God's promises for the future to be realised now. For example, we are promised that one day, there will be no more death, mourning, crying, or pain (Revelation 21:4), so when we or a friend suffers with a physical or cognitive disability, we can be tempted to question God's goodness. We are expecting the promises for the future to be true now. Some may even point to Jesus' healing ministry, heralding the start of the kingdom of God, and expect all illness or disability to be healed by God now. God is able to heal our physical bodies and tells us to pray for the sick (James 5:14–15).

However, the New Testament makes it clear that we are not promised physical healing this side of the new creation. Although we are told to pray persistently, lack of healing does not point to insufficient faith or lack of prayer. Paul speaks to the Corinthians of a 'thorn in the flesh', which he pleaded with God to remove (2 Corinthians 12:7–8). He is not being punished for sin, nor is he lacking in faith, but God wants to use this weakness to stop Paul relying on himself.

Another way we can act as if God has already renewed heaven and earth is when we claim that there is no disability, only difference. When we do so, we fail to recognise that we do still live in a broken world, maimed not only by the ongoing sinful choices of humanity, but also by the curse on creation. We undermine the struggles of those living with disability and fail to recognise their pain. We should expect all our bodies, to a greater or lesser degree, to bear the impairments and limitations imposed on them by our bondage to decay. This side of the new creation, every human's body is decaying. Our 'imperishable' bodies are a promise for the future, not for now. This book will explore many ways in which aspects of 'difference' cause 'disability', but this does not mean that we are denying the existence of disability.

UNDER-REALISED ESCHATOLOGY: 'NOTHING WILL BE BETTER THIS SIDE OF HEAVEN'

However, it is also possible to fall into the trap of relegating all God's promises to the future, and thereby denying the work of the Spirit in our lives now. When all we can say in response to disability in our church is that one day it will be gone, we fail to recognise the work of God in that individual now. For many, whether they have a neurological difference which negatively affects the way they experience the world or a physical disability which limits their body, these differences are part of who they are now. God has promised to be working in each member of his covenant community, conforming them to the likeness of Christ (Romans 8:28). God doesn't need to ignore their disability as he does so, but can make beautiful and God-glorifying even those limitations which seemed to be negative.

Whether we are currently disabled or not, we can lean so heavily on future promises that we do not feel any pressure to make changes now. We fail to expect real growth in ourselves in love towards our fellow Christian. We have a wonderful Saviour who offers us grace to cover every failure, but who calls us to make real change now. We can grow in love towards others in the body of Christ, recognising that there is forgiveness when we fail, but expecting to see growth and sanctification now.

DISABILITY IN THE NEW CREATION

So what should we expect of the new creation? We see both continuity and change in our expectations of the future.

CONTINUITY

We have already seen that Jesus' resurrected body offers a picture of striking continuity. His body was generally recognisable as him, bore the scars of his crucifixion, and was physical, being able to eat and drink (Luke 24; John 20). While we cannot necessarily assume this for our own bodies, and 'what we will be has not yet been made known', we are told that 'we shall be like [Christ], for we shall see him as he is' (1 John 3:2).

It is important to recognise that many aspects of life which seem important to us now, such as marriage, will not continue into the new creation (Luke 20:34–36). We cannot assume something will persist into the new creation because *we* think it's important. Some people have argued that their disability will remain in heaven, as it is so key to their identity. We are not told enough to be sure what aspects of the present will continue into the new creation, and thus we should approach the topic with humility. However, the example of Jesus' resurrection body certainly does not rule out, and indeed encourages, the idea that aspects of disability and difference will continue in a glorified state.

For example, the extra sensitivity of the autistic person to sensory stimuli may become a glorious gift to be shared with others in the new creation, where we can revel in the full beauty of the perfected physical world. As we experience the praises of God sung by people of every tribe, race, and tongue, it makes sense to us that some of the languages used will be those currently used by the Deaf community around the world, such as British Sign Language. The contagious joy of a child with Angelman syndrome will be shared by everyone as we see Jesus face to face.

We don't have an explicit answer about the continuity of particular disabilities in heaven, but we can look at what we do know. We know there will not be death, mourning, crying, or pain (Revelation 21:4), so we know that the *disabling* effects of disability will be gone forever. This is a great hope for those experiencing pain now. We know that there will be a bodily resurrection, not simply a continuity of the spirit (1 Thessalonians 4:16–17) and that each of us will still be ourselves, keeping some form of physical continuity. Without continuity, there is no real resurrection.

CHANGE

It is also clear that we should all expect radical change to our bodies in the new creation. In one of the longer passages of the New Testament on this subject, Paul addresses the concerns of the Corinthian church. Influenced by the culture of their day, they saw 'spiritual' things as good, but physical things like our bodies as intrinsically evil. For this reason, they were starting to teach that only a person's spirit would be resurrected. It seems that they accepted Jesus' bodily resurrection, but were having difficulty accepting their own. Paul first has to persuade them that the two resurrections – Christ's and their own – must stand and fall together: 'If there is no resurrection of the dead, then not even Christ has been raised' (1 Corinthians 15:13). Having made this point, he moves on to discussing the nature of these resurrected bodies in the following passage:

> But someone will ask, 'How are the dead raised? With what kind of body will they come?' How foolish! What you sow does not come to life unless it dies. When you sow, you do not plant the body that will be, but just a seed, perhaps of wheat or of something else. But God gives it a body as he has determined, and to each kind of seed he gives its own body. Not all flesh is the same: people have one kind of flesh, animals have another, birds another and fish another. There are also heavenly bodies and there are earthly bodies; but the splendour of the heavenly bodies is one kind, and the splendour of the earthly bodies is another. The sun has one kind of splendour, the moon another and the stars another; and star differs from star in splendour.
> So will it be with the resurrection of the dead. The body that is sown is perishable, it is raised imperishable; it is sown in dishonour, it is raised in glory; it is sown in weakness, it is raised in power; it is sown a natural body, it is raised a spiritual body.
> 1 CORINTHIANS 15:35–44

Paul wants to make it clear that the body is raised, but that there is a radical difference between our earthly body and its risen counterpart. He uses a series of analogies to help us understand this change.

The first is that of a seed. When we plant a seed, it 'dies' – it goes under the soil, and many must experience cold temperatures, which break down their outer shell and allow them to germinate. The seed contains a miniature undeveloped plant, containing all the genetic information required for the growth of the plant. And yet which of us ever thought that a sunflower bore any resemblance to the seed? The seed is small and insignificant, where the plant is majestic and beautiful. If we had never seen a sunflower, we would not be able to guess what one might look like by looking at the seed!

Paul's second analogy appeals to the variety within the physical created universe. He points out that even in the physical world we can see, there are many different kinds of body. Even seeds are each different from each other – even if we are not farmers or gardeners, a quick trip through the nuts and seeds section of the supermarket will show us that! We can think of many insects which undergo some kind of metamorphosis, like a caterpillar turning into a butterfly (astoundingly, the caterpillar does not simply grow wings, but completely breaks apart within the chrysalis into a kind of DNA soup before re-forming as a butterfly).

The natural world should be our first clue that something can have physical continuity and yet be utterly different. Paul begins to enumerate a few of these differences in verses 42–44: our new creation bodies will be imperishable – they cannot die or decay. They will be glorious – we will no longer be ashamed of any part of our body. They will not be weak, but powerful – every one of us will experience freedom from the limitations of our weak bodies, not just those who experience some kind of physical disability now.

In another letter to the same church, Paul compares the difference between our bodies now and our bodies in heaven to tents being replaced with buildings.

> For we know that if the earthly tent we live in is destroyed, we have a building from God, an eternal house in heaven, not built by human hands. Meanwhile we groan, longing to be clothed instead with our heavenly dwelling, because when we are clothed, we will not be found naked. For while we are in this tent, we groan and are burdened, because we do not wish to be unclothed but to be clothed instead with our heavenly dwelling, so that what is mortal may be swallowed up by life.
> 2 CORINTHIANS 5:1–4

While it may seem very important to us to nail down exactly what aspects of our current identities will continue in heaven, it is a bit like someone who's never seen a brick-and-mortar house discussing whether their new tent will have the same blackout lining and extra-strong guy ropes or not. We all underestimate what God has in store for us. Our categories are simply too limited to imagine how we can still be 'ourselves' and yet utterly transformed. Perhaps Paul means us to think of the difference between the tabernacle 'tent' of the post-exodus years and the beautiful temple built by Solomon. Both were works of art, both represented God's presence; they even had a similar layout. Yet the temple built by Solomon was a greater and truer reflection of God's glory, to be surpassed only by the heavenly reality to come.

It's helpful for us to realise that this change is something *all* of us will undergo in the new creation. Often we speak as though disabled people will be healed but the rest of us will be just as we are now, giving the impression that we are somehow better than them or that God has more work to do for them. This can lead to people with disabilities feeling hurt and misunderstood, not accepted as they are now. Instead, we need to present a biblical picture, which is one of both continuity and change for *every* believer.

Jesus' resurrection body – able to disappear and reappear in another place, enter a locked room and yet also be touched and eat and drink – gives us an idea of how this continuity and change might look. Some commentators describing Jesus' resurrection body suggest that it was *more* substantial than the physical world around it – he doesn't walk through a wall because of some ghostly lack of form, but because he is more real, more solid, than what is around him.[2]

The Corinthian church had an over-realised eschatology. Some were denying the resurrection of the dead, and mocking the possibility of a physical resurrection as being ridiculous. It led them into all kinds of sin and failure to love one another. Paul shows them that their vision is too small, too limited: what we can expect in the future is beyond our ability to describe, but utterly wonderful. In one sense, the scale of the change we can expect to our bodies in the new creation is so great that those who speak only of physical and cognitive disability being healed in the new creation give too small a vision of what is to come. When we describe our heavenly bodies as being just like our bodies now but at peak physical fitness, we do ourselves a disservice – and we are also reducing the glory of our risen Saviour, as we are told that our bodies will be transformed to be like his (Philippians 3:21).

Even from what we see of him in the New Testament, the eternal, risen Lord Jesus is far more than a particularly athletic man.

THE BANQUET FOR THE WEAK: GOD'S HEART FOR THE HUMBLE

We also see that many of the images of God's kingdom contain references to physical disabilities:

> One of the people at the table with Jesus heard him say those things. So he said to Jesus, 'Blessed is the one who will eat at the feast in God's kingdom.'
> Jesus replied, 'A certain man was preparing a great banquet. He invited many guests. Then the day of the banquet arrived. He sent his servant to those who had been invited. The servant told them, "Come. Everything is ready now."
> 'But they all had the same idea. They began to make excuses…
> 'Then the owner of the house became angry. He ordered his servant, "Go out quickly into the streets and lanes of the town. Bring in those who are poor. *Also bring those who can't see or walk."'*
> LUKE 14:15–18, 21 (NIRV, emphasis added)

We repeatedly see a picture of God bringing scattered, weak, broken people into his kingdom. As Jesus' ministry showed, those who are blind and those with mobility difficulties are not the only ones God has in mind with these promises, but those who recognise their weakness and spiritual blindness and turn to God. Those who are too proud, self-sufficient, and reliant on their own strength to come to God, like the Pharisees, end up excluded from the banquet. However, this isn't 'just' a metaphor for spiritual dependence. Jesus tells this parable immediately after he has said:

> 'For all those who exalt themselves will be humbled, and those who humble themselves will be exalted.'
> Then Jesus said to his host, 'When you give a luncheon or dinner, do not invite your friends, your brothers or sisters, your relatives, or your rich neighbours; if you do, they may invite you back and so you will be repaid. But when you give a banquet, invite the poor, the crippled, the lame, the blind, and you will be blessed. Although they cannot repay you, you will be repaid at the resurrection of the righteous.'
> LUKE 14:11–14

Jesus ties together our expectations of the future – that God calls those who are poor and those who can't see or walk (physically or spiritually) into his eternal kingdom, and that those choosing to follow God should set out to honour those who are physically poor, unable to walk, and blind now. In doing so, we reflect the heart of our heavenly Father, who specifically seeks out the weak and humble.

DISCUSSION QUESTIONS

1. How does Jesus' focus on the heart challenge the way you see and relate to people with disabilities or differences?

2. Where might your view of healing or the new creation be 'over-realised' or 'under-realised'?

3. Who is God calling you to welcome to his 'banquet' today?

4. How could embracing your own weakness change how you serve others?

5. What's one step you can take this week to reflect God's heart for the overlooked?

Introduction to part II

Over the rest of the book, we'll be considering many kinds of 'additional needs'. Most of these are considered disabilities because they make day-to-day life more difficult.

You may want to use the next section of this book in different ways.

Some may wish to read it from cover to cover. If that is you, we hope and pray that not only will you find the content and real-life experiences interesting, but that this book will also provide you with a broad understanding of the various types of additional needs you may encounter within Christ's church. We hope it will give you some practical ideas to support those around you as you seek to make your Christian community fully accessible to those with additional needs. You may start to spot needs you were not even aware of before!

For others, you may have already encountered a particular area of need within your church and you are looking for advice as you seek to meet that need. Each chapter in this section works as a standalone piece of writing, so please feel free to skip ahead to relevant chapters. We would ask, though, that this second section of the book is not read without the context of the first. The theology and thoughts explored in part I really are the heartbeat of the book which underpin all we are about to discuss in this second section.

However you choose to use the rest of the information in this book, we pray that it will bless and equip you as you serve wherever God has placed you.

As we dig a little deeper into different diagnoses and the barriers or obstacles that individuals may face, there will probably be some terminology and abbreviations we use that you have not come across before. We hope this does not put you off! We have created a glossary at the back of the book which you can use as a reference point (page 223). You will also find an appendix which will signpost to different organisations and resources that might be relevant to you and your context (page 227).

A THOUGHT ON DIAGNOSES

When we start to group individuals into categories, we can run into some challenges. Isn't every person's situation unique? What if they don't have an actual diagnosis, but some very apparent needs? Is the label a help or a hindrance?

When someone receives a diagnosis, it means an expert in that area has examined their traits, symptoms, and experiences of life and used this to identify a condition. For neurodevelopmental conditions, the presence of traits is not sufficient for a diagnosis, but they must be 'severe' enough to impact their daily life. For a physical condition, an individual may undergo tests, which a doctor or specialist uses to work out the reason for their experiences. With both, there is an element of human fallibility involved. Sometimes people spend years going from one test or assessment to another without an answer. Sometimes they get a diagnosis, but it doesn't answer all the questions. Whether for a physical or neurodevelopmental need, the diagnosis itself is a human construct, but describes an underlying reality. We need to recognise both these things as we approach the subject.

Humans have observed, researched, discussed, and developed sets of descriptors which make up a 'diagnosis'. This means diagnoses don't necessarily stay the same. For example, the ICD-11 (the current classification system for diseases devised by the World Health Organization) removed Asperger syndrome as a separate diagnosis, instead including its description as part of autism spectrum disorder.[1] Our understanding of physical disabilities also changes over time, as changes to medical understanding or available technology allow a different analysis of causes and underlying features of conditions. Many of the diagnoses we describe in this book will change over time, be reframed, or be rearranged. Neurodevelopmental conditions will be absorbed into one another or separated out into further categories. Fallible humans decide what level of hyperactivity is 'beyond the norm for a typically developing child' just like they decide what blood pressure is 'too high'. Psychiatrist Allen Frances acknowledges the weakness of diagnoses of neurotypes: 'Our categories are no more than tentative approximations and are subject to distortion by personal whims, cultural values local to time and place, ignorance, and the profit motive.'[2]

This is not to undermine or dismiss the diagnosis, but to recognise that we need to look beyond the label (or lack thereof) to the person. If we see someone with a need, we can be part of meeting that need, of removing any barriers to their belonging at church. We can do this regardless of whether we know their diagnosis – the label should not be a key to unlocking support. Parents may be trying to understand their child who they think is a bit 'different' or awaiting the results of medical tests to explain a physical disability. If this is you, don't feel you have to wait for a diagnosis to ask for support for your child. We want answers, labels, or scientific names for conditions to validate our experiences. It's natural to seek out these answers, but we shouldn't allow them to distract us from getting to know the individual and supporting them as best we can.

Is there any benefit in a diagnosis? Yes! Many diagnoses allow medical professionals to treat an individual properly – two conditions with the same symptoms may be treated entirely differently when the cause is understood. Names for neurodevelopmental conditions, which are not illnesses to be treated or cured, can also be useful. A football game has rules not to satisfy the designs of an arbitrary rule-maker, but to make the game work. The rules are devised because they work. People receiving a diagnosis may get a better understanding of themselves, as it connects together several features of their life. Although there may be great variation within any given diagnosis, there are also common features. The 'label' can be a shortcut to explaining that there is a need and helping others anticipate challenges.

As churches, it is not our job to make medical diagnoses. What we can do, however, is be alert for needs which may create barriers. We can ask questions, and be observant and loving. We can be imaginative about how to make changes which reduce or remove those barriers. This isn't a job for one person. This isn't only a responsibility for the 'able-bodied' or 'neurotypical' people. This is a ministry which we can all do – because we're all members of the family, of the body of Christ.

In part I of this book, we've seen the basis for this mutual responsibility. It is not founded in human categories, which shift over time, but in God's design for humanity. Made in God's image, we are created for relationships, with one another and with God, and created to work, to serve one another and take care of the world. In the church, we can serve one another and build community based around our relationship with God and because of our shared status as image-bearers. God has shaped his covenant community over time, showing us what it looks like to serve one another, to consider others' needs, and to recognise the unique value every individual brings to the body.

We know this won't always be easy; we live in a fallen world. We live in a world where sin – a selfish, rebellious attitude which rejects God as king – shows itself in our unwillingness to put ourselves out for other people; a world where the brokenness of creation means that some of our needs will be in tension with other people's needs, where everyone will need to make sacrifices; a world where the solutions are seldom simple or efficient. It won't be easy, but we have been given a means and a hope. We are not Victor Frankenstein, patching up a body out of incongruous parts; we are working within a body created by God. His Holy Spirit lives in us as we change to become more like Jesus in our love for one another. We have been given glimpses of his plans for every member of his church, glimpses so wonderful that they change how we live now as we anticipate the new creation.

⑤
Physical disabilities

LOIS BUNYAN AND CLAIRE WOOD

Despite this being one of the longest chapters in this book, we will hardly be able to scratch the surface of the vast range of physical disabilities you may encounter in the church. The term 'physical disability' encompasses many conditions, some visible, some hidden. There is no way the authors of this book can claim to be an expert on all, if any, of these conditions. We also recognise that there will be many conditions we have not been able to include. Rather, we hope the chapter will give you a more general awareness of the challenges those with a physical disability may face in your Christian community and equip you to make adaptations to meet their needs and love and serve them well. We hope it acts as a springboard, introducing some common themes and getting you thinking about what would work in your own context.

Unlike a learning disability or neurodivergence, a physical disability may not be lifelong. Sometimes people are born with a physical disability due to a foetal abnormality or trauma during pregnancy or birth, but it is also common for people to develop physical disabilities later in life. This may be because of an illness, post-viral fatigue or infection, or the result of an accident. It is also inevitable that as we age our bodies will suffer and begin to stop working in the way they once did, meaning that physical disabilities will be a reality for most of us at some point in our lifetime.

Such changes can be life-altering and unexpected. With them will come grief: for the activities once enjoyed which are out of reach, for the dreams we may have held for the future which will never happen as we had planned. Anyone who has experienced even a short-term injury leaving them unable to carry out everyday tasks will have experienced some of this frustration and pain.

It is right to pause here and 'mourn with those who mourn' (Romans 12:15). When mourning with friends their loss of abilities they once had, we can be tempted to go straight to what we perceive as encouragements – things they can still do or ways the situation could be worse. We need to give our friends time and space to grieve what they have lost and be comfortable to share in this process with them. However, not everyone who has mobility difficulties will be experiencing this grief. Some may see their condition as an intrinsic part of who they are and embrace the identity which comes with this disability. Sometimes, the grief and the joy in their condition may coexist.

In this chapter, we will explore different conditions in depth and the impact that living with a physical disability may have for those within your church community. We will go on to consider conditions affecting mobility, followed by conditions affecting the senses. However, we are first going to zoom out and think broadly about disabled access in the building where your church or Christian group meets.

ACCESSIBILITY

One of the easiest places to start is with a tour of your building: this is a simple activity that any member of your church can organise, where one or two individuals gather and assess risks in the building, noticing anything that might pose a hazard or obstacle to someone with a physical disability.[1] Ideally, include someone with mobility difficulties in this activity. You don't need to be the group leader or one of the church trustees to organise this, though everyone will benefit from keeping lines of communication open with those who may be in a position to spend money or make changes. Putting together a report on your space will provide a valuable resource for those in decision-making roles, and you may spot things which can be immediately changed with little effort and no cost.

Before you even enter the building, consider: are there enough disabled parking spaces? If there is no possibility of on-site parking, you can always write to your local MP or councillor and put in a request for disabled parking spaces to be added to the street your church is on, allowing blue-badge holders (in the UK) to have priority parking.

Leaving the cars behind, what is it like as you approach your building? Are there uneven paving slabs or steps? Could a ramp or handrails be introduced? Are wheelchair users able to use the same entrance as everyone else? How wide is the entrance? Is it wide enough to get a wheelchair through? Is the door made of glass? If so, would it benefit from the addition of glass manifestation or a bold sticker to make it stand out to those who are visually impaired? As you move around your meeting place, continue to notice doors, steps, uneven ground, and obstacles. If there are level changes, are these marked in some way to be more obvious to the visually impaired? A strongly contrasting colour painted along the edge of the step can make it much safer.

If you have a welcome desk or a place to serve refreshments, is there space around it? Are signs and noticeboards clear or cluttered and full of notices in small print? If there are service sheets or other printed materials (hymn books, Bibles, and so on), do you have large-print versions available? If you spot that there are no large-print Bibles available, why not buy one for your church in the same translation you regularly use (if possible, with the same page numbers)?

Consider the layout of the sanctuary: does the way the seating is laid out allow room for a wheelchair user to sit comfortably with their friends or loved ones in a service? This may be harder with fixed pews, but can be managed by adding an extra row of chairs at the back or front of the church. Likewise, is there enough legroom for those with walking sticks, walkers, or a broken leg to stretch out? Do you have an accessible toilet? If so, is it clear from obstructions (for example, objects under the rails which can prevent them being moved up and down or prevent the wheelchair user moving alongside the toilet)? Is the emergency pull-cord at its full length or has someone looped it up out of reach? As you walk through the building, consider all the activities which happen there. Can a wheelchair user get onto the stage, if you have one? How many side rooms (such as rooms in which children's groups may meet) are accessible? Where food is provided, are allergens clear?

As well as conducting this kind of review of the space, it can be helpful to sit through a service with the needs of physically disabled people in mind. If pictures are being used (for example, projected on a screen or pinned on a board during a talk), are they verbally described? Is the language used inclusive? For example, 'stand if you are able' or an equivalent is likely to make someone unable to stand (the reason for which could be unseen) feel much more at home in that service. If possible, test the hearing loop system. Does it work consistently throughout the meeting space? Is the lighting bright enough to read printed material easily?

SOME THOUGHTS ON TOILETS

Toileting facilities can be an unseen burden for disabled people. It is a legal requirement in the UK when doing renovation work on buildings open to the public to include at least one wheelchair-accessible unisex toilet.[2] It is also a requirement for all public buildings, even those built before the days of accessibility laws, to include 'reasonable adjustments' towards accessibility (what is considered 'reasonable' depends on the nature of the building and the money available).

The exact disabled toilet requirements (in the UK) depend on a variety of factors relating to the size and layout of your building. However, our discussion in part I should increase our motivation for making our churches accessible and be a driver towards a much higher standard of what we consider 'reasonable' than is required by law. Instead of 'getting away with' the minimum possible, we should try to provide amenities that are as thoroughly equipped and spacious as possible, placing the dignity and comfort of those with a physical disability as a top priority.

There are three categories of accessible toilets. The most basic is referred to as an 'ambulant accessible toilet' or 'enlarged cubicle', including things like variable-height toilet seat risers, lever taps/paddle flush, an outward-opening door, and grab rails. These toilets are useful for walking disabled people, but are not large enough for a wheelchair.

'Wheelchair-accessible toilets' are larger and should allow for a full turning circle for a wheelchair user to move around easily. They also include a lower basin and shelving for colostomy bag users, as well as an emergency assistance pull-cord located within reach of the toilet. Although accessible toilets provide enough space for wheelchair users to move around easily, they do require the wheelchair user to be able to transfer independently onto the toilet to be able to use it. Many wheelchair users in the UK will not be able to use an accessible toilet.

'Changing places toilets' are larger still; they include all the above, as well as a hoisting system and adult-sized changing bed and curtain. Toilet seat colours, automatic lighting, and Braille signage can be added to any of these three options to make the toilet facilities friendlier to those who are visually impaired.

It may be that you are not in a position to make these changes, such as if your group meets in a building you don't own or you have an old church building and limited funds.³ Why not put together a wish list, working from aspects you can control (such as the language used or print size on printed materials) and including a longer-term plan for how you hope to resolve other difficulties. Don't assume that changes are not possible within a listed building: both the Church of England and Historic England publish documents with many examples of innovative changes made to make listed buildings accessible without impacting their visual appearance.⁴

We will now consider a variety of conditions individuals may experience and think practically about how we can support and meet their needs. The first part of this chapter will centre around disabilities that affect someone's mobility. The second will focus around those disabilities that impair the senses (while recognising that there will inevitably be crossover for many).

MOBILITY
LOIS BUNYAN

Within any Christian community there will be some who encounter mobility issues. Sometimes these issues may be temporary – for example, when someone sustains a sport-related or accidental injury – while for others they may have a lifelong condition. Others may find their mobility decreasing over time, possibly because of an illness like multiple sclerosis (MS) or Parkinson's disease. We may have adults or children in our congregation whose mobility is affected by a physical disability. Here is the story of one boy and his family, told by his mother.

> ### DOROTHY'S STORY
>
> Our son has a life-limiting neuro-muscular condition called Duchenne muscular dystrophy. It's a progressive condition, meaning his muscles will get weaker as he gets older, to the point of paralysis. It affects all the muscles in his arms and legs and as a result at the age of 10 he is no longer able to walk and is dependent on a powered wheelchair. As he gets older, he will slowly lose the ability to move his arms. The muscles of breathing and the heart muscles are also affected and over time he will mostly likely need ventilation, first just at night and then 24/7. He

will also most likely face heart failure, and this is generally what limits life in Duchenne.

We don't know how many years we have with him on this earth, but it's not expected that he will live into his 30s. It is a brutal condition to watch, as slowly, rather than growing in independence, our child is growing in dependence, and activities that we take so much for granted are slowly robbed off him.

Duchenne not only affects our son's life, but it affects all our lives. As our time becomes more and more taken up with caring for our son, our time with our daughter is affected. Going out as a family can become a mission. Will there be disabled parking where we are going? Will we be able to get into the place we are going? Will there be an accessible toilet? Will there be things that our son can do? Nevermind the increasing list of equipment needed to go anywhere, particularly overnight. Talk about killing spontaneity!

How do we cope? Many times, we have said, 'We couldn't do this without Jesus!' What a joy it is to know he's in control of all things and he promises that for those who love him, he is working all this for our good. Not only that but he's done something about the mess of this world. At the cross the Lord Jesus took the curse of this broken world so that he can offer resurrection hope to all who trust him: a wonderful hope of resurrection life in the new creation, where there is no more need for wheelchairs or disabled-parking bays, and where our son who knows and loves our Saviour will be in his presence forevermore running and jumping with abandon!

However, even with this wonderful hope, it's tough!

How can the church help? Don't shy away from lamenting with us as we struggle through day by day. Pray for us and grieve with us as we watch our precious boy decline and at the appropriate time, point us to the wonderful hope we have. Be sorrowful yet rejoicing with us (2 Corinthians 6:10).

Yes, please make access to the physical church possible, but inclusion is so much more than that. Think through how our son can be enabled to fully participate in the life of the church body. Not only serving him in that way, but allowing him to serve others. Paul in 1 Corinthians describes the church as a body with stronger and weaker parts, but that each part has a vital role to play. Allow him to play that role.

One way we see him serve others is by enthusiastically answering questions during the children's slot in the service or throwing himself into memory verses or quizzes at camp or at holiday Bible club. This encourages the other kids and challenges the adults. Although our son is getting weaker every day, it has been such a joy to see him grow stronger in his faith, which can often be witnessed in things that he says. The Lord uses the weak to shame the wise! Although none of this would happen if our son wasn't allowed to fully participate in all these activities.

However, my husband and I have had the great privilege to be in full-time ministry, my husband as the church pastor and I help with children's work, etc. We are leaders on a Christian camp for children and teenagers. This has meant that we've been able to adapt activities ourselves to fully include him or be there to help others see what can be done to make it possible for our son to join in. Not everyone is as blessed as this!

If you are a leader of any of these activities, first chat to the parents of the children in the group with additional needs. Ask them what would help or ask them for ideas on how to adapt activities to make them accessible for their child. You'll find they know their child and their needs best and are constantly adapting how they do things to 'make it work'!

Make sure the Sunday school room/camp or holiday club venue is accessible and has accessible toilets, etc. When doing craft, is there room for a wheelchair to pull up to a table? Are the materials all within reach? Does the child need adapted scissors or pens? Do the children all sit on the floor? Would chairs make it more accessible? What about games? How can they be included? Is there a role in the game which doesn't involve running around? One example is chair ball where the 'nets' are two people seated with buckets who catch the ball on opposite ends of the hall. For any sort of hunt (e.g. an Easter egg hunt), put the items at waist level (on windowsills, etc.) or provide a litter picker for those who need one. It may also help if parents or leaders encourage their children to think about the interests of others so that they are more willing to play games that include those with disability, rather than just football!

There are many ways the church family can bless a family like ours, such as looking after our daughter or cooking us a meal when we need to be at medical appointments with our son, sometimes four hours away. We have been so blessed by Christian friends who have come and stayed with us so that we can all spend time together in an environment that means our son is fully included. We've been blessed by friends coming to stay in the house once our son is in bed so that we as a couple can get out and get some time together. One Christian friend has taken our daughter out once a month and spent time with her having a hot chocolate. It gives her a chance to chat about how things are for her and to do something not affected by her brother's disability. If you ever wanted to show hospitality to us and don't have an accessible house, you'd be very welcome to bring the dinner to us and eat it with us!

DIFFERENT WAYS MOBILITY MAY BE AFFECTED

For some, *fine motor skills* are affected: this can make simple activities that one often takes for granted more difficult – for example, turning the pages of a Bible, writing, or helping yourself to a cup of tea or coffee. When supporting an individual who has difficulty with fine motor activities, it is important to ask if they would like support rather than just assuming and taking over. It may be okay for a task to take a little longer if it encourages someone's independence and sense of dignity and achievement. We can ask, 'Can I get you a cup of coffee?' or, 'Would you like to share my Bible?' rather than stating, 'I'll go get you a coffee,' or forcing assistance on someone. Try to communicate that you are ready and willing to support should help be required, while not overwhelming an individual and taking over in a way that might leave them feeling upset or useless.

For others, their *gross motor skills* are affected. This makes whole body movements hard, such as walking, jumping, or running. At the extreme end, someone may have *paralysis*, where movement and/or feeling in some or all of one's body is lost entirely (for reference – quadriplegia is when the upper spinal cord is damaged, affecting all four limbs and the torso, while people with damage lower down the spinal cord are referred to as paraplegic). Where movement is affected, it is common for tools and aids to be in place, such as walking sticks, mobility scooters, wheelchairs, or walkers. Ensure there is sufficient space and storage for such tools and aids in your meeting place and designated seating with extra room for those who need it. Consider activities such as Communion or prayer ministry – can we adapt these activities in a way which requires minimal movement for those with mobility issues?

It is also worth briefly mentioning some etiquette around mobility aids: many long-term disabled people see them as something akin to an extension of their body. It is not rude to look at them, but it is usually considered rude to touch or move these aids without explicit permission, just as we wouldn't pick someone up without asking them first.

Let me tell you about my friend Merryn. When Merryn was 18, she travelled from her hometown in Cornwall to London for an audition to study music at university. On the train home, she randomly suffered a spinal bleed, which left her quadriplegic. She was transferred to the spinal unit in my hometown (as it was the best and largest in the south-west of the UK). Some friends at her church knew of my local youth worker, who went to visit her a few times and then introduced her to my friend Grace and me. We soon became good friends. Grace and I went in to visit her at the spinal unit weekly throughout her rehabilitation. We bonded over talking about our celebrity crushes, teenage heartbreaks, Taylor Swift, and eating meatball marinara from the local Subway. We prayed together on occasion and as Merryn's rehabilitation progressed, we were able to meet her at the hospital bus stop and travel on the bus together to church.

That youth leader did not do anything groundbreaking, but he knew that Merryn had lost her home, church, school, and friends, and he knew that she was living far away from her family (all before you even begin to comprehend the grief of losing control of your body and dreams for the future). So that youth worker did his best to bring these things to her.

No two examples are identical, and we will know individuals with different lives and needs. However, the principle is the same. Just as Jesus, in the gospels, actively seeks out and spends time with disabled and unwell people, we should go out of our way to support our friends with mobility issues. We should actively look for ways to allow them to be a part of our Christian communities – adapting the building you meet in, changing the location of the church lunch or picnic, offering lifts to those who need it, or making pastoral visits to people's homes. This cannot and should not be done entirely by the ministry team – this is something every member of the church can be involved in.

Brain injury and strokes affect everybody differently. People who have suffered a brain injury may experience problems with their mobility, communication, cognition and memory, fatigue, and emotional health and well-being. Brain injury can occur through a variety of causes, including trauma to the head or illnesses such as meningitis. One common cause of brain injury is a stroke, where a disruption to the blood supply causes long-term injury. Brain injury is often sudden, and can completely change an individual or a family's life in an instant. There is great pastoral need to minister to individuals and loved ones under such circumstances. Friends and church family will need to draw round to support them through the grief of losing the life or skills and abilities they once had, to walk alongside them as they process and accept what life now looks like and to point them to how God might be calling them to serve now.

I was privileged to be put in contact (via the charity Through the Roof) with Louise and hear her story and her experiences of developing a brain injury, after an infection in her gut went undiagnosed for a long time and sadly spread to her brain. She spoke of how, in the early days, she found it very difficult to accept the impact that the infection had caused and the resultant brain injury and eye conditions. She was overwhelmed by grief for the healthy body and active lifestyle she once had and struggled profoundly with her mental health as a result.

In her Christian journey, she spent over 20 years seeking and pursuing physical healing, encouraged by well-meaning Christians who wanted to see her physically and mentally healed and returned to the life she once knew. However, in more recent years she has come to understand and accept her brain injury, largely through the contact and support of the charity Headway, who work nationally to support people suffering with brain injuries and their families. They have put her in contact with others who have had similar experiences, provided her with a key worker (who has become a great friend), and helped her to build strategies to support her. These include managing her fatigue and memory loss, as well as suggesting solutions for everyday tasks that she was finding difficult.

This, alongside the love and support of friends at church, has made a big impact to her spiritual walk. She has realised that God is her strength, and he wants to use her, just as she is now, to grow and serve his kingdom. This transformation has given Louise new confidence to serve at her local church; she plays the ukulele in the worship band, helps to administer Communion, and now uses the extra moments of time she has in her week (she is no longer working) to focus on building and deepening relationships. She says her prayer life has been transformed, realising the power of prayer and the privilege to have periods of time resting in which she can commit to lifting others up in prayer. She spoke of how her experiences have given her new empathy to walk alongside others who have suffered and point them to Jesus.

You are likely to encounter individuals with *chronic fatigue syndrome* or myalgic encephalomyelitis (ME). This is a long-term condition, affecting different parts of the body, but causing extreme tiredness. While the cause is unknown, the experience of someone with ME/CFS is real – they are not simply being lazy or need a bit more sleep. ME/CFS can affect anyone, including children, and can result in such extreme tiredness that the individual is temporarily unable to walk and may need a wheelchair. It is important not to make assumptions if we see someone using a wheelchair one day and not the next – they are not necessarily 'getting better', but may have better and worse days.

ME/CFS often affects those who have been extremely active and busy, meaning that groups and churches will need to be thoughtful about reducing responsibilities, without removing opportunities to serve or experience fellowship altogether. If someone is unable to leave their house, arranging with other friends to take turns to visit them and perhaps watch part of a church service together online, can be a great help in an otherwise bleak time. This condition has become even more common recently, with a large number of people suffering from long COVID, a form of chronic fatigue. This is the case for Lis, who shared her story with us.

LIS' STORY

I am 55 years old, married to Ian. The COVID infection came to our village in January 2020, though no one knew what it was then. Both Ian and I got it – Ian got better in 6–8 weeks, but I contracted long COVID; at the time, it was simply called post-viral fatigue.

I found myself having to use a wheelchair to get about, and with a near-constant brain fog. With long COVID, you have to make your week work for you; work out what will fit in, what the priority is. For example, if I want to meet up with a friend, I will deliberately leave time to sleep for some of that day to prepare, then leave my diary empty for two days afterwards to allow myself time to recover. It took time, initially, to work out what it meant in reality. I can't stand: COVID has affected my nervous system, leaving me with PoTS (postural tachycardia syndrome, which means that the automatic nervous system is no longer able to compensate for changes in posture by balancing heart rate and blood pressure). I get about with walking sticks and frames at home and a wheelchair elsewhere. I am not able to work or do the charitable work I had done previously. I find it hard to be out and about.

We live in a small village and were attending a little evangelical church, which has steps up to the church. Before my PoTS diagnosis, I tried to walk up the steps, but eventually the doctors decided that I needed to use the wheelchair outside the house. This raised the question of whether the church would spend £100 on a portable ramp for me. There was a wheelchair-accessible entrance, but it was via a back path with nettles, which was unlit, so it couldn't be used in the evenings. You needed to knock for someone to let you in. However, because they had that, they felt that their church was accessible enough. It was particularly awkward because the most recent accounts had shown a relatively large sum of money unused from the previous year. Eventually, we decided to move to a bigger church, which had recently done a big building project to make the church fully accessible with ramps, lifts, and disabled toilets. They also have online services (live-streamed), so I can join in when I'm too tired to attend in person.

I have experienced the transition from being very involved in church – running a charity, tutoring, preaching, leading worship, running a house group, serving in various committees – to not doing any of that now. For the first year, I was asking, 'Lord, what am I doing?', though not 'Why me?'; I knew God was journeying with me through it. I would listen to the radio, but felt isolated. It was hard for Ian, who suffers from some mental health problems of his own, to attend church without me. As we're still fairly new to our church, we are just getting to know the people there. It is isolating and scary – you can feel you have no purpose, you have no worth. You have to do mental gymnastics to remove the sense of failure, guilt, and lack of self-esteem. I wouldn't have thought it was part of my sense of self-esteem, but I realised that I took a lot of pride in being able to do these things, I loved doing these things, I felt called to do them. However, I've recently got to the point of being able to accept that I'll never be the same as I was, and pass on some of the materials from my charitable work to others.

Our daughter got married last year, so we invited old school friends and friends from our old city to the wedding. Sixteen of us ended up staying together in a house at the wedding venue. It was a healing, invigorating, restorative experience. I met face to face with people I hadn't seen for a long time, and they were supportive. I was able to say, 'I'm alright where I'm at. It might not be where I wanted to be, but I'm alright.' We sat together on the Sunday to pray and sing together. This moment felt like a taste of heaven, a moment I'll never forget.

We have recently joined a Through the Roof 'Together at Home' Bible study, which meets online twice a month. It has been a good opportunity to meet people with similar experiences. You can just join, you don't need to contribute, which is great when you're feeling exhausted. Ian and I led the last one together. I slept for seven hours afterwards and took four days to recover, but it felt really good.

We're also seeing opportunities to serve our church: we're hoping to share some of the work of Through the Roof at an event. The minister has also asked us both to put together an article about faith as someone with a disability. We've also had the opportunity to have lots of conversations, particularly with other people with long COVID.

We're in a partnership with Jesus – we can't just make something happen and see if Jesus blesses it. We have to be open to him challenging us or saying, 'Not yet.' That's where we are at. I hope I'm behaving like an ox, sharing a yoke with Jesus; I don't need to push or pull, but to respond to Jesus' calling.

To others with disabilities, I would say: you need your voices around you, people who can talk even if you can't. Grab your allies, use their voices. Be clear about what you need in order to be involved.

UNSEEN PHYSICAL DISABILITIES

There will also be a whole range of disabilities which won't be visible from the outside – no mobility aids or special equipment to make them obvious but still causing daily challenges to individuals. Ideally, an accessible toilet should be set up to enable someone with a stoma to change their bag;

a clean shelf, bin within the toilet cubicle, and full-length mirror make this a much easier process. This is just one example; other conditions which affect someone physically but are not immediately obvious include endometriosis, epilepsy, diabetes, functional neurological disorder, irritable bowel disease, lupus, haemophilia, and many more. Some of these will be managed by the individual with relatively few adaptations needed, while others may require more support. Without being intrusive, try to find out how someone could be supported. Don't judge them when they are less reliable in attendance or seem to leave the group frequently. Not everyone using an accessible toilet or parking space will have a disability which is visible from the outside; this does not make their need any smaller.

ANN'S STORY

I was diagnosed with ulcerative colitis (UC) at the age of 23. UC is one of several inflammatory bowel diseases. These are different to irritable bowel syndrome, although sometimes there can be similar symptoms. UC is an autoimmune disease where the person's immune system attacks the cells in the bowel – essentially my own immune system is trying to kill me! The main symptoms are bowel pain and urgency, but like many UC sufferers, I also have regular joint pain from inflammation and extreme fatigue.

Although I was diagnosed in my 20s, I had been ill throughout my secondary school life, passing from doctor to doctor who could not explain my symptoms. The result is that I became isolated and stopped going to church and my youth group. The mental toll of building up the courage to leave the house, knowing that I might not get to a toilet in time and have an accident, was too much for me and I developed some significant mental health issues. At that time my church's toilet facilities were limited and only accessible through the crèche. Opening the doors during a service was very noisy and everyone in the congregation would look to see what was going on. Frankly, it was embarrassing and humiliating for a teenager, and I couldn't face it any more.

While at university in London, I found it difficult to fit in at church. Without a diagnosis, people can be dismissive of your symptoms, and I would urge all Christians to look out for those in a congregation who appear to be finding it difficult to integrate. The Christians I made friends with were those who were understanding and willing to have chats in smaller groups away from the crowds. They weren't pushy for me to join in with everything, and were genuinely pleased to see me when I was able to make it.

When I left London, finding a suitable church for my husband and me was difficult. Negative experiences included people practically jumping on me as I walked through the door and insisting on me being involved in everything, which made me feel really uncomfortable. A senior pastor at a church chose to share my new diagnosis with someone else without my permission, and indeed incorrectly relayed the condition that I had. This was particularly difficult for me to accept, as I was dealing with the bombshell of my new diagnosis. It made me very untrusting of telling other people, so if you are told about a disability or illness, make sure you know the person's wishes on whether they want that information shared, and who with, and always make sure you have your facts right.

It has taken me a long time to settle into our current church, but for the first time in my whole life, I finally feel like I am part of a church family who love me and accept me for who I am. I don't worry about what people will think if I do not turn up, and a seat is always arranged at the back for me so that I can get out to the toilet when needed. No one questions me if I go out for some fresh air when I feel overwhelmed, and the online streamed service means that when I feel too ill, I can still watch from home or just listen if I am too tired to open my eyes. My minister has been particularly supportive, meeting with my husband and me on our own when I have found things difficult in my walk with Jesus.

It's important to say that there are still some very difficult times. Knowing that I am not judged for this by my church family is very important to me. My minister has also helped me to recognise that my job as a secondary school teacher has enabled me to support teenagers struggling with physical and mental challenges with far more discernment and Christian love than any other staff member can offer, and we have been able to use my teaching skills within the youth and adult ministry at our church.

One thread which came out in many of the stories we heard was the benefit of live-streaming, or at least recorded services available online. While there can be a danger of live-streaming leading to church members feeling uncommitted to one another on a personal level, it offers a wonderful solution for those who would love to be with us in person but are not able to be there every week. We can find ways of making this experience as personal as possible and work on in-person relationships beyond the Sunday service. It might be possible for someone from the church to visit an individual's home and watch the live-stream with them each week or for someone to visit regularly during the week.

Often, people with disabilities have family members caring for them: a spouse, parents, or their children. It is enormously helpful to be aware of these people who are shouldering this additional responsibility and supporting them where needed. A group of friends could agree a rota of evenings to allow parents an evening out. A family in church could draw alongside a young carer to offer some of the experiences he or she may miss out on due to caring for a disabled parent: going ice-skating, for a country walk, or simply having a guilt-free rest. Asking a spouse adjusting to caring for their disabled husband or wife how they can best be supported can make a huge difference.

DIFFERENCES IN SIGHT OR HEARING
CLAIRE WOOD

Some physical differences particularly affect the senses, such as vision and hearing impairments. Sight and hearing differences happen for a wide range of reasons – they may be genetic, the result of injury or illness in childhood, or due to old age. Not everyone's experience of hearing or vision difficulties will be the same; some may see shapes or hear some sounds, while others may see and hear nothing. Vision difficulties may be particularly associated with low light conditions or periphery vision. Hearing difficulties do not necessarily mean that an individual can hear nothing. Someone who has experienced low or no vision or hearing for the majority of their life is likely to be managing in a completely different way from those experiencing the degeneration of sight or hearing which frequently comes with old age, so we will explore the latter separately in the following chapter, though many accommodations could be relevant to both groups.

SIGHT

If you are blind or partially sighted, your experience of church may be very different from that of others in the congregation.

Entering a space for the first time can be difficult, whether you use a cane or rely on limited vision. The welcoming smile may not be visible and the route to enter the building may not be obvious. Maybe the space is familiar, but you enter a room of people chatting without being able to see any faces.

The service progresses, relying on song and liturgy words projected onto a screen, often with moving images behind the words, making them impossible for partially sighted people to read. Again, the talk relies on projected images to illustrate the points; the pastor assumes that everyone can see them and so uses them without describing their content. The Bibles are printed in tiny font on thin pages, and even large-print Bibles are usually only 12-point font, hardly large enough for someone with significant visual impairment to use. The mood lighting used to illuminate the building only contributes to your challenges.

After the meeting, children are milling around underfoot, making getting a cup of tea a precarious process. Even when someone comes over to chat to you, you may not be entirely sure who they are at first, making conversation more challenging. You long to participate fully, but end up slipping out early, tripping over the pile of buggies parked by the door as you do so.

During the week, it can be hard to get to other events: perhaps the newsletter explaining activities is only available as a printed piece of paper, so you don't know what's running unless you can find someone to read it to you. Attending midweek groups may be equally challenging. Following a conversation when you cannot see faces, especially one where people are likely to speak across one another, is very difficult. It is hard to know whether you are interrupting other people as you cannot clearly see the body language others use to show that they are about to speak.

While it's good to realise the challenges someone with reduced vision may experience, it is also important not to underestimate their capabilities. Especially when people have been blind or partially sighted their whole lives, they are usually able to do normal jobs, parent their children, get around, and negotiate life. They may use technology like text-to-speech readers for computers and phones, audio labellers, and magnifiers. Guide dogs and canes can allow blind people to get around safely. Not only this, but their practised reliance on other senses allows them to gain a lot of information about their environment which sighted people might miss. There is even evidence that non-visual senses are actually enhanced in those who have become blind before the age of three.[5] It is therefore important not to have preconceptions about what visually impaired people will or won't be able to do.

While those who are blind or partially sighted are likely to operate well in familiar environments, the challenges of negotiating a new environment may put them off coming to church. The ways in which Christians can support those in their church communities with visual impairments are varied.

Some support will be at an organisational level: notices delivered orally or via email (which can then be read via adaptive technology); high-contrast words and text on screens, without moving backgrounds; having large-print handouts or a digital device/tablet with the passage or song words available; changes to the building such as contrast strips on stairs and railings; pictures used as illustrations being verbally described.

Other changes are more of a cultural shift. Every Christian can be involved in making their group a friendly place for someone with a visual impairment. We can greet them verbally – not just with a wave and a smile, but a clear greeting. If we see someone we think may need help, we can ask what kind of help is needed. In this situation, we can introduce ourselves (rather than assuming they will recognise our voice) and talk directly to the individual. If they have a guide dog, approach them or walk on the side away from the dog (to avoid distracting the dog).

Some people with visual impairments may wish to be guided verbally: explaining which way to turn from their perspective or what hazards might be ahead of them. Others may be happy for you to offer your arm or have them place a hand on your shoulder. When guiding, always explain what you are doing as you go, and ask permission if you are going to touch any part of their body. You can tell the individual about any steps or turns as you approach them, and which way doors open. Maybe you're guiding someone to a seat in the church; if so, place their hand on the back of the seat before they sit down, so that they can work out where they are. Even if you're in a rush, don't walk away without telling the person first, as they may not realise you have gone.

If you have a blind or partially sighted person in a smaller group with you, it is helpful if everyone can say their name aloud at the beginning of the conversation, so that their positions around the room are clear for the rest of the conversation. If you bring over a hot drink, make sure you tell them where you're putting it. They may need help to find their coat when they leave the meeting.

For churches seeking extra support in being a 'sight-loss friendly church', the Torch Trust[6] runs training and keeps a database of churches committed to welcoming those with vision impairments well.

CHICH'S STORY

I was born and grew up in South Africa. I have been ordained now for over 45 years, half of that being in South Africa and half in the UK. My wife, Gill, and I came to the UK in 2000; we thought it would be for only a couple of years, but our daughters followed and we are still here. I served in two parishes in the Manchester diocese before retirement, and it was at the time of transition between the parishes that my story begins.

In April 2008 I began to lose eyesight in my left eye, and nobody could figure out what was happening, especially as the eye itself appeared normal. The ophthalmologist did many tests, but nothing showed up. At the end of the year I felt a change of ministry would be right, probably a 'God-incidence' as I look back. In early January 2009 I went for an interview for the new post and wondered that day if the right eye was quite okay. I was appointed to the post and then came three traumatic weeks. A new indication in the original eye led to a special DNA blood test, which revealed a rare genetic condition. It is one that shows up in younger men, and I consider myself fortunate to have had normal eyesight up into my 60s. The right eye deteriorated much faster, and by the end of the month I had been registered blind. The condition is non-degenerative, and has stayed static for 15 years. It should not get worse, unless another condition appears. I have hazy peripheral vision, but no centre vision, so I can see shapes and outlines, but no detail. That put an end to reading words or music and driving.

Every five minutes someone is declared blind in the UK. Over 90% of those registered blind have some slight degree of sight, so if someone using a white cane, as I do, seems to show some degree of vision, it does not mean that they are trying to deceive. My cane is essential in unfamiliar areas.

I was appointed to a new parish with eyesight, and arrived in ministry blind. I had to adapt very quickly, especially as to how to read aloud long passages of scripture or liturgy without knowing Braille. There is amazing technology available: I speak from a full text (rather than notes), listening to the text as I speak it aloud.

I can't take a service at the last minute if it involves reading. Time is needed for preparation. If I am prepared, the conducting of worship is more straightforward, as I am in charge. It is before and especially after the service that life is more challenging. At coffee time after the service, I can't recognise people, and I can't detect body language between people to know whether to join them or not. If there is a buffet afterwards, and no one to help, goodness knows what I am putting on my plate. I know my way around my own church, so that is not a problem for me. But what about the blind or partially sighted person who comes to a new church for the first time?

Before my eyesight loss, I thought all that was needed in church was a disabled ramp for wheelchair users and a loop system for those hard of hearing. I feel ashamed when I think of the small-print leaflets I produced to get as many words onto a page as possible, with no thought about those losing eyesight.

I know a young man who sings in a cathedral choir. He reads Braille music, but is also given service details ahead of time so he can participate fully. Obviously there are some things a blind person cannot do, such as anything involving driving, but there is a lot more that person can do than others might assume. Never make assumptions. I was previously involved in race awareness training in the diocese, and the leaders assumed that I would have to stop being involved after I lost my eyesight. Not true. I remained involved even beyond retirement.

HEARING

We will use the capitalised 'Deaf' to refer to the whole Deaf community, including hearing members: d/Deaf is a commonly used abbreviation to cover both the Deaf community and other deaf individuals.

People who have been deaf or hard of hearing all their lives will have developed different strategies for communication from those whose hearing has degenerated in old age. Some will be proficient lip-readers, and many will use BSL (British Sign Language) as their first language. The Deaf community includes both deaf people and others who speak BSL, such as children of deaf adults (CODAs). They have their own culture, including ways of getting one another's attention, shared jokes, and patterns of behaviour.

Many Deaf people would prefer to be seen as a minority group rather than within the framework of disability, but whichever lens we use, the Deaf community (like any other) is a group of people in need of the gospel. There are some churches that worship entirely in BSL, as well as many churches with BSL interpreters. The process of translating the Bible into BSL is still in its early stages, meaning that members of the Deaf community are still without a full Bible in their first language. Those who use BSL as their first language, even if they are also able to read and write in English, often find English word order confusing and slower to process. However, some deaf or hearing-impaired people do not see deafness as a primary identity, particularly if they have been born to hearing parents. They may not be fluent in BSL, but may have developed other ways of communicating, such as lip-reading or using hearing aids or cochlear implants.

While a d/Deaf adult may have the ability to choose to attend a Deaf church, this is not a reason to avoid considering ways to make our churches deaf-friendly. Families with both deaf and hearing members should not have to attend different churches, and the relatively small number of churches conducting services only in BSL means that many do not have one nearby.

When we meet someone who is deaf, we can use gestures and speak clearly. Show them that they are welcome. Ask them if they can lip-read, pointing to your lips and using short phrases. If they still do not understand, write your message. Staying with someone and offering to sit with them and have a drink together can be a way of making someone feel welcome even if you are not able to communicate much with one another. If the individual asks for an interpreter, there are Christian organisations[7] to help you find an interpreter for the next time they visit the church. If possible, they should be a qualified interpreter, not just a member of your church who knows a bit of sign language, to allow for clear communication. Alternatively, you may choose to employ an interpreter for a special event or one-off meeting. If the individual wants to be a member of your church, why not raise money to pay for a regular BSL interpreter? Not only will this allow this one person to know they belong in your community, but it will also open the door to others exploring Christianity who may previously have been unable to access your services.

Prayers for healing have been discussed in chapter 4. We know that Jesus healed deaf people in the Bible, enabling them to be reinstated to community in a context in which deafness was a barrier to the majority of life. In contemporary culture, many of these barriers have been removed, and so many deaf people do not consider themselves to be disabled. They may be surprised or even insulted if you assume they want prayers for their healing.

MIRIAM'S STORY

I was diagnosed as partially deaf at age 7, and I had my first hearing aids then. Over the years my level of deafness has worsened – I now wear two hearing aids. There is deafness in the family (although I am the only one who uses sign language), so there is a strong chance that my deafness is hereditary.

I attended schools for Deaf children from the age of 10 and having lots of Deaf friends and peers has enabled me to develop a strong sense of Deaf identity – I'm not ashamed of my deafness and enjoy using BSL (British Sign Language). I became a Christian at 13 years of age and started regular church attendance then. Over the years, as my deafness has worsened, I have found following church services has become more difficult, and now rely fully on BSL interpreters/communicators.

Church provision for Deaf and hard of hearing people has improved over the years – e.g. installing (and advertising) induction loop systems which link up with the appropriate setting on hearing aids, and providing BSL interpreters for church meetings. My own church has a BSL interpreter every Sunday morning, who is funded by the church.

> I feel very blessed. My church has also provided basic BSL courses for members who were interested.
>
> As I wasn't born deaf, I can communicate one-to-one easily with hearing friends in church. However, my profoundly Deaf friends experience greater barriers. Involvement in group activities can be hard, due to lack of communication support. People who can't use BSL tend to either stay away from Deaf people or just have very superficial conversations, making friendship-building difficult. They may 'push' Deaf people to develop only a tight small circle of friendships. Other Deaf people may have to travel some distance to find a Deaf-friendly church. There is also the challenge of insufficient funding for all meetings to have a BSL interpreter, and it can be hard to find Christian BSL interpreters/signers to cover all church services.
>
> Churches wanting to help me and other Deaf people can provide BSL interpreters at all church meetings or as much as funding allows. There can be reserved seating in the front row with good lighting. Where appropriate, Deaf people should be involved in church services.
>
> In my church, I have been involved in arranging basic BSL courses (including a bit of teaching myself), and arranging BSL interpreters for our Sunday meetings. I have also organised and led a monthly meeting for Deaf people to provide teaching, discussions, etc. for the local Deaf community.

As mentioned earlier, sight and hearing loss due to old age is also covered in the following chapter, though many of the accommodations mentioned above will be applicable to both groups.

You may be feeling somewhat overwhelmed by the number of possible conditions to consider. You want to love those with additional needs and disabilities, but it all sounds so complicated. We want to encourage you to keep going! Each chapter will have practical tips which anyone can try. Why not pick one and pray that God would help you make this change?

TOP 10 FOR EVERYONE

1. Keep your church's accessible toilet clear of clutter so a wheelchair can actually get in there. If you see the alarm cord looped out of reach, put it back where it should be.

2. Keep an eye out for people with mobility difficulties before the service and offer them a cup of tea or help moving a chair if needed. Putting out a table with space for wheelchairs can be a great way of promoting conversation at eye-level.

3. Allow people agency and independence in your offers of assistance. Ask, don't assume.

4. Be respectful of disabled people's space and mobility equipment.

5. If speaking to a blind person: tell them your name first and let them know when you are leaving.

6. Sit with someone and be friendly, even if you are not able to communicate much with them.

7. Learn a few signs in BSL so that you can greet those who use this language. The BSL fingerspelling alphabet is easy to learn and could allow you to communicate in a limited way.

8. If guiding a visually impaired person: take time to find out how they want to be helped.

9. Offer to read/describe things out loud if someone can't see them.

10. Be careful not to overemphasise prayers for physical healing, making it seem more important than other ways God is glorified through your friend with a disability.

⑥
Age-related disabilities and impairments

LOIS BUNYAN

In recent years, I have started to spot a few grey hairs appearing on my head and the first signs of wrinkles on my face. I have been reassuring myself that these changes in my physical appearance are just the outward evidence of life experienced, lessons learned, and wisdom gained and shared. This is not only wishful thinking to soften the blow of my youthfulness gradually evaporating: we read in Proverbs 20:29 that 'the glory of young men is their strength, grey hair the splendour of the old'.

Nowhere has this been more evident to me than on a summer camp my husband and I run for young people aged 13–16 each August. As part of the camp, we have a young leaders' programme that encourages 17–21-year-olds to serve on camp, by giving them additional input and mentoring throughout the week. This programme has been increasingly successful in recent years since Ruth, a godly friend of ours, has come onboard to help lead it. Ruth is in her 70s and has three daughters and an army of grandchildren. She has known and loved the Lord for a long time now, and she has many insights and helpful wisdom to share about what it means to live a faithful, gospel-hearted life, continuing in Christ. I am utterly convinced that this is what makes her one of the best people to equip and support our young leaders on camps. The diversity of Christ's body, the church, is beautiful, and a massive strength of that diversity is our varying ages and lived experiences.

The Church of England statistics for 2022 show that 35.6% of regular church attendees are aged 70 or above.[1] If we assume a similar picture across all church denominations in the UK, then it is important to consider the ageing population of our Christian communities. While many aspects of ageing are beautiful, it can also be very hard. The results of the fall of Genesis 3 cause our bodies to decay, to become worn out and stop working as they once did. Frailty and suffering sadly come hand in hand with old age, and this means that old age can be a difficult and lonely time for many. In old age, it is common for people to experience mobility issues and hearing loss and to lose their sight. Daily tasks which were once second nature become challenging or need to be done by others. For example, in the UK, 4% of adults aged 41–60 have disabling hearing loss, whereas the rate increases to 80% of adults over 70.[2] Since many factors may come together with age, we will consider this category with a wider lens, bearing in mind the challenges and joys of our ageing bodies.

HEARING AND SIGHT LOSS

Some of the most common age-related disabilities and difficulties are hearing loss and visual impairment. Some of the tools suggested in the previous chapter will be relevant here, but many will not, as someone experiencing hearing or sight loss due to old age is less likely to have learnt British Sign Language (BSL) or Braille or become familiar with some of the adaptive technology available.

There are some practical resources and tools churches and Christian groups can have on hand to aid those who are struggling with age-related sight and hearing loss, such as large-print service sheets and printouts of the Bible passages for the service or session. Chairs with arms provide added support to an older person experiencing vision loss, allowing them to feel for the chair more easily when sitting or standing. Evening meetings can be a challenge to older people for a number of reasons, but one of these may be because of poor eyesight. Older people who are still able to drive in the day may be unable to see well enough to drive at night. Putting on lunch clubs and daytime opportunities to gather may be helpful, or offering a lift may solve their difficulties. None of this is rocket science, but it will make a big difference to someone's experience of church.

For those planning activities, it is important to ensure that there is an induction loop system for hearing-aid users and that there are transcripts of talks available and subtitles on any videos that are used. There are some limitations to loops: they may only work in some parts of the building, and they only pick up voices speaking into microphones. Be aware of these limitations when planning. This isn't just a consideration for those planning activities, however. We will all have been in the situation where we are talking to someone who is unable to hear us properly, often due to age-related hearing loss. This is exacerbated by noisy rooms, which make reliance on a hearing aid (which amplifies all sounds equally) problematic. We can be patient when conversations appear to take unexpected directions, and offer to continue the conversation further away from other people if possible. Older people with hearing loss may feel a bit on the edge of things, but often have great wisdom to impart, so often being ready to listen to them without necessarily being able to have a two-way conversation is mutually beneficial.

MOBILITY CHALLENGES

Another common way in which older people can become disabled is through loss of mobility. Older people may become less steady on their feet, relying on walking frames to help them walk longer distances. They may have less stamina for getting around than they once did. Many experience or fear a fall, which can have further negative consequences due to the loss of strength during time spent recovering. While equipping our buildings for wheelchair access may be the realm of trustees and buildings committees, everyone can be involved in helping older people with reduced mobility to get about. We can offer lifts, carry bags, bring cups of coffee, or go and sit with someone after the service rather than expecting them to come and stand somewhere else.

In British culture, it is often the case that older people, brought up in a generation much less willing to make demands on others, will not advocate for their own needs. One person shared with me that they were struggling to walk to church, but would not necessarily have felt able to ask for a lift there, so felt blessed when someone said they were 'passing her front door anyway' and would stop by to pick her up. Knowing this is the case, we can be proactive in asking how people are, and whether there are any changes which would help them get to church or midweek groups.

Meals can often be a lifeline for older people: decreased appetite, perhaps combined with the challenge of cooking for one, may mean that they struggle to motivate themselves to cook. Chatting to her grandmother, Claire heard how a meal rota organised by individuals at her church had reminded her afresh of God's abundant generosity to us, not just giving us food but such a rich variety of different dishes. She told Claire how some of them were brought by people she didn't know well, and what a blessing it was to spend time in conversation with these people, sharing the 'little' things God was doing in her life. We have no doubt that this will have also blessed and encouraged her visitors in turn! She also valued people bringing her baked goods, which were hard for her to make in small enough quantities for herself.

We talked to one couple about their experience of Parkinson's, a condition which affects motor skills.

MIKE AND WENDY'S STORY

Mike: For me the biggest problem is balance and movement. Involuntary movement is embarrassing. I sit at the back of church for that reason, to not put others off.

Wendy: Yes, he finds it embarrassing for him, but other people don't really seem to mind. The church we go to is lovely – it's a witness to the Lord really.

Mike: I like that people accept me as I am and don't make extra arrangements for me, they treat me as a normal person. They are lovely and friendly. My son drives me to the men's breakfasts on the first Friday of the month. It's a chance of fellowship you don't get the rest of the time, especially living a bit away from the church and not being able to drive anymore. We get to church on a Sunday, but we can't be as involved.

Wendy: We've made friends with people who have come over to our home and had lunch with us. My daughter will also take us to see them. One young couple who have a one-year-old are particularly close friends, and happy to come to our house, which is much easier for us. At church, we often look after the one-year-old after the service, and it gives the parents freedom to mingle and know we are watching their little one.

We have carers coming in to put on Mike's stockings and they all know we are Christians. There's a Muslim carer, and he asked us about the difference between being a Musim and a Christian and we explained it to him. When he applied for a promotion, he asked us to pray for him because he said we get answers to our prayers! We also have a carer

> who was a Hindu, and he wanted to become a Christian. Every time he comes here he asks us for a verse to study, and he will come back and talk about it the next time he comes.

SERVING

It may be especially frustrating for someone who has served in a particular way for a long time, who may be very gifted in a certain area, to find that they are no longer able to serve as they once did. My grandfather was a very gifted preacher who worked for many years as a pastor and as the general secretary of the London City Mission. He found it incredibly hard when in his early 80s he had to stop preaching, not because his ability or desire to teach the Bible had changed, but because his vocal cords could no longer sustain the projection he needed to deliver a sermon. He continued to minister in the lives of his family and friends through his wisdom, prayers, and participation in Bible studies, but I know he found this transition extremely difficult. At times, he even felt hopeless and a little useless.

The diversity of Christ's church means that we each have areas of service that particularly interest us or at which we are gifted. Let's try to be sensitive to people's grief and feelings when the time comes for them to step back from serving in certain ways because of age-related disabilities or difficulties. Let's try our utmost to advise and help them to find other areas of church life to get involved in where they continue to feel valued, useful, and that their skills are being used well. We came across one lady who had previously been actively involved in many areas of service, but was struggling to feel part of things now that she had stepped down from most of these responsibilities. She was able to run the registration for the church's holiday club, sitting on the front desk to sign people in, which allowed her to continue to play a valuable role in a team which she had once led.

ISOLATION

By the time my grandfather was in his early 90s he was mostly housebound (due to poor vision and physical limitations in mobility); he had also lost my grandmother and was feeling very low and isolated. One of the things that really lifted his spirits was discovering TBN UK (a Christian television channel on Freeview). My grandfather belonged to the reformed tradition of the

Anglican Church; a lot of the content on the channel reflected a far broader spectrum of the local and international church than he was used to, but he was deeply encouraged by it. Not only did he have access to a wide variety of talks, sermons, and worship music, but it gave him a way to evangelise from his living room. Any visitors who came to the home or people who rang him on the phone were told about the wonderful ministry of TBN UK and how they could watch the channel when they got home. Some were even invited to watch it with him!

It is worth us considering how one's perspectives can change when unable to leave the home. When one is isolated suddenly, it can have a great impact not only on emotional and physical health, but also on spiritual health. When you are not seeing the fruit of gospel ministry in the lives of those around you because you cannot attend church or are unable to be involved in Christian groups or ministries, the encouragements of ministry may feel further away. One might be tempted to think there are not any encouragements and become disillusioned by it. Gathering with other Christians is extremely significant for fellowship and discipleship. We must therefore be creative in how we bring the gathering of believers to those who are unable to leave the home. This is something that has been hugely advanced with the normalisation of live-streaming services and video calls since the COVID-19 pandemic, but these may not be accessible for those with age-related sight or hearing loss. Pastoral visits can make a real difference in people's lives, a lifeline when their current experience of fellowship and teaching is sparse. These visits could include sharing Communion, reading the Bible aloud, and praying with one another. They could simply be an opportunity to discuss the work of the Spirit in their lives and the life of the church. There can sometimes be a tendency to think that these pastoral visits are solely the responsibility of clergy or church elders. However, the New Testament is full of instructions to every member of the church to serve and love each other, for example:

> You, my brothers and sisters, were called to be free. But do not use your freedom to indulge the flesh; rather, serve one another humbly in love.
> GALATIANS 5:13

> Do nothing out of selfish ambition or vain conceit. Rather, in humility value others above yourselves, not looking to your own interests but each of you to the interests of the others.
> PHILIPPIANS 2:3–4

The churches of Galatia and Philippi were being reminded to love one another and set their own needs to one side for different reasons. However, both groups – not just their leaders – are told to reject selfish desires in favour of love and humble service.

It is noteworthy that when the church was in its early days, even as we see the church meeting together daily and sharing as anyone had need (Acts 2:42–47), one of the first practical challenges which arose was around care for older people. We read in Acts 6 that the converts from a Greek background felt that Greek-background widows were not being looked after as well as the widows who were ethnically Jewish. The apostles take this seriously – they gather a meeting of all the Christians. They are practical about it – they realise that time taken to bring food to all the widows will take time out of their preaching and teaching ministry. They therefore appoint seven men 'known to be full of the Spirit and wisdom' to be responsible for the food distribution (Acts 6:3). The task is taken seriously, and the group of seven, who all have Greek names, are publicly commissioned for this important work of service.

Within the structure of Acts, these important practical considerations are given prominence. The section describing this challenge to the early church begins 'In those days when the number of disciples was increasing' (v. 1) and ends 'So the word of God spread. The number of disciples in Jerusalem increased rapidly' (v. 7). Growth both precipitates the need for practical provision, and practical provision enables further growth.

Some may fear an older person becoming too reliant on them as an individual, and shy away from adding an additional commitment to their already busy lives. If our churches have an organic culture of love and service towards one another, then this relational 'burden' is one that we can all bear together. If we are unable to visit due to our own work or family commitments, making time to go and speak to an older person in the church gathering is also appreciated. One person told us, 'I know I am precious to them when they ask how I'm doing.' She commented that they especially noticed that it was not just the women but also the men who took time to see how she was doing; she saw that the whole church, not just her friends, cared for her.

DEMENTIA

The World Health Organization describes dementia as 'a term for several diseases that affect memory, thinking, and the ability to perform daily activities'. It also states that it is currently the seventh leading cause of death and one of the major causes of disability among older people globally.[3] Alzheimer's disease is the most common cause of dementia.

Dementia is more common in women. It tends to affect those over the age of 65, although younger people may experience early-onset dementia. It is a progressive condition that will worsen over time; for some this happens slowly over many years, while for others the deterioration can happen much more suddenly.

The physical and cognitive impairments that an individual will experience because of the condition are now recognised as a disability under domestic law in the UK. Those suffering with dementia in the UK may be entitled to benefits such as PIP (Personal Independence Payments) or attendance allowance (for those over state pension age) to help support themselves and their families. Applications for state benefits can be challenging for both practical and psychological reasons and so an offer of assistance may be much appreciated.

Day-to-day memory loss, confusion, difficulties with concentrating and organising thoughts, and lack of awareness of where one is in one's space are all common symptoms for people living with dementia. Sometimes people with dementia experience hallucinations and heightened emotions or mood swings. These things make it difficult for a person with dementia to advocate for themselves, especially when it comes to medical appointments, arranging a care package, and claiming support and benefits. Be aware of those within your church with dementia, and ask if they would like someone to accompany them to appointments and assessments. Be conscious of those who live alone or who are isolated from family members, who may need extra support in the home or administrative help and emotional support to relocate to a residential care provision.

At church or your Christian group, a person with dementia may have difficulty understanding their surroundings, following the sermon or other aspects of the service, or following instructions such as turning to a passage in the Bible or coming forward for Communion. It would not be unusual for somebody with dementia to get up and walk around during a service or meeting. Familiar patterns and liturgy can be extremely helpful in a time of collective worship, as they are simple to follow and can help someone to reorientate themselves if they become lost in their surroundings or become confused. Think carefully about the music that is used. Music is a powerful tool, as it evokes past memories, emotions, and brings comfort to those who hear it, so old, familiar hymns can be of enormous benefit to those with dementia. It may even be worth asking if someone with dementia has a favourite hymn or prayer that you can include in your regular time of worship. Church services of less than half an hour are ideal for those with dementia to attend, and some churches choose to run extra services specifically with this need in mind. Ensure your meeting place is well lit (shadows can be confusing!) and there is not lots of outside or external noise that might be disorientating.[4]

One important practice in the life of the church which is likely to be familiar to those with dementia, feeding them spiritually long after they are able to articulate why, is Communion. Some people with dementia may need a spoon or easy-grip cup to support them to take Communion. Towards the latter stages of the disease, it is common for people to need care in a residential care provision or hospital. It is a real blessing if the church can bring Communion to them. Those who are near the end of life may not be able to swallow, so consider bringing a clean cloth to dip into the wine or a puréed substitute for the bread.

It can be difficult to care for someone with an age-related disability or difficulty, especially when that person is your parent. We can have grace and flexibility when someone's capacity changes due to increasing pressures of caring for an older relative. We can also intentionally make time to spend with them and be a listening ear and pray with them.

CAROLYN'S STORY

I sat down for a coffee and a chat with Carolyn, who spent many years supporting and caring for her mother with vascular dementia. She said the thing she found most difficult was the toll it took on her emotionally; she found it hard watching the deterioration in her mother's health and ability to look after herself. The toughest point was when she was no longer able to recognise Carolyn. She recalled another time when her mother was adjusting to a new care home and was struggling with this transition, which manifested in an angry outburst (this was very against her nature). Carolyn recalled feeling so overwhelmed she burst into tears in front of all her mother's carers.

I asked Carolyn how friends supported her through these emotional stresses. She said that it was enough for her that people at church knew about her mother's situation. She also said that it was brilliant when people asked open-ended questions, like 'How are things with your mum?' This gave her the option to go into detail on days when she felt able and wanted to chat and process all that was going on, but it was also vague enough that she did not feel pressured to talk on days where she was too overwhelmed and close to tears.

Carolyn's experience is such a helpful reminder of the impact disability can have not only on the individual but also on those close to them.

TOP 10 FOR EVERYONE

① Include both young and old people together in church ministries, so that those at every stage of life can serve each other.

② Think creatively about new areas of service for those stepping down from ministries they are no longer able to do.

③ Ask your church leaders to print out a large-print copy of the passage and songs. You could even offer to print this at home.

④ Chat to an older person in your church this week and find out how God is working in their life.

⑤ If you haven't seen an older person at church for a while, ask them what's making it hard for them to attend. It may be something you can solve.

⑥ If someone is struggling to make it to church, offer a lift, make plans to visit them, or phone them up instead.

⑦ Offer assistance (sensitively) with forms, hospital appointments, and practical needs like shopping and gardening.

⑧ If you cook a meal or bake cakes and have more than you need, consider putting together a 'meal for one' for someone living on their own.

⑨ Ask family members how things are going as they take on more care for their older relative.

⑩ Plan ways to communicate and stay in touch with those in residential homes, especially if they are no longer able to come to activities in the church building.

Learning disabilities

LOIS BUNYAN

'Learning disabilities' is a broad term that encompasses many different experiences and conditions. A learning disability is lifelong; it is not something that can be 'treated' or 'get better' with time, although with the right level of support an individual's quality of life can be considerably improved. Learning disabilities can present as mild, moderate, or severe, and each person's experience is unique. Mencap, a charity in the UK which campaigns and provides support for individuals with learning disabilities, has a helpful definition:

> A *learning disability* is a reduced intellectual ability and difficulty with everyday activities – for example household tasks, socialising or managing money – which affects someone for their whole life. People with a learning disability tend to take longer to learn and may need support to develop new skills, understand complicated information and interact with other people.[1]

The level of help and support that each person with a learning disability will need varies. For some whose learning disability is severe, they will almost certainly need help with all aspects of life – support in communicating, everyday tasks, and personal care. For others with a mild or moderate learning disability, they will need less support and live seemingly 'normal' lives. They may live with relatives or in supported living, they may need adjustments in school or the workplace, or help with finances.

Some people have profound and multiple learning disabilities (PMLD). This is when they have a severe learning disability and other physical impairments that hinder their sight, hearing, speech, or movement. People with PMLD are likely to need a high level of support from family and carers.

Sometimes people with a learning disability have a co-occurring condition, such as cerebral palsy or autism. However, it is important to remember that not all people with these conditions have a learning disability. Learning disabilities should not be confused with specific learning difficulties, such as dyslexia and dyspraxia – a learning difficulty will impact the way in which someone learns and processes information, but it does not impact their intellect, unlike learning disabilities. (Specific learning difficulties are covered in the following chapter.)

Learning disabilities can develop for a variety of reasons. Sometimes it is due to a chromosomal abnormality while a child is developing in the womb, occurring randomly or as the result of genetics. Down syndrome is a well-known example of this. In other cases, it can be due to complications in pregnancy or birth. Sometimes a learning disability can develop because of an injury or illness in early childhood, such as meningitis. We may also encounter learning disabilities resulting from developmental trauma, such as foetal alcohol syndrome or shaken baby syndrome.

People with a specific condition and a learning disability often have shared behaviours, physical features, or challenges; for example, people with Angelman syndrome will be likely to have trouble walking or have issues with balance or coordination, may be known for frequent laughter or smiling or for becoming excited easily, and may be more prone to epilepsy. Each condition has shared characteristics, but each person will be unique in their physical appearance, temperament, interests, and giftings. Each person with a learning disability uniquely and beautifully displays God's image and points to his glory.

It is beyond the scope of this book to do a deep dive into all the conditions that are associated with learning disabilities; the list is long and some genetic conditions and chromosomal abnormalities are so rare that some people may never receive an official diagnosis. However, we hope this chapter will help inform the way we can care for and support people with learning disabilities and their families in our churches: not just so that we can welcome and include them, but also so that they experience the joy of belonging to God's people.

A WARM WELCOME ON A SUNDAY

There are many things we can do as churches to make our gatherings on a Sunday accessible to those with learning disabilities and their families. Here is how one young adult with a learning disability described his involvement in church, emphasising his joy at the friendships he experiences there:

> ### TRISTAN'S STORY
>
> Being part of a church is nice. You get to pray; you get to meet new people. I'm getting baptised to be more part of the church. You get to meet new people; you get to sing; you get to be social. You get to be part of the Lord and Jesus. You get to read the Bible; you get to meet new people. And being baptised is going to be the best part of all of it, bringing you closer to the Lord.

SERVING

> It is more blessed to give than to receive.
> ACTS 20:35

Serving is a great place to begin; we saw back in chapter 1 that humans were created to serve one another. When we serve alongside other Christian brothers and sisters, we share in fellowship with one another. We learn more about what it means to sacrifice for others, and we can use the gifts and talents God has given us to build up and equip the church. Sometimes we may be hesitant to allow those with learning disabilities to serve in our teams at church, as we fear it will lead to more work for the existing team members or it will be an inconvenience. However, we should not think in terms of efficiency, but how together we are reflecting Christ's body.

Perhaps it may mean that the hospitality team needs to allow a little bit more time on a Sunday morning to prepare tea and coffee as they support their friend with a learning disability to complete the tasks. Perhaps the worship band might not sound as polished or the welcome might be a little more enthusiastic than normal. However, when we make room for an adult with learning disabilities on our serving teams, we enable them to share in the great joy and privilege that it is to serve Christ's church. We show them that they are a valued part of the family, and we encourage them in pursuing their spiritual gifts. We know of a couple of churches where individuals with PMLD serve on the welcome teams. We have been told about the joy their enthusiastic greeting gives those arriving at their church buildings.

We talked to an adult with moderate learning disabilities, Rebecca, about some of the different parts of church life in which she serves:

REBECCA'S STORY

I help with the coffees on fourth Sundays. And I help with the Sunday school there. At one congregation, I help with the group for three- to four-year-olds.

What sorts of things are you doing in those groups?
I help with arts and crafts. Also I help set up and pack up for one congregation, meeting in a local primary school.

What aspects of going to those things do you like, are there bits of them you particularly like? Say, with the three- to four-year-olds?
I wanted to help... I like being with the children.

Can you tell me a little bit about what you do at the church youth group on a Monday evening?
Monday evening, I help to set up and pack up. I help with refreshments each time and I do the whistle at the end of the tea time and activity time. So kind of moving on between each activity.

And at the midweek church group for preschoolers on a Thursday? Tell me about this group. What do you do there?
Like help. Yeah, help set up. And yeah, and help with the games.

And what do you enjoy about these groups?
I like being with the people.

You go every year on a church youth group camp. What do you enjoy about camp?
I enjoy just being with the people, and I enjoy the meetings as well.

> *What do you like about the meetings?*
> We learn about God's word.
>
> *And do you have particular jobs on camp?*
> I make sure that we've got the stuff we need for mealtimes out. And if we need more stuff I can get it out. And also I check that the loos have got enough loo paper and baby wipes and things are clean.
>
> *I expect that's an unseen but really important part of camp, right? These things don't work well if the toilets don't have any wipes!*
> *We both laugh.*

Rebecca's story shows us just how important it is to make time and space for people to serve in a range of ways. The time she spends setting up and packing away, putting out refreshments, washing up, and completing other predictable, routine tasks not only supports the service of others, but also enables her to form relationships and flourish in them.

THE SERMON

> They devoted themselves to the apostles' teaching.
> ACTS 2:42

Something significant happens each week when we gather around God's word and hear it read and preached. As we hear the words of scripture taught, the Holy Spirit reveals truth to our minds (1 Corinthians 2:10) and directs our heart towards holiness (Ezekiel 36:27). Preaching the word of God is not done simply for entertainment, to make us feel good, or even to share information. It reflects our belief that it is God who shapes us through his word, by his Spirit. If we believe this, we should find ourselves considering how accessible the teaching is to those with a learning disability.

This is an area where we need to carefully balance two truths. We know that the Bible is 'God-breathed' (2 Timothy 3:16) and that as we hear God's word read and faithfully taught, it is the Holy Spirit who teaches the believer (e.g. John 14:26). We might therefore say that the manner of our delivery doesn't matter – we can let the Spirit do the work. However, we can see human limitations – God chooses to work through humans, and we recognise the importance of speaking the same language as our listeners or using our God-given skills to present truths clearly. Choosing to think about the accessibility of our sermons to those with learning disabilities is not denying the ability of the Spirit to work in their hearts. It is following in the footsteps of Paul as he tailored his message to his hearers (for example, in Athens, where he chose to quote Greek poets to draw his listeners in; Acts 17). It is following in the footsteps of Jesus, who used tangible, multisensory tools to remind his disciples of spiritual realities (the Lord's supper being an obvious example). Prophets like Jeremiah and Ezekiel acted out their messages with bold and physical representations of spiritual truths.

If you are a larger church with multiple services, it might be worth considering stylistic variation in how teaching is presented across services. If you're a smaller church, this variation could be across a month or term. Do you have a service with a sermon that is designed to be shorter and less academic? Could you provide visuals (via a projector screen, a flipchart, or physical objects used to highlight key points)? Multisensory visual aids, such as food, sounds, scent, or real-life props, ground the teaching in known realities and can allow more people to engage with the message. Even a handout with an easy-to-follow overview of the main points can be a useful support. All these things can help those with learning disabilities to keep engaged and follow along with the sermon. Caring about how the Bible is taught does not indicate a lack of belief in the Spirit's work, but rather a conviction that God's word really matters in the lives of all believers.

THE WHOLE SERVICE

There are various ways we can make all the elements of our patterns of worship accessible to those with learning disabilities. There may be individuals in our congregation who use Makaton, a language programme using signs, symbols, and speech to support communication. This is known as an 'AAC' (alternative/augmentative communication system) – also discussed in our chapter on autism. If so, we may wish to learn the signs to some key parts of the service, such as the Lord's Prayer. Count Everyone In, a charity working to support churches in welcoming adults with learning disabilities, has developed a Makaton training workshop (Know and Grow Makaton), to teach churches signs they may find useful.[2] Makaton used alongside songs, prayers, or repeated elements of our services helps to highlight key ideas for those who use it. Makaton also has symbols, which are useful for signage around the building if it is the familiar communication tool for someone in our congregation. Makaton is not the only communication aid used by individuals with learning disabilities – some may use PECS (picture exchange communication system), for example, on a tablet or board. We can ask an individual or their carer what would be most helpful for them.

Some churches choose to make certain services 'all-age'. These services, when carefully planned to meet the needs of *all* ages, can be a powerful tool in ministering to those with learning disabilities in your congregations. We are tempted to view this kind of service as hard work: it is often a lot of effort for the staff, children are restless, parents are stressed, and those without children are in danger of switching off or not attending at all, because they assume it is not aimed at them. However, an all-age sermon at its best can be a beautiful tool for the whole congregation as we learn together. It is often in these moments, as the simplicity of the gospel is displayed, that the Holy Spirit convicts and challenges us the most. For an adult with learning disabilities in your congregation, the all-age worship service provides an interactive environment with more music, movement breaks, and visuals. This environment is far more suited to allowing an individual with a learning disability to learn and engage in what is being taught.

In delivering these services, everyone involved should be clear on the aim: not to speak only to children, but rather to offer a simple and interactive exposition of a passage that is accessible for all. This extends beyond the talk into notices, corporate prayer, *and* Bible readings. Often liturgies are available with simpler vocabulary, a dramatic reading may be appropriate to a passage, and notices can be turned into sketches which are more memorable and accessible to all. Even where all aspects are well planned, it is also important to keep all-age services to a strict time schedule, as it is easy for them to become too long.

While we all have some kind of pattern to our services, some churches place a high value on variation, inventing new phrasing every week for 'call and response' elements, prayers, and other parts of the service. Many people with learning disabilities find it much more helpful to have phrases which they can learn, especially if they are unable to read. Consider how you can balance the needs of those who value spontaneity and variety with those who will learn and grow through carefully phrased elements repeated from week to week. A combination of the two may be helpful, such as using the Lord's Prayer after corporate prayers which are likely to change.

YOUTH AND CHILDREN'S PROVISION

As we have briefly touched upon above, the term 'learning disability' is very broad and encompasses a great deal of variety. Two children may have exactly the same diagnosis on paper but need drastically different levels of support. There will never be a one-size-fits-all approach, and flexibility is key for any youth and children's team. The best place to start is connecting with the family; when we befriend them and get to know them, we will find out how we can best meet their children's needs.

Most children with a diagnosed learning disability in the UK should have an education, health, and care plan.[3] (If the child does not, you might want to point their family towards the local authority and see if they can get one in place.) This document describes the child's special educational needs and the type of supports and aids that should be in place in their educational setting, as well as other provisions and activities they attend. It details the support the local authority provides to the individual and family – this support may include things like respite care, a motability car, adaptations to the property the family are living in, activities and therapies, as well as their eligibility for different benefits.

This document is also a good guide and starting point for youth and children's workers and volunteers. It can be helpful to put in place similar strategies and support at church and in a midweek youth group, to build continuity for the child across school, church, and home life. Ask if the family is willing to share this document with you. If this is not possible, a chat with the family about the strategies, approaches, and care they have in place for the child at home will help to determine how the child can be supported within church youth and children's work.

ONE-TO-ONE SUPPORT

If a child receives one-to-one support at school, you may wish to consider replicating this at church, rather than expecting a parent to stay with the child in groups. This may seem like a massive undertaking: most churches already struggle to find enough volunteers to run the rest of the group; how can they expect to find a volunteer for just one child? However, in our experience, people often rise to meet the need in this situation and are excited to do so. There are many times in church ministry when we feel the truth of Matthew 9:37: 'The harvest is plentiful but the workers are few.' What does Jesus tell us to do in this situation? 'Ask the Lord of the harvest, therefore, to send out workers into his harvest field' (Matthew 9:38).

When some volunteers come forward, it is helpful to run a training session for them with the family, so that they can learn how best to support the individual. You may also create a care plan with the parents with information about the child's needs and a description of how to support the child, as well as their likes and dislikes. When one-to-one support has been established, you may consider putting this in place for the entire service, if your church has children in the main church for the beginning or end part of the service. This often eases the transition into or out of children's groups and can also give the parents more freedom to speak to others in the church family and to enjoy this part of the service with any other children they may have, knowing that their child is fully cared for and supported.

CHALLENGING BEHAVIOUR

There may be some occasional circumstances where you come across behaviour which causes harm or danger to the individual or the people around them. This might look like:

- hitting, kicking, pinching, or pulling hair
- throwing objects
- inappropriate language, swearing
- destructive behaviour (damaging objects, punching or kicking walls)
- spitting or eating inedible objects
- running off
- inappropriate behaviour of a sexual nature (for example, stripping or masturbating in a public place).

Not everyone with a learning disability will exhibit challenging behaviour, and when it appears it is usually infrequent. In this context, challenging behaviour is often a result of the individual's inability to express themselves or communicate a need; it could be a sign of distress or discomfort. The individual may lack understanding of what behaviour is and isn't appropriate in certain contexts.

Helpful questions to ask yourself may be:

- What triggered the behaviour?
- Is the individual in pain? Or discomfort? (Do they need the toilet? Are they hungry/thirsty/unwell?)
- Do we need to change the environment (move somewhere quieter or work with a different group of peers)?
- Does the individual require privacy?

If an individual known to you regularly exhibits challenging behaviour, it is likely that their family or care provision will have strategies in place to manage the behaviour and this will vary depending on the individual and the behaviour. It is important to have open communication with families and care providers. But here are some general principles that may be helpful.[4]

- Stay calm. This is hard, but the calmer you are, the more likely you will be to prevent the behaviour from escalating. This also communicates to the individual and the rest of the group that you are in control.

- Pre-empt triggers to reduce the likelihood of behaviours. For example, sitting the individual in a space where they are comfortable, keeping craft materials out of reach, encouraging regular toilet and water breaks.

- Consider your environment. Does the individual need to leave and return when they are calmer or if they are unable to leave, does the group need to move somewhere safer?

- After an incident of behaviour, remember the dignity of the individual and be mindful of them in the ways you speak to others about the incident.

We always strive to include an individual wherever possible, even when that is difficult and costly (see chapter 3). However, there can be situations when we do not have the resources or experience to guarantee the safety of the individual, the rest of the group, and our volunteers. This is a painful and heartbreaking position to be found in. Whether or not we know and love the individual and their family, feeling at a loss about to how to meet their needs can leave us feeling guilty and unsure how best to navigate the situation. We don't want to isolate people in this position further, and even with the gentlest approach in the world, we know that conversations about this can leave them hurting and disappointed.

This is hard, but there are occasional instances when some challenging behaviour requires specialist training, and if we try to overextend our capabilities we could end up causing harm. We can recognise our limitations, and yet there may be other ways we can discuss the individual being able to access your Christian community with their family or care provider. For example, this could include home visits or an employed personal assistant accompanying them to an event or service. In complex situations, it may be helpful to seek advice from organisations such as Mencap, who offer a helpline service,[5] or the Challenging Behaviour Foundation.[6]

ADAPTATIONS TO CONTENT

When considering how to tailor teaching content to an individual with a learning disability, the starting principle is the same as for the rest of the group. If we could choose one thing that we wanted the child or teenager to learn or take away from this session, what would it be? Perhaps it is a memory verse or a theme sentence. Being clear about our key message helps us present this clearly to everyone. How can you use the time you have with that child to present this 'one thing' to them?

Maybe it is singing or signing a memory verse together while running around the church garden with a football. Perhaps you might look at a picture book of the Bible passage together. Perhaps you could use Lego or playdough to reinforce or retell the Bible story – the whole group is likely to benefit from this kind of presentation. Perhaps it is sitting at the side or the back of a group alongside the child or young person while they play with some fidget toys or engage in some sensory play, allowing them to observe and be included in whole-group activities or discussion.

Ideally, support should be used to enable the child or young person to be included in the whole group, with the option of working separately with them where that is needed. Many Bible teaching resources aimed at children have suggestions for adapting games, crafts, or teaching to make them accessible: using these can be helpful as we get to know what sort of adaptations will help the individuals in our church.

AGE-APPROPRIATE SETTINGS

There is sometimes an argument that it is beneficial to keep a child back in a group that is below their age range if they have a learning disability. At first glance, this may sound logical, especially if the child's intellect does not appear to match their peers. We fear the child may fall behind and not understand the teaching, or worse, they may be disruptive and prevent others from learning. However, we would like to suggest that there are great benefits in keeping the child with the rest of their cohort.

While a child with a learning disability may take longer to learn new skills and may have a reduced level of intellect, spiritually, physically, and emotionally they are likely to develop alongside their peers. An example of this is puberty; a teenager with a learning disability will hit puberty the same as any other teenager and will experience all the same feelings, emotions, and changes that puberty brings. When you consider this, it feels much more appropriate for them to be in a group with the other teenagers at church rather than being held back with younger children.

They might, of course, need some accommodations to remain in the group with their peers. Perhaps they will continue to have one-to-one support or a buddy, or they might have an 'easy read' version of the worksheet or a sensory tray linked to the Bible passage you are studying. The NIrV Accessible Edition of the New Testament works well for this purpose – it has shorter sentences, single-column text and illustrations. Flexibility is key: having one-to-one support will give them the freedom to come in and out of the session as required safely.

Keeping the child with their peers is not only beneficial to the child themselves. It is good relationally as well; it encourages lasting friendships to form over time as children with learning disabilities grow up alongside their peers. Good friendships with others in their age group will also help as the individual grows up and is no longer able to attend activities for under-18s. It also helps to model inclusion to the rest of the youth group. Two young men, one with Down syndrome, both shared their experience of such a friendship with us.

JOHN AND JAMES' STORY

James: The summer Christian camp I grew up on was intended for the ages of 13 to 16, but since my parents were camp leaders, I started attending before I could walk. Being a 'camper' under the age guidance could have had its challenges – the activities and trips were not intended for my participation, and any 'real' campers I befriended were guaranteed for only four years or less. Thankfully, however, there was always one familiar face waiting for me every summer.

John's parents were the camp's overall leaders at the time, so John and I would spend one week a year growing up together. I have no recollection of our introduction; we have simply always been in one another's life (although technically John is 13 months older, a fact he often likes to remind me of).

I find it hard to describe someone's disability on their behalf – simply out of respect, and to avoid any misrepresentation – but in simple terms, John has Down syndrome, with a notable affectation to his speech. For those meeting John for the first time, it can be a challenge to catch his words or conversation, but having grown up alongside him, I could have a conversation with John almost as easily as anyone.

As a result, I've always known how funny John is. We thought of ourselves as a bit of a double act, and we were rarely seen apart. I think, in small ways, I could help other young people our age who were meeting John for the first time. I could relay John's humour and jokes, and help open up John's conversations for others to be included. And not because John depended on me to do so, but because I wanted others to be blessed by knowing John's genuine and passionate character in the same ways that I have.

One tradition of the summer camp (at a time when John and I were old enough to be actual campers) was that the evening worship was followed by a round of hot chocolates. One such evening, after a particularly stirring worship, I wanted to stay a bit longer to reflect and pray. I told John – who, for context, is often first, third, and sixth in line for a hot chocolate – he could go, and I'd catch him up.

Instead, John remained next to me and prayed aloud over me. He thanked God for me, our friendship, and our time together at camp. I cannot pretend that I caught every word that John spoke, but I didn't need to. His words were genuine and heartfelt, his thankfulness to the Lord pure. John's relationship with the Lord reminds me of Matthew 18, in which Christ calls us to have childlike faith – the challenge of putting aside our will and pride and depending on the Lord's provision wholeheartedly.

I cannot begin to comprehend how John perceives each day, and the challenges he may face. But the faith and trust he has glorifies the Lord, as does the love he shows his family and friends. I am truly blessed to have had such a long friendship with John, in which there has been so much joy, personal growth, and true fellowship shared.

In conversation with John:

What do you like the most about being a leader at camp?
I like everything.

Everything?
Yeah!

Can you tell me about some of the different things you like?
I like the fun duties. Yes, I like it, so it's fine. I like cooking, I do. I like movies as well; I like hot dogs as well.

Can you tell me a little bit about your friends at camp?
My friends, I've got one friend, James, because he really likes me, because I do.

Did you meet at camp or somewhere else?
Both.

How have James and your other friends helped you love Jesus?
I'd say everyone, yes.

How do they do that? Do they encourage you? Do they pray for you? Do they talk to you about Jesus?
I would say yes, because everybody loves me, yes.

And how do you help them love Jesus?
I like friends and everybody makes me be better with friends to me, James and [another friend] he is on my list. And then to everybody ask questions about how they're doing with God.

And that's encouraging for them?
Yes.

And do they ask you questions about how you're doing with God?
Yes, they do as well, yeah.

And how does that make you feel?
I feel good, it makes me happy, I think a funny guy, like me.

As we had this conversation with John, the delight he had in this friendship was evident in everything he said. This friendship with a peer had continued and grown beyond their teenage years, and allowed both of them to encourage one another more in Christ.

TRIPS AND OUTINGS

One of the most enjoyable things about being part of a church youth group can be the trips, outings, camps and activities that you get to do. This can become complicated for youth and children's workers and volunteers when a child has an additional need. Here are some useful things to consider.

How accessible are the venue and activities for all those in your youth and children's groups? For example, if you have a child with a learning disability that has mobility issues, does the swimming pool you are attending for the Friday night youth group trip have a hoist and disabled changing facilities? Does the venue you are attending for your weekend away have a fully accessible bedroom and wheelchair access? Can the activity holiday cater for your young people's physical and behavioural needs and, if not, what can you implement to change this? Thinking carefully about who their assigned leader is and sharing key information with them in advance is crucial. Chat to the family beforehand to think of a strategy for the young person to attend. It may be that carer support will enable them to take part. Showing that you want the child or young person to take part and are willing to make changes for them is one way we can show radical love. This is often a huge load off families who are used to having to do all this work and forward-planning themselves.

There may be times when an activity or trip is not practical or accessible for every individual. This does not necessarily mean you need to cancel the trip; it may still be the case that the benefit to the rest of the group outweighs the inaccessibility for the one. However, in these situations, consider how you might make a future outing more inclusive. Visiting a bowling alley is often an excellent option as they usually have accommodations available to make it a fun experience for everyone.

John and his dad shared with us just how valuable his youth camp was to John, both spiritually and relationally.

JOHN'S STORY (CONTINUED)

Dad: Camp, his birthday, and Christmas are the three things he really looks forward to. I would say he fully engages in the celebrations, because he's always at the front. Aren't you, John?

John: I like that!

Dad: Seeing him at the front of the camp celebration is amazing.

John: And for me, I did this before, like in worship; I like dancing, to do a bit of fun dance, in worship, so yeah; I do, yeah.

And camp is really good because it's free to let you do that, isn't it?

Dad: He does do it at church as well, but he's got more freedom at camp. And you became a Christian at camp, didn't you?

John: Yeah.

Anything else you want to tell us about camp?

John: For camp it has been many years ago for me. I love this camp, because I love camp porridge – it's as good as my birthday for me.

MIDWEEK

SUPPORTING INDIVIDUALS THROUGH ACTIVITIES

Many churches around the country have midweek groups for adults with learning disabilities. These groups are a precious and valuable ministry; they provide an opportunity for fellowship and community as well as accessible teaching. Not only this, but they also serve others beyond the church; local authorities are often underfunded and therefore provision and activities for adults and children with learning disabilities can be limited. A free activity run by a local church can meet a genuine need and can be very appealing to care homes and supported living facilities. Attendees often bring along family members or carers to support or assist them at the groups, which means we are in a unique position to minister to not only the individual with learning disabilities but also their carers. By running a group like this, we serve individuals not only in our congregations, but also those outside the church. While it is a wonderful act of love and care to provide a group of this nature purely to meet a practical need, we do not need to neglect the spiritual needs of those attending.

You might want to look into running a Messy Church, 'a way of being church for people of all ages involving fun'. They provide lots of session material and other resources on their website.[7]

Count Everyone In[8] also offers a wealth of resources to support such groups. They say:

> We long for the day when every adult with a learning disability, regardless of where they live in England or Wales, has less than 5 miles to travel to a church that is intentionally accessible and welcoming so that no one misses out on Jesus![9]

Some adults with learning disabilities may attend activities at more than one church. If this is the case, it is important to have an open dialogue with the other church to ensure that no one slips through the gaps of pastoral care which this situation can produce.

SUPPORTING INDIVIDUALS THROUGH FRIENDSHIPS

We should not see these groups as the sole discipleship and fellowship for those with learning disabilities in our church congregations. Where appropriate, those with learning disabilities should be invited to participate in all areas of church life: they should be active members of our home groups and prayer meetings, and they should be included in formal and informal social church gatherings. We should see our friendships with our brothers and sisters with learning disabilities in the same way as anyone else in our church family. We can actively pursue reading scripture and praying together, holding each other accountable, sharing our lives and spending time together in our homes and socially at places like the local pub or cinema.

As a society we tend to value things like career success, financial stability, intellect, and outward appearance. It can be easy, therefore, to look for these attributes when seeking friendships with others. We tend to gravitate towards people who are like us or even sometimes those whom we wish we were like. It is therefore not a surprise that sometimes adults and children with learning disabilities can get overlooked socially or even bullied by those around them.

Is there a culture of building meaningful relationships within your congregations and if so, does this extend to our brothers and sisters with learning disabilities? As Christians, when we befriend someone with a learning disability, what is our motivation and expectation? Do we see it as an act of service or even sometimes a chore, something we should do to be kind and Christian? Do our friendships go deep or do they stay surface level?

When speaking to someone with communication difficulties (whether they are using a form of AAC or have less distinct speech), it is easy to slip into using 'baby' language, thinking this is all they are capable of understanding. This is absolutely not the case and can be boring or insulting to the individual. Start from the assumption of speaking to the individual as you would anyone their age.

Rebecca gave us some examples of her friendships with others in her church:

REBECCA'S STORY (CONTINUED)

I go to the pub after the evening service.

Are there other things that you do with people from church? Do you sometimes go out for meals with people or go and eat at people's houses?
[She refers to a friend who has since moved away.] We did occasionally, we have been doing that, but now we've stopped.

There have been some people haven't there, who've been really good at making that happen?
[She mentions another individual.] She is good at that.

There have been some friends who've really invited you to things.
Yeah, on Sundays after church, I've gone round to people's houses for a chat.

And would you do that with other people sometimes or just you?
Yeah.

What does your friend normally organise?
We used to go, we've been to her house. We've done [another family's] place and lots of people's places.

You don't have an email address, your phone is at home. So how do people let you know what's going on?
They text me, and I check when I get home.

I guess people know that they can't change their plans last minute, because you won't necessarily know what the change to the plan is, is that fair?
Yeah.

Tell me about your home group. So you said you go most weeks to a home group. Is that somewhere local?
It's local, I get a lift. [A local couple] take me there because it's at [a location at the far end of town].

And in a normal home group meeting, what sorts of things do you do with the other people there?

> We read the Bible and then we talk about it. And then we pray about the Bible and then we pray for each other.
>
> *Do you find that helpful?*
> Yes.
>
> *Have you got good friendships with the other people in your home group?*
> Yes.

Rebecca's story reminds us of the value of individuals being supported by a network of different friends. It can be hard if an individual they were previously very close to leaves. Rebecca was very grateful for the many people who each played a small part in helping her feel a loved and valued member of the church family. She also reminds us of the importance of communication. Many adults with learning disabilities do not have access to the internet or a phone they bring out of their homes, as this could be unsafe for them. It is easy for churches to lean too heavily on technology in their communication (both official and social), which leaves people out unintentionally.

SUPPORTING FAMILIES

On their best days, parents of children with learning disabilities experience the joys common to many parents: the excitement of watching their child master a new skill, the fun of spending time with them in the playground or going out for a picnic as a family. Some of the wonderful parts of parenting a child with learning disabilities will be watching their other children grow in mature and compassionate consideration for others and getting to know the unique personality of their child with a learning disability.

On their hardest days, however, these parents may be grieving their child's diagnosis or the life they dreamed their child would have, while simultaneously adjusting and forming new hopes and dreams for their child's future. They may be struggling with financial pressures as they strive to renovate their home to make it more accessible or fundraise for the equipment, education, or aids they feel they need to improve their child's quality of life. They may be tired – tired because their child does not sleep well, tired of managing their child's challenging behaviour or complex needs, tired physically from lifting and caring for a child with limited mobility as they grow. They may worry they are failing their other children because their child with a learning disability needs so much of their attention. They may feel resentful – because they had to give up their thriving career, they do not get to have any child-free time with their spouse or friends, or even because they never get to hear a full sermon on a Sunday or finish a cup of coffee.

Siblings, too, face challenges. They may have increased levels of responsibility in the home or have witnessed their peers make fun of or pick on their sibling in the school playground. They may feel like their sibling monopolises all their parents' time, and they may worry about the future and what will happen when their parents are no longer able to care for their sibling.

Families of children with learning disabilities will face many obstacles and challenges in life, which can sometimes lead them to retreat and draw back from social groups. They often build great networks and bonds with other families in similar situations. It can be helpful for them to have a small circle of friends and family who they trust and who understand the unique challenges and pressures they are experiencing.

The local church can be well placed to support families as they face these challenges. Churches may be in the position to offer pastoral support or biblical counselling as families work through feelings of grief or resentment. Members of the church may be able to provide babysitting or respite care to allow the rest of the family a break or some quality time alone for the parents, either to spend together or with the child's siblings, allowing them that time uninterrupted with their parents. There may be practical support in the form of cooking meals, helping siblings with homework, or even providing administrative support to help the family apply for various benefits or grants. As you support a family in this situation, encourage them to take rest where possible, both physical and spiritual rest. There might be opportunities to access local authority funding for respite care, which can be used in a variety of ways to get this much-needed rest.

It is important to recognise the unique challenges family members of those with learning difficulties will encounter and consider how we might best love and serve them. Alongside this, we must not forget the unique joys and privileges that come with parenting a child with disabilities. Emily Perl Kingsley describes this beautifully in her essay 'Welcome to Holland':

WELCOME TO HOLLAND

I am often asked to describe the experience of raising a child with a disability – to try to help people who have not shared that unique experience to understand it, to imagine how it would feel. It's like this...

When you're going to have a baby, it's like planning a fabulous vacation trip – to Italy. You buy a bunch of guide books and make your wonderful plans. The Coliseum. The Michelangelo David. The gondolas in Venice. You may learn some handy phrases in Italian. It's all very exciting.

After months of eager anticipation, the day finally arrives. You pack your bags and off you go. Several hours later, the plane lands. The flight attendant comes in and says, 'Welcome to Holland.'

'Holland?!?' you say. 'What do you mean Holland?? I signed up for Italy! I'm supposed to be in Italy. All my life I've dreamed of going to Italy.'

But there's been a change in the flight plan. They've landed in Holland and there you must stay.

The important thing is that they haven't taken you to a horrible, disgusting, filthy place, full of pestilence, famine and disease. It's just a different place.

So you must go out and buy new guide books. And you must learn a whole new language. And you will meet a whole new group of people you would never have met.

It's just a different place. It's slower-paced than Italy, less flashy than Italy. But after you've been there for a while and you catch your breath, you look around... and you begin to notice that Holland has windmills... and Holland has tulips. Holland even has Rembrandts.

But everyone you know is busy coming and going from Italy... and they're all bragging about what a wonderful time they had there. And for the rest of your life, you will say 'Yes, that's where I was supposed to go. That's what I had planned.'

And the pain of that will never, ever, ever, ever go away... because the loss of that dream is a very very significant loss.

But... if you spend your life mourning the fact that you didn't get to Italy, you may never be free to enjoy the very special, the very lovely things... about Holland.

Copyright ©1987 by Emily Perl Kingsley. All rights reserved. Reprinted by permission of the author.

A WORD ON SAFEGUARDING

An adult with a learning disability is recognised as a 'vulnerable adult'. They are likely to be vulnerable for a variety of reasons. It could be due to a physical disability or sensory impairment; they may be vulnerable because their learning disability makes it harder for them to understand social situations, communicate their needs, or look after themselves adequately.

We must be aware that those in our congregation with a learning disability are more likely to be taken advantage of and vulnerable to abuse. They may at times present a danger or risk to themselves or be at risk of harm or exploitation from others. We should bear in mind the possibility of unintended exploitation – for example, they may happily use all the money they had for groceries for the week to buy everyone a drink in the pub after church or indeed accept more drinks from others than is right for them. Ideally, there would be responsible individuals keeping a careful eye on their well-being, and their wider circle will be alert to the possibility of unintended exploitation.

It is good practice for anybody providing one-to-one support for a child or adult with a learning disability, providing pastoral care, or leading a home group to have completed a safeguarding course. They should have an enhanced DBS check, not just a basic or standard-level DBS check. Your church network or denomination may also provide specific training for working with vulnerable adults.

Other training qualifications may be useful in keeping vulnerable adults physically safe, such as first aid and epilepsy training.

This chapter could feel like an intimidating list of hard-to-implement changes, but the reality is that this is something most churches are already doing well. This was apparent from all the contributors for this chapter, who were positive about their experiences of love from their Christian communities.

TOP 10 FOR EVERYONE

1. Encourage those with learning disabilities as they serve: thank them for what they are doing, no matter how small it may seem.

2. Engage someone who uses a form of AAC in conversation.

3. Over coffee, ask a person with a learning disability what they did last week.

4. Include people with learning disabilities in invitations to social events, even if it involves visiting them to invite them in person.

5. Support parents of children with learning disabilities by offering to get relevant training (e.g. first aid) to enable you to care for their child from time to time.

6. Love and celebrate the person rather than seeing them only as a project.

7. Offer to help with applications for PIP (Personal Independence Payment) from the government, grants for equipment, or other support services.

8. Volunteer to serve at an event at your church for people with learning disabilities. If you don't run anything, why not form a group of people to pray and plan towards setting something up, maybe in partnership with another church?

9. Volunteer to act as a one-to-one so that a child with learning disabilities can take part in children's work at your church.

10. Look out for people with learning disabilities in your Christian groups: take collective responsibility for protecting them from harm and reporting anything suspicious to a safeguarding officer.

Specific learning difficulties

CLAIRE WOOD

Specific learning difficulties include dyslexia, dyspraxia, and dyscalculia. Maybe you're breathing a sigh of relief as you get to this chapter. These are the 'easy' difficulties to solve, right? Most of us have a vague awareness of dyslexia having something to do with being bad at spelling. Surely this is one for schools to worry about, not churches and Christian groups? Many people with specific learning difficulties manage without extra support or have found their own solutions over the course of their lives to overcome the challenges they face. However, specific learning difficulties can encroach on all aspects of life, and at the very least, understanding how someone we know may experience life will help us to love them more.

If you've ever been for a walk in the countryside, you may have experienced the challenge of trying to work out where the path that's marked on your map is. You're climbing up a hill and you see a worn track heading off in what seems to be the right direction, but it soon turns out to take a circuitous route back to where you started. It's at this point that you realise that it's a path worn smooth by sheep, and not the right of way you were looking for. You might eventually make it back to your campsite, but hours after someone who followed the correct path!

The pathways in the brain of someone with specific learning difficulties can be a bit like this. The brain will naturally try to follow these routes, even after the correct 'path' has been pointed out. These 'thinking preferences' are not chosen by the individual, but wired into the way their brain works. However, just as the circuitous sheep path might take us past a spectacular view other walkers missed, there are also advantages to unorthodox thinking. This chapter will explore what specific learning difficulties are, how they may affect people, and what we can do to love them better. We also want to take some time to explore how our Christian communities can make the most of the skills and talents God has given many.

WHAT ARE SPECIFIC LEARNING DIFFICULTIES?

First, it's worth taking a moment to dwell on the name. It's confusingly similar to 'learning disabilities', especially as specific learning difficulties fit the requirements to be classed as disabilities under the Equality Act 2010. The key difference is that they are not linked to intelligence – someone with a specific learning difficulty could have any IQ. Although they can make learning difficult (hence the name), they do not mean that an individual cannot learn skills or knowledge. Many people would prefer that they be called 'specific learning differences', to reflect the fact that the 'difficulty' is often significantly lessened when different methods of teaching are used. We will use the abbreviation SpLD through the rest of this chapter.

There are a few commonly diagnosed SpLDs, though in practice many of their characteristics co-occur and overlap, with many being considered 'spectrum' diagnoses – each individual presenting their own unique combination of strengths and weaknesses. SpLDs often co-occur with each other and with diagnoses like autism and ADHD, which means that the best approach will always be one tailored to the individual concerned.

DYSLEXIA

Dyslexia is a neurological condition affecting many aspects of life. Most people are aware of the tip of the iceberg, so to speak – dyslexia's effect on reading, writing, and spelling. However, it also affects many other areas of life, such as working memory, spatial awareness, and even organisation and time management. As a result, dyslexic people may suffer from low self-esteem or anxiety. However, these challenges don't give the whole picture. Many of these difficulties derive from a skill in another mode of thinking. There are many influencers trying to shift public perceptions towards appreciation and making space for these ways of thinking in educational settings and workplaces. The reality is that with dyslexic people in the minority, much of the apparatus of life is set up for the 'typical' brain's way of thinking. This means dyslexic people often don't get to see and appreciate the God-given gifts of their way of seeing the world – they just experience the roadblocks.

Dyslexic people are often very good at visualising things, imagining them in three dimensions. By the time they are learning to read in school, their brains are so naturally accustomed to flipping images around to decode their meaning that they struggle to remember the difference between letters with similar shapes, like p, b, d, and q, or easily muddle reversible words like 'was' and 'saw'. This can make the experience of reading more challenging for many dyslexic people. Reading God's word should be like water to a thirsty plant; we read in Psalm 1 that 'blessed is the one… who meditates on his law day and night. That person is like a tree planted by streams of water, which yields its fruit in season and whose leaf does not wither' (Psalm 1:1–3). And yet accessing this life-giving water can be considerably harder for some dyslexic people.

Researchers have found that weighted fonts, which give additional cues about which way up each letter should be seen, are much easier for dyslexic people to read. Reducing the chance of words showing through thin paper (often a feature of Bibles!) and increasing font size can also make a difference. Buying a friend a Bible printed in a dyslexia-friendly font on high-quality paper could make a huge difference to their experience of reading the Bible.[1] If they have a smartphone, some Bible apps now have an option to change the typeface to the OpenDyslexic font.[2] Listening to the Bible as an audiobook or using a journalling Bible, which encourages the reader to annotate the text, may also support the way a dyslexic person most naturally accesses a text. Pictures or objects can also help in visualising events in a narrative.[3] In a group setting, such as a small group Bible study, it may be beneficial to act out the events of a story together. Reading through a passage in a different translation or paraphrasing with a friend in advance can also be valuable.

Reading aloud can cause high levels of anxiety to dyslexic people, especially if they have learned to associate reading with negative experiences at school or growing up. Many dyslexic people wrongly consider themselves lacking in intelligence as a result of these experiences. Loving our dyslexic brothers and sisters may involve a bit of forward-planning. If you are leading a small group discussion, try to find out in advance how each member feels about reading aloud. Some may prefer never to be asked, whereas some would love the opportunity with some advance planning. We had a dyslexic member of our congregation deliver the Bible reading entirely from memory one Sunday, but she was delighted to be asked, as she really loves God's word, and the passage chosen that week was one which had particularly impacted her life.

Some dyslexic people are great readers but struggle with writing, particularly spelling. While it's a temptation to engage in some jokes over spelling mistakes, the recipient may not find it as funny as you do. As with all our relationships, it is helpful to come back to the many verses in the Bible about being careful of our speech. When teaching the Ephesian church how to relate to one another, Paul says: 'Do not let any unwholesome talk come out of your mouths, but only what is helpful for building others up according to their needs, that it may benefit those who listen' (Ephesians 4:29).

We may also find ourselves falling into making unfair judgements of others. If we tend to associate poor spelling with low intelligence, we may subconsciously form a low opinion of our friend's abilities, meaning that they are overlooked for serving opportunities they may have excelled at. Not only is this assessment simply wrong, as good spelling is not an accurate measure of any ability other than spelling, but it is also one way in which we may fall victim to our culture's idolisation of education. We are reminded in 1 Corinthians that 'the foolishness of God is wiser than human wisdom, and the weakness of God is stronger than human strength' (1 Corinthians 1:25).

Reading, writing, and spelling are often referred to as the visible part of the 'dyslexia iceberg'. We may have compassion and understanding regarding these well-known aspects of dyslexia, but fail to recognise other aspects of life which may cause challenges. Many dyslexic people find aspects of social interaction much harder. Some struggle with poor self-esteem; we can remind them of the gifts which God has given them, and even more than this, we can point to their identity as people made in God's image (Genesis 1:26) and dearly loved children of God (Ephesians 5:1). Relatively unfamiliar social situations, like going to a Christian conference, may cause extreme anxiety for a dyslexic person: they may struggle with directions getting there; they have to remember a time and place that is not in their normal routine; and they have to make choices about where to sit and with whom. If you know someone who experiences some of these social anxieties, why not offer to meet them for a coffee and arrive together at the venue, or if that's not possible, arrange in advance that you will sit with them. When having a conversation with a dyslexic person, you may need to allow more 'thinking time' so they can process what has been said and formulate a response. It's easy to think a pause in conversation needs to be filled with us talking more, when we actually just need to be comfortable with silence.

Organisation and time-keeping are also common challenges for dyslexic people. We don't want this to be a barrier to taking part in the life of our church or other Christian community, so whether we are setting the timetable of events or just attending, we can think about how to help those who find this aspect more difficult. This could involve sending a quick message to a friend to remind them about the event on that evening or being patient with the friend who's always late when you've arranged to meet. If the church calendar is available online, this can allow all events to be fed directly to a personal calendar, one of many ways in which using technology well can support dyslexic people.

Dyslexic people are often skilled in seeing lots of little details as part of a bigger whole, seeing links and patterns between things which others may not spot. This often means that it is easier for them to process small pieces of information if given in a framework, connected to the whole. I am constantly amazed by God's word, and how seemingly insignificant details turn out to be threads running through the whole, teaching us a bigger truth about God. There are many books which teach frameworks within which we can understand any passage from the Bible,[4] which may be particularly helpful reading for a dyslexic person seeking a better understanding of God's word. When we have worked to remove some of the barriers they may experience, we are also likely to experience the blessing of insights coming from our dyslexic brothers and sisters who are able to see connections neurotypical brains are less able to spot. Building and being part of a culture of discussing what God is teaching us at the moment will allow us to benefit from these gifts more.

Asking dyslexic people to be involved in communicating information to people in your church or Christian group can be extremely beneficial. In preparing to write this chapter, I have found the guide written by Aurora Betony[5] to be both a rich source of information and eye-opening in terms of the ways in which she presents information. Her dyslexia allows her to see information in a completely different way, which she is then able to communicate through flow charts and graphical representation. Many of these themes are evident in Bethanie's story.

BETHANIE'S STORY

I received a formal diagnosis of dyslexia when I asked to be assessed at the start of university, but had found real challenges and realised something perhaps wasn't quite right when I was doing my GCSEs at school.

My family began to wonder if it was more than just the stress and increased workload of GCSEs when I started to have daily tension headaches that would see me head-down in my lunchbreaks with my eyes closed and returning home to sit in a dark room as the lights were too bright, just wanting to go to bed. When the doctor's attempt at giving me codeine for the pain, as over-the-counter painkillers weren't helping, left me spaced out, there needed to be an alternative solution. Fortunately for me, my mum worked in a primary school, and they had recently been doing some dyslexia screening with pupils, so she brought one of the kits home to test it out on me. From this, we felt it was possible that I may have dyslexia and went about contacting my school for follow-up.

From the three hours (!) of assessment I later undertook, they deemed that I did have dyslexia, with my greatest challenge being the processing and comprehension from what I was reading and some visual stress that is improved by using colour, sometimes referred to as Irlen syndrome. This began to make some of my experiences make more sense. For example, my friends at school being much further ahead when individually reading chapters in class and then seeming to get so much more out of it when we had to discuss what we had read in pairs. Of course, their insights helped me learn the text or story, but it would often leave me wondering why I hadn't taken that from it, as after all, we had read the same thing. Part of the visual aspect for me is when there is a big chunk of text, I can often struggle to follow this while staying on the same line of text or without being distracted by the spaces and gaps between words, sometimes referred to as 'rivers'.

Putting these thoughts into the context of life for a Christian, one of the challenges I face is reading the Bible and being able to understand and grasp what it is saying, not in relation to anything else yet, but firstly the meaning of what I am reading. It may require me to read over a section a few times to begin to process it. So, for me, being in a small group or Bible study session can be a bit unsettling, as I never really feel I can contribute much to a discussion, as I am still trying to process what we have read and maybe talked about so far, trying to connect things together.

Another aspect that I can find daunting or uncomfortable is when someone will turn to you to discuss or ask you a question after the service in relation to the sermon that you've just heard and expect you to be able to engage in a good conversation about what was said and your thoughts on it. However, for me, I haven't yet processed it all enough to be able to say what I thought of it, more than just a shallow response of 'Yeah, it was good, wasn't it?' or 'Yes, there were definitely some points to think about.'

As you might imagine from what I have mentioned so far, church Bibles are not the easiest thing for me to access. If I've been asked to do a reading or perhaps a prayer in advance, then I would likely print this out on coloured paper in a decent-sized font or use a tablet where I have been able to alter the colour of the background. One of the other main areas that remains a source of headaches for me is the use of screens for words. Often the contrast of the colours used will, after a few songs or during a sermon, leave me with the beginning of a headache or eye ache. I appreciate the challenge it is to be accessible to a range of ages and to partially sighted people, so generally I won't say anything.

During a sermon or a talk, I can find it helpful to have a notebook and make notes of key points being discussed or perhaps things I want to explore further myself, and then I can refer to these at a later point to go over what was said. There will inevitably be some doodling as well which helps to keep my mind active.

More recently, I have found colouring during the service to be helpful, and I have a particular author of Christian colouring books that I like to use. Colouring in helps my brain to stay active and more focused on the sermon than if I were to sit there listening, when my thoughts wander off to what we were having for lunch or something that happened during the week.

My background is in education, and my current work is supporting young people, so the main way that I serve at my church is in the children's work. I am part of a small team of leaders and helpers who plan and run

> the kids' sessions while the sermon is happening. I think my training and personal experience have made me aware of including different aspects within a session, as I know that we all learn differently and will enjoy different things.

DYSPRAXIA (DEVELOPMENTAL COORDINATION DISORDER)

Dyspraxia is another neurodevelopmental condition which affects people's everyday lives but is a relatively unseen disability. Its 'official' name (as used by the NHS or World Health Organization) is developmental coordination disorder (DCD), but dyspraxia is a widely used alternative and is often preferred, as it includes the wider range of challenges those with the condition may face. The word dyspraxia means 'difficulty in doing'. It encompasses difficulties with coordination, both fine and gross motor skills, as well as additional problems common for dyspraxic people, like difficulty concentrating, following instructions, and being organised. As with dyslexia, problems like difficulty making friends, behavioural problems, and low self-esteem probably follow their experience of life rather than being inherently a part of the condition.

A diagnosis of DCD will always include a motor assessment, looking at evidence that the individual's level of coordination is below expected developmental levels. Children with DCD are likely to have difficulty playing sports which require coordination, control, and balance. They may find tasks like getting dressed and eating neatly with cutlery much more difficult. Adults with DCD may continue to be clumsy, have poor handwriting, or struggle to use tools. They may be unwilling to try new physical tasks, partly through finding them more challenging, but also through being long-accustomed to failure in this area. Some find that it affects their speech, sometimes called 'verbal dyspraxia', as their motor control over the muscles used for speaking does not allow for clear and fluent speech.

As with dyslexia, there are a number of secondary difficulties associated with DCD: organisational difficulties, low self-esteem, and difficulties in social interaction. Some difficulties overlap with other neurodevelopmental conditions like autism: dyspraxic people often experience sensory sensitivities and have difficulty sleeping. The way we approach loving those with DCD in our church families will depend on the individual. Many of the strategies mentioned above for supporting those with poor organisational skills will be relevant here, as well as those in chapter 10, which focuses on sensory processing disorder.

One way we can be considerate of those with dyspraxia in our congregations is by encouraging a range of different social opportunities. It is common for our youth groups, weekends away, children's activity holidays, and even informal get-togethers to be dominated by sports, particularly for the men. This may not be a problem – not all those with dyspraxia are unable to take part in sports – but particularly for young people, who may be less willing to join in with something if they're less competent than their peers, it can be good to have a range of activities for different skills and interests. Why not have a Mario Kart race on a games console or play some board games together? Meeting up with a group to go for a run in the park may be a way of including some physical activities without a competitive element.

DYSCALCULIA

Dyscalculia has not been given as much recognition as other SpLDs. This is partly because definitions and causes of dyscalculia are still under discussion and partly because it can be confused with general difficulty with mathematics. While someone may struggle with mathematics for a whole range of reasons, dyscalculia is considered a neurodevelopmental condition, because a difference in brain wiring (not intellectual ability) affects individuals' ability to work with numbers as well as wider abilities, such as working memory and visual and spatial awareness. In everyday life, an adult with dyscalculia will be likely to struggle to write down a phone number, remember their own phone number, know the relative values of different coins, or understand directions. They may struggle to read the time on a clock or understand what it means. They may take longer to find a verse in the Bible when given a numerical reference, and might find it helpful to have a spatial instruction as well, such as 'halfway down the page'.

DEVELOPMENTAL LANGUAGE DISORDER

Developmental language disorder (DLD) is a lifelong condition which causes difficulties with speaking and understanding words that is not explained by any other condition. It is relatively little known compared to other difficulties, but it is thought to affect 1 in 15 children, continuing to affect individuals into adulthood. In many cases, the difficulty with language may be seen in challenging behaviour or difficulty making friends, particularly in childhood. DLD limits an individual's ability to understand:

- the sounds which make up words and then the words which make up sentences
- the meaning conveyed by words
- the goals or intention of the speaker.

Let's consider an example to clarify these three aspects of language. In the phrase 'Jesus is the king of kings', we hear words, made of syllables and sounds, each of which we understand and can decode. We may also recognise a truth claim – that Jesus Christ is a ruler over all others. Finally, we might infer the speaker's purpose – they are praising Jesus. We do all this without thinking, even if we do not know the technical terms for all these elements which go together to produce meaning. Someone with DLD may have difficulty with receptive language (what is understood), expressive language (what the individual is able to communicate), or both.

A child with DLD may struggle to communicate what they want clearly. This can lead to frustration, both with peers and adults. They may struggle to sit calmly while instructions are being given or a story is being told, as they are finding it hard to follow the words. As they get older, the difficulties may affect their ability to understand non-literal phrases, jokes, and slang. Children with DLD may have a stammer or feel self-conscious about talking in front of others.

Whether we're engaging a child in conversation after a church service, teaching them in a small group, or joining their family for a social meal, we can show them love by listening well. We can take time to listen to what they have to say, getting down to their level if necessary to enable them to get the full benefit of the meaning conveyed by our face. We can repeat back what a child has said, not to correct them, but to establish that we are listening and trying to understand. We can be careful not to make comments about their language skills which may make them feel more self-conscious. If we are really struggling to understand a young person, we can apologise (if possible, take the blame yourself!) and ask them for help: can they say it in another way? Can they show us? If their difficulties are particularly in understanding, the problem may be less obvious in their speech, and may come out as 'poor behaviour' as the child misbehaves to cover up for their lack of understanding.

We may not know the diagnostic background of every child in our church community – the child may not even have a diagnosis yet – but we can be slow to judge and quick to support, help, and love, knowing that 'bad' behaviour is often the child's way of communicating a challenge they are experiencing. Families may benefit from help in finding out what speech and language therapy is available in their area, as waiting lists are often long and applications require persistence and advocacy.

DLD is a lifelong condition, so we are likely to come across adults with difficulties in the same area, although they may not have a diagnosis of DLD. Research suggests that adults with DLD are much less likely to be able to drive (they struggle to pass the theory element of their test), will have had lower academic achievement and therefore more limited employment options, and will continue to struggle with aspects of expressive and/or receptive language. It is easy to dismiss someone with poor language skills as less intelligent, unworthy of our conversation, or uninteresting. However, if we take time to get to know them and support them as a friend, we will find the gifts God has given them. Some of the adaptations mentioned above for dyslexia will also be valuable in small groups or to allow adults with DLD to benefit from talks and Bible readings.

AREN'T THESE JUST EXCUSES?

These labels aren't just a way of saying someone isn't very good at something, but describe a fundamentally different way of thinking and seeing the world. Loving our friends with SpLDs starts from understanding them better and trying to see the world as they see it. However, if we have a SpLD, it is easy to fall into the trap of thinking that God can't use you in particular ways because of your difficulties in that area. This can easily lead us into a self-centred way of seeing our gifts and our service to our Christian communities.

Throughout the Bible, God uses people who don't necessarily seem well equipped for the tasks ahead of them – and as a result, God is glorified all the more. A well-known example is Moses, who tries to duck out of the task of speaking to Pharaoh on behalf of God's people, saying:

> 'Pardon your servant, Lord. I have never been eloquent, neither in the past nor since you have spoken to your servant. I am slow of speech and tongue.'

The Lord said to him, 'Who gave human beings their mouths? Who makes them deaf or mute? Who gives them sight or makes them blind? Is it not I, the Lord? Now go; I will help you speak and will teach you what to say.'
EXODUS 4:10-12

God uses Moses in spite of his challenges, and gives him what he needs to do the job God has given him. In the same way, God is able to use both the strengths and weaknesses of our neurotype for his glory.

We met Reuben, who shows us how God has used him through and in spite of his dyspraxia:

REUBEN'S STORY

I am the youth and children's lead at a wonderful church in London. I've been greatly blessed by how the Lord has filled my life with faithful churches who have discipled me in the faith with Christ-honouring teaching.

I've heard a saying: 'Head, heart, hands.' I tell it to the children I work with. Paul tells us in Titus that a knowledge of the truth leads to godliness (Titus 1:1), and so our belief impacts our actions. Jesus tells us that the mouth speaks what the heart is full of (Matthew 12:34). It is difficult for us, in our theology, to imagine a world where someone's actions are not connected to, or impacted by, their heart.

So as someone with dyspraxia, what does that mean for my everyday ministry work?

What does it mean when I ask the same organisation-related question many times, when my daily priorities are all over the place, when I take a day to complete the planning time for Sunday school sessions that others would think to be simple, and send it off full of spelling mistakes?

What does it mean when I'm not asking the right questions or structuring my time in such a way that looks as if I'm not taking ownership of my ministry, when I forget to bring the key components necessary for that day's Sunday school, or when I'm asked to do one thing and then I return a different result entirely?

What does it mean when there are simple tasks that any ordinary person would have done, and I seem to fail?

I believe (mostly) in 'Head, heart, hands.'

Does this mean I am being lazy? Sinful? Callous towards my ministry area? Is this a heart problem?

I wonder if we sometimes put 'Head, heart, hands' in the wrong order. I can have the best heart intentions, and my hands can work absolutely according to what those are, but in the middle is my head.

If you want to know how dyspraxia can feel, it's like if the entire catalogue of information you have in your head regularly undergoes being shot through with a gun. Holes could exist in any information that I think I understand perfectly, and (although sometimes I know what I don't know) I often have no idea that the holes are there.

Imagine that your to-do list, priorities, and goals are all written on a deck of cards. At any time, and you're not sure when, that deck shuffles itself. I can (and do) maintain a rigorous structure, calendar, and to-do list. I am (and try to be) self-organised as much as I possibly can. I can have the purest heart attitudes. And still, I won't know.

In your churches, it would surprise me if the dyspraxic didn't look like something similar. It would surprise me if they could accurately tell you their reasoning for doing something that looks stupid, lazy, poorly thought through, or disorganised. It would surprise me if they felt comfortable in the work they were doing, if they weren't anxious that they could drop the ball at any time and felt that they were managing mostly on improvisation and luck.

It would surprise me if they wouldn't benefit from a large helping of patience and an acknowledgement that their hands don't necessarily portray the whole picture of their heart.

TOP 10 FOR EVERYONE

① Specific learning difficulties/differences are not illnesses; be careful how you describe them.

② Try not to equate challenges in a particular area with low intelligence, even in your mind.

③ Research what technology or printed material might help a friend.

④ Challenging behaviour from a child or young person may be their way of communicating that they are struggling; react with compassion, not anger.

⑤ Be patient with poor organisation and time-keeping; offer support not criticism.

⑥ Try to keep social activities varied and step outside your own comfort zone.

⑦ From the front of church/children's groups, give clear instructions and time to process them.

⑧ Remember not everyone processes information at the same speed.

⑨ Give people with SpLDs opportunities to serve if they want to.

⑩ Help friends with SpLDs remember they are dearly loved by God and made in his image when they are tempted to feel low self-esteem.

Autism

TRIONA BRADING

AN INTRODUCTION TO AUTISM

Autism is a lifelong neurodevelopmental disorder. It is not a disease; it means your brain works in a different way to other people. It is something you are born with, although sometimes it may not be noticed in childhood. The differences in the way the autistic brain works will mean that autistic children and adults will have 'additional needs' – a bit more support or acceptance than we would expect a 'typical' person to need. Some will have much higher support needs than others.

Throughout this chapter we use 'identity-first' language over 'person-first' language when referring to autism; that is, 'autistic' rather than 'person with autism'. This choice has been made because it is the preference of the majority of the autistic community. Although this is the choice of language we will use, it is always worth checking with an individual about their preferred language.

There is much discussion about whether, as a society, we should recognise autism as simply a difference or as a disabling condition. Part of the confusion around this comes from the diversity within the spectrum itself. For some, it is vital that autism is a recognised disability, as they need that label to access vital support, care, and services. For others (particularly those with lower support needs), 'difference' seems to fit better. And yet, even for those who may appear to have 'typical' lives, there is still suffering. For example, the rate of suicide in autistic people is as much as eight times that of neurotypical people.[1] The overlap between autism and mental health struggles is staggering, with the phenomenon of 'masking' (altering your behaviour to appear more neurotypical and blend in) taking a real toll.[2] A study conducted in 2022 found that 90% of autistic women had been victims of sexual assault and autistic people across the whole spectrum are at greater risk of abuse due to their social communication difficulties.[3]

Whatever the level of support needs of an individual, to have received a diagnosis, there is a recognition that this person is facing barriers and experiencing a level of suffering. As Christians we understand suffering as part of the fall, as discussed in chapter 1. However, there are also elements of the autistic experience that can lead us to praise God. Caleb's story, as told by his mother, illustrates some of this beauty.

CALEB'S STORY

Caleb is 12 and is severely autistic, has ADHD, and is non-verbal. He's not hung up on his 'social standing': he's very loving and affectionate, so will go up to people, often people on the margins, and give them a hug or show an interest in them, and it breaks down a lot of barriers. He makes people laugh, and he's just kind of a free spirit. And I think people really like giving to him. I always felt guilty asking others to look after him, but people have told me that it gives them a lot and they enjoy spending that time with him. It's easy to talk about the last being first, but you don't often see that in the congregation. As he goes to the youth group, the other children will learn about service and caring for others. Even if it's just teaching them to give him a high five, going to play with him, discovering he's a really fun character, they will learn the joys of service and love.

While certain autistic traits may leave us vulnerable to suffering, they may simultaneously point us to God's design for humanity. For example, while it may be the social norm to be able to tell a white lie, we can all learn from the genuine pain it can cause autistic people when truth is not expressed precisely or literally. A rigid love of order can be debilitating, but also reflects the God who brings order out of chaos. A special interest, although sometimes tedious for others, allows a depth of understanding in one area. While some sensory experiences can be painful for autistic people, others can bring a corresponding level of joy and delight in God's creation. It's important not to use language that may suggest autism is 'as a result of the fall'. See chapters 1 and 4 for more thoughts on this.

Autism is characterised by differences in social communication and social imagination (how we communicate, interpret what others say, and understand their perspective), as well as repetitive and/or restrictive behaviours and interests. Autism is a spectrum condition, which has often been misunderstood as linear, ranging from mild to severe. However, the autistic spectrum is more like a circle or colour wheel, with a unique profile for every individual. This means that each autistic person will present differently; for example, communication difficulties can mean being non-speaking, but it can also mean difficulties in understanding metaphorical language or tone of voice or not understanding non-verbal communication.

Many people will see themselves reflected within areas of the autistic spectrum, but there is research that the shape and size of particular areas of an autistic brain differ to a neurotypical brain. People recognise themselves in traits, because autistic traits are human traits, but that does not make everyone a little bit autistic; it makes all autistic people human. It is when this specific combination of criteria comes together to a sufficient degree that one can be diagnosed as autistic.

Caleb's story shows one presentation of autism, where the impact of communication difficulties is so great that he is unable to speak. His sensory-processing difficulties also make church a challenging environment to be in, but his parents and church family are working together to meet his needs.

CALEB'S STORY (CONTINUED)

It's been really hard since Caleb was born; he has severe sleeping difficulties, and I would say it's really only in the last years that I've felt comfortable going to church. However, the first time we went to our church, the senior minister noticed that Caleb was really struggling with the music, and asked if we would like them to turn it down. I was just completely stunned that someone would have that consideration.

Previously, it was just very difficult to take him to church, because I felt like people were judging us, and he's quite disruptive. He's quite noisy and he does a lot of stimming [self-stimulatory behaviour]. He can't really join in with the activities that they are doing at Sunday school, so often one of us would stay with him and he would just run around, and it just felt kind of pointless and eventually we stopped going. But now at our current church, we've got a rota set up, so two weeks out of four we have two people helping him. We're also trying to come up with a curriculum and activities for him to do. He's also got cognitive impairments so he can't read, so the level of activities he can do in a church context needs to be very basic. It makes it difficult for him to be in a Sunday school with children of his own age – they are now quite advanced and he's still playing. He will run around and jump on the trampoline. So at the moment he is in a room on his own with one or two carers, so that we can go to the service.

He's very dysregulated a lot of the time, so it's quite hard for him to keep calm and he needs to do particular things to keep himself calm. He's constantly running around, so a typical Sunday school setting was quite difficult for him. It's really only since being at this church that I've felt comfortable or felt that he was welcome, because before I just felt that he was disrupting everyone or making noise. He also finds really noisy kids quite difficult, so that was quite hard. In order to stay calm, he flaps and makes noises and other children don't understand these behaviours.

He wears ear defenders because of the noise, and he needs a very calm, low-arousal environment. We tried to take him in to the start of the service before the kids went out, and that works some of the time. And then he goes out to his room and he will spend some time jumping on the trampoline and then roaming around the room, but what we are trying to do is to start to read him some stories, and build some Christian input into his little Sunday school.

I think it's been a journey for me because it's also something that's changed in me. I've realised what God's heart for church is and that actually Caleb has every right to be there, and I mustn't feel guilty for asking churches to make some concessions.

AUTISM AND ACCESSIBILITY IN CHURCH

When thinking about accessibility, it is worth pointing out that autism often has co-occurring diagnoses or conditions. In this chapter, we are specifically focusing on autism itself, not the co-occurring conditions. If you are seeking to consider how you can make church accessible for someone with autism and a co-occurring condition, we recommend you use information from this chapter alongside information from our other relevant chapters. There are many excellent resources you could use in parallel with this information to support access to church for those who are struggling with their mental health.[4]

When seeking to make church an autism-friendly environment, the priority should be knowing your autistic church family members well, and creating an environment in which it is comfortable to have discussions around their individual strengths and struggles. This is something all of us can be part of as we share our own difficulties.

MASKING

Autistic masking is where an autistic person learns, practises, and performs certain behaviours to appear more neurotypical in a social setting. It is this phenomenon that has led to years of misunderstanding of the female presentation of autism, as women and girls are more likely to mask than their male counterparts. Masking can be suppressing or changing behaviours that feel natural or soothing, such as stimming. This might mean twirling your hair rather than flapping your hands. Masking can also include copying the non-verbal behaviours of others or developing what is known as a 'social script' in order to survive social situations without others thinking that you are weird or abnormal.

While adapting to different settings is a normal human behaviour, it can cause a far greater mental load to an autistic person and is used as a survival strategy across more settings. It can even be detrimental to an autistic person's well-being, as it can feel as though you are always trying to hide your true self, as it would not be acceptable or well received by those around you. We are not saying that autistic people should never have to mask, but rather that we can meet them halfway: the neurotypical person could sacrifice their own desire for eye contact, for example, while the autistic person works hard to have a social conversation with them. We should, however, realise that for some, masking is not an option. An individual who is non-speaking, for example, cannot start speaking in order to mask their disability.

THE SENSES

The sensory processing experience of an autistic person differs to that of a neurotypical person. Each sense can be either hyper (over) or hypo (under) sensitive, and autistic people can show either sensory-seeking or sensory-avoidant behaviour. The autistic sensory experience of the world is one of intensity and vibrancy, which can bring joy, but can also be overwhelming. When the intensity of a sensory experience is overwhelming, it is known as sensory overload. Sensory overload can be difficult to manage and can show itself in the individual as anything from irritability to shutdown or meltdown (see below).

If there are known autistic members of your church family, it can be good to learn and understand more of their sensory profile. Are there any sensory experiences that are hugely uncomfortable or even painful for them? Is there a sensory experience that they gain great joy from? The more that you know someone, the more easily you will be able to pre-empt barriers to worship and work together to make church an accessible environment. We often leave this kind of conversation for someone else to have – a church leader, for example. However, we can show love by our interest in another person, and we may find ourselves in a position to help! In one church we have visited, a congregation member decided to put together some little 'sensory packs' (containing some fidgets and tactile materials) to leave by their church door with a sign inviting anyone, adult or child, to borrow one for the service if needed.

The following chapter will deal in more detail with sensory processing difficulties, as these are not unique to autism.

MELTDOWNS AND SHUTDOWNS

Any and all of the stresses mentioned above – additional vulnerability and emotional struggles, the intensity of masking all day in social settings, and the constant onslaught to the senses – can push autistic people into meltdown or shutdown. The reaction will depend on the individual, but both shutdowns and meltdowns are extreme, uncontrollable reactions to a level of stress which has exceeded the individual's capacity to tolerate. A meltdown can be thought of as being an 'explosion', often with tears, shouting, and physical outbursts, while a shutdown is more of an 'implosion', when the individual may be unable to talk or move and may physically withdraw. Both reactions are outside of the individual's control and are not limited to children – they should not be seen as being like a tantrum, even if externally there may be similarities.

Supporting an individual during either a meltdown or shutdown will mean keeping them and others safe. They may need space and reduced or increased sensory input to help them regulate. A meltdown will climax relatively quickly, while a shutdown is a lower state of energy that can last for hours, days, or even months. As regulation strategies will vary so much person to person, the most useful thing you can do is make the dignity of the person your priority. We can redirect others away from the situation, help the person to a safe and quiet space, or even take them home if needed. We can model in our speech how we talk about meltdowns and shutdowns with others, lovingly correcting those who may describe them as 'tantrums' or 'attention seeking'.

LANGUAGE AND COMMUNICATION

In Christian life we do a lot of communication. We exchange emails, texts, and WhatsApp messages. We chat over coffee and meals. We have sermons and seminars. We pray, we sing, and we might even have some all-age action songs! As communication differences are central to the autistic experience, this is a key area to address.

1 Figurative language

We use figurative language a lot. Every culture has its own idioms and our language (even in this book) is scattered with metaphors. For an autistic person, who is more likely to take things literally, this can sometimes cause confusion.

2 Sarcasm

Sarcasm is frequently used but can be hard to detect. It's not about avoiding it entirely, just being mindful of when and how it's used and offering clarification if needed.

3 Rhetorical questions

Rhetorical questions are common in sermons and discussions, but literal thinkers may not realise a response isn't expected. Clarifying with phrases, like 'I don't need an answer' or 'Just think about this', can prevent confusion.

4 Non-verbal communication

A huge amount of our communication is done non-verbally. Non-verbal communication can be difficult for autistic people, where there could be a tendency to take what is spoken at face value. They may also use unexpected body language themselves. An awareness of this, while being clear in what you are saying, can help minimise confusion.

THOSE WHO DO NOT SPEAK

While some autistic people can have very clear spoken communication, there are some autistic people who are non-speaking. This may be their choice or the result of a co-occurring learning difficulty, but being non-speaking does not always equate to a lower level of cognitive function or understanding. The BBC's *Inside Our Minds*[5] showcases this very clearly as we meet Murray, who shares his experience as a non-speaking autistic man through creating a film with Chris Packham. Someone unable to speak may be able to understand fully, so we should not assume they are unable to comprehend our words. As with all disabilities and difference, we must treat everybody with the respect and dignity due to an image-bearer. It is common for people to speak to those who are non-speaking or who have a disability as though they are children or even babies. Interacting with somebody in an age-appropriate way (while using clear, simple vocabulary) is an important way to show them love and respect.

Alongside this it is worth finding out an individual's preferred method of communication. Some people may use Makaton or a similar sign-supported speech system, while others may use AAC (alternative/augmentative communication system). AAC could be a book with symbols or an app on a tablet. It could be that an individual types what they wish to say, and it is read by an automated voice. Some autistic individuals are sometimes non-speaking and at other times verbal. Some are able to speak but find it easier to communicate through writing or text.

Communication can take many forms and spoken words are not the only way for someone to express themselves.

If you know you have someone in your church or other Christian group who uses a form of AAC, it may be hard for them to join group conversations. Inviting them to pick the topic of conversation, and advocating for them by asking others to wait and not interrupt can make a huge difference. We might need to change our expectations of non-verbal cues and speed of conversation; even one person modelling this to others will help more members of your group catch on to how to include them.

Mark shared with us what life looks like for his son James, who has almost no spoken communication.[6]

JAMES' STORY

James is 22 and was diagnosed aged 2 as autistic and with a learning disability. At 15, he was also diagnosed with epilepsy and social anxiety, and there are other undiagnosed additional needs that James journeys with. We are a church family (we also have a daughter, Phoebe, aged 25), and since they were little we have always taken our children to church. James has almost no spoken communication, and needs one-to-one support wherever he goes, so from an early stage we needed to have support in place at church. Thankfully, our church was keen to provide that support, with James attending the church preschool during the week and the crèche and then Sunday school at church, typically with the same people supporting him at both. On the whole, the church accepted James for who he is and got to know him and how to support him best. That often involved tailored activities that James would take part in, focused on the things he likes to do (he has always enjoyed art and craft, for example).

The church congregation were great with James; of course, there were times when James might make a loud noise in the middle of a quiet moment in a service and some people would look and frown (I call these the 'meerkats'), but most of them were kind and supportive, understanding and caring (I call these the 'additional needs lions').

As he grew and became a teenager, that support continued with a small team of one-to-one helpers, one of whom would always be there for James when he was at church with us on a Sunday morning. When James was 15, epilepsy arrived along with associated social anxiety and James' attendance at church reduced significantly, to the point where he isn't able to go at all currently. He finds it too busy, too loud, too much. A couple of people from church still support him at home, though, and he is regularly asked about and not forgotten.

The support given to James over the years has enabled the rest of us to be able to actively participate in church. Our daughter, Phoebe, was in the worship band before she married and moved away; my wife, Clare, is still involved in the children's work; and I get to preach and lead sometimes or occasionally help with the youth work. None of this would have been possible if the church, and certain individuals in particular, hadn't stepped up to support James. Of course, there is always more that can be done; in our case, James was well looked after while at church, but there wasn't much that was geared towards his ongoing spiritual development.

There is often a misconception that non- or minimally speaking autistic people (of any age) are intellectually lacking. While James has minimal speech (a handful of words), he can, and does, still communicate in other ways, such as sounds, gestures, facial expressions, body language, and sometimes signing or symbols. Seeing him navigating to something he wants on his iPad, whizzing through lists and menus faster than I can keep up with, shows that there is a keen mind at work there.

I believe that James is able to have a spiritual relationship with God, and this is evidenced in several ways. Since birth, I have sung over James each night that old chorus 'Jesus loves me, this I know'; there have been adaptations to the words over the years, with the line 'little ones to him belong…' becoming 'teenagers to him belong…' and more recently 'twenty-somethings to him belong…', but the song has remained part of our bedtime prayer and worship time routine. James' limited repertoire of spoken words comes in here as he can join in with 'Yes! Jesus loves me!' and often finishes with a resounding 'Ah-men!' During this time of prayer and worship, I often see a look of joy on James' face. Yes, in part, it is because he enjoys these consistent times together, but I also believe that God is there with us, ministering to

James in those moments, and that James is responding. Does James have a deep theological understanding of the things of God? No. Does he know that Jesus loves him? Absolutely yes!

As James is unable to get to church currently due to social anxiety, the visits from church members help him and us to feel that he is not forgotten, but is still part of the church family. We hope that we will be able to support James to come back into church again in the future, but until then we are encouraged by the support we are given and the encouragement James receives to be an influential part of the wider church, as it continues to strive beyond accessibility and inclusion to reach true belonging for all.

PREDICTABILITY

Predictability and routine are key factors in encouraging an autistic person to thrive. This does not mean that you must always follow an unchanging structure, but there are ways you can add predictability to your Sundays and midweek activities. Some aspects of church life may be outside our control, but sometimes offering your time to work towards a solution is a great way to encourage leadership teams in the right direction.

Website

What does your website communicate about your church life? Does it give an accurate impression of what someone might experience when coming to your church? Photos that show the spaces clearly are helpful in visualising what it could be like to come to your church. Do you say roughly how many people attend the services or groups? Do you give a general sense of the components of a service or club? If you wanted to be more proactive, you could write a social story that can be downloaded from your website about coming to a service or group. Maybe you could offer to take photographs of different areas of church life for the website manager to add. Or write a 'member's eye view' of what happens in your group.

Orders of service/programmes

An order of service, setting out the order of events (such as prayer, singing, Bible teaching), is a brilliant resource to help someone to know what is coming up in a service. If you want to save paper you could include an order of service in your weekly email or have a small number printed out at the back of church available to those who find them helpful.

Communicating around change

If you know that there is a change coming up for an autistic member of your congregation, small group, or youth group, communicating this in advance is very helpful in giving them time and space to prepare for it. There are many ways this could be done: letting people know through a bulletin email, phoning the individual, or putting up a notice on a notice board. It is not that autistic people are unable to cope with change, it is that change can be a particularly hard thing to process when routines and predictability bring such a sense of safety and comfort. Knowing a change is coming, or even better, being included in the change, can make it much more comfortable.

In friendships

Perhaps most of these options feel outside your control as a church member, but you'd still like to show love to your autistic friend in this area. Think about what you can communicate ahead of inviting them round for dinner: are there any things they might find helpful to know in advance? If you are anticipating a big life change which you know will have an impact on your friend, think carefully about how you can communicate this ahead of time.

YOUTH AND CHILDREN

MAX'S STORY

Max has a 'classic' presentation of autism. If you look at him or watch him interact with others for five minutes, you'd see that there's something different about him. He knows the burden of his challenges more than I do as his parent, in a world that doesn't quite fit with the way his brain thinks. I can't imagine how difficult it is for him just to function on a day-to-day basis, and how difficult it is for him to do things which I just think are basic.

Despite this, he always comes across as very positive and full of joy. Especially now he's a teenager, it's becoming more obvious. Because of his social-emotional wiring, he has a 'simple' view of the world, a childlike trust and honesty. People are always saying 'what you see is what you get'; he doesn't mince words, which can be tricky sometimes! People say that they find it very refreshing. He is very black and white in a world where a lot of people try to make things a lot more complicated.

He's also not inhibited or embarrassed. In worship, he'll do the actions with exuberance, he doesn't have the barrier that a lot of people will have, worrying about how other people see them. With that comes some challenges: he doesn't understand social cues in a way that most people do. So that if he has a comment or a thought in the middle of a service, he will say it in a normal, or even slightly louder, voice, which can be disruptive.

The church has been really wonderful, welcoming us however loud or exuberant he wants to be during the worship time. I've never felt like I got dirty looks or people wondering why this giant, six-foot-two teenager is being so enthusiastic. It is something that we have been so blessed by. He does find it challenging to be quiet, for example when the pastor is speaking or in the prayers or any time when the congregation isn't expected to speak. Luckily, our service has lots of toddlers running around, so if somebody is noisy, it doesn't feel too out of the ordinary. That's really helped me not to feel embarrassed!

He definitely has some sensory challenges. He'll stim, he'll clench his hands when he's excited and happy or sometimes when he's anxious. You might see him fidget and move around. The biggest challenge he has is in the after-service coffee time. When there's a lot of unstructured activity, he can get very overwhelmed very quickly. There are often lots of people milling around at this time, and there's no clear expectations or structure. That's when he'll do a lot of stimming, he will wander around the outside of the sanctuary and not really engage with others. It's not a problem, he's not distressed and so if people recognise that that's just how he behaves, it's fine. Sometimes people don't know whether he's upset or whether they should talk to him. It's great if people understand that there's nothing wrong and they can approach him. Often he will then come out and engage in conversation.

> When he first started attending the children's groups at our current church, I also attended as an adult helper. He needed additional support, and it's difficult for the main leader to be able to always have to talk to him or get him back when he's wandering away. I helped until they got to know him and he got comfortable in the space. I also spent a lot of time talking to the youth leader about how he could best be supported. The leader was very open, and not fazed at all. They didn't see his needs as a problem, but wanted to ask how they could best make him feel comfortable. Their concern was always more about helping him feel part of the group rather than worrying about him being disruptive. It really blessed me, because I know that he is disruptive and can be difficult, but that was never a negative; he was never treated as a problem.
>
> He participates enthusiastically in welcome alongside us. Anytime there's something concrete and usually physical that needs to be done, he is very happy to help. So if we need to empty the baptismal pool or straighten the chairs, and give him clear instructions, he's very happy to do it. He struggles to anticipate a task which needs to be done, and the more complex and more interpersonal a task is, the more challenging it is for him.
>
> If I was trying to think about what Max contributes to the body, it is definitely more through his joy and his enthusiasm than physically carrying out tasks. It is a hugely comforting and humbling thing when people comment on how encouraged they are by his joy and how we interact as a family. It's just an amazing way that God uses him, and it seems like the church would be missing something without people of all different types. Just being able to see how he contributes in that way is really beautiful and is part of his service.

If you have youth and children's groups or clubs running at your church, having an awareness of how to include and support autistic children will be invaluable. This is not only for members of your church family with a diagnosis, but an inclusive and clued-up group is an exciting prospect for children attending your group for the first time. All of the previously mentioned accommodations will be relevant in a youth and children's setting, and in the same way as communicating with autistic adults about their experience and preferences, it is important to get to know the children and young people in your group. If you are speaking to the parents, you could ask what sort of support is in place for their child at school as a starting point for thinking what you can offer at church. Collaborating with families around supporting the child is key, as it will help to create consistency for the child.

General ways you can begin to make a children's group autism-friendly are:

- use a visual timetable
- be aware of the noise levels in the room
- give clear instructions, and say what you mean
- incorporate movement breaks
- be curious about the causes of particular behaviours.

If your church doesn't have groups for children on a Sunday or midweek, some accommodations are still possible. Flexible seating with space to move around or offering a quieter zone of the building can give autistic children space to self-regulate and feel comfortable in the service.

It is also worth noting that for some families, the journey to diagnosis and support for their child may have been far from straightforward, and they could be learning about autism for themselves for the first time. Have compassion towards these parents. Imagine a world where your church is their oasis – where they are able to come, knowing that they and their child are valued, loved, and their church family will go out of their way to meet their needs; where they are welcomed and wanted, loved and cared for. Listen to the parents and carers; if they say their child needs something, believe them. You may not see the fallout of that lack of provision, as the child or young person may appear 'fine' in your group – but they could well be masking, and at home, all the pent-up emotions come spilling out. It is difficult living as an autistic person in a neurotypical world, especially for children, who may be less equipped to advocate for themselves.

Remember Caleb's family? This is how they felt:

CALEB'S STORY (CONTINUED)

I've had a lot of pain from being rejected from churches; whether they meant to reject us or not, we were not made to feel welcome. Caleb didn't conform, and I felt like I was being judged for his behaviour – it really put me off church for quite a few years. I think there are a lot of

> special needs families in our position that just sit at home because they feel, 'My child's behaviour is not acceptable to people and I'm not going to put myself through that and put them in that position.'
>
> Going through a long journey towards diagnosis is normal; there are a lot of medical appointments and diagnoses. It's not just the children but also the parents who have been through a really hard time, and parents want to feel understood and accepted and part of the family. It's okay if it's all a bit mucky and messy and the kids make a bit of a noise in church on Sundays. When it's all about being polite and well-behaved, we can lose sight of the truth that we are all imperfect.

A story like this will almost certainly raise a number of emotions: grief for the families who feel excluded, guilt for our own past failings or lack of awareness, and perhaps some defensiveness. The first step towards loving people better is understanding them and their needs, so reading this book is a wonderful place to start. You may wish to ask people you know to share their own experiences of raising autistic children.

We don't have to be part of the youth and children's team to care well for autistic children and their parents and carers. It is worth encouraging neurotypical children to grow in their own understanding of autism and other disabilities and neurodivergence, so that the whole church family can capture the vision of what it means to love and include those who seem different to ourselves. Talk to your children, godchildren, and friends' children about neurodiversity and disability and the inherent value of humanity. Be considerate of any sensory needs or preferences that an autistic child may have, and don't assume rudeness if they react in a way that you do not expect when you interact with them. Speak to the parents and see if there are practical ways you can come alongside the whole family. Perhaps it is harder to find a babysitter who understands the specific needs of an autistic child in your congregation. If you have a positive relationship with this child, could you offer to babysit? If you have a family with an autistic child over for a meal, are you willing to cook something that feels safe for the autistic child to eat? Or perhaps it would be easier to meet at the child's home which is more familiar to them. Flexibility and communication are wonderful gifts to an autistic individual and their family.

PATHOLOGICAL DEMAND AVOIDANCE

There is a specific profile, widely considered to be within the autism spectrum,[7] known as pathological demand avoidance (PDA). This is where any perceived demand placed on an individual creates such anxiety that the task becomes impossible – even activities that the individual loves and wants to do. This is not simply demand avoidance, which is a feature of many neurotypes, but is specifically 'pathological' or 'pervasive'. An individual with PDA can go into 'fight, flight, or freeze mode' even in response to implied demands, such as being asked how they are (which implies a demand for a response). They might avoid normal self-care tasks like washing themselves and getting dressed. Self-imposed expectations can also be a challenge for someone with PDA, leading to extreme emotional dysregulation. Jo's story will help us understand what this looks like.

JO'S STORY

My daughter has taught me the true meaning of wonder and delight. She is forthright, determined, kind, sensitive, creative, and artistic. She brings joy every day and has taught me so much more about the nature and grace of God. She was diagnosed as autistic with a PDA profile when she was 8, in the middle of the COVID-19 pandemic. Even if my daughter really wants to do something, if she feels overwhelmed then she can't. A demand can apply to all sorts of things: praise is a demand; social expectations are a demand.

She went from surviving to not being okay at all. She was regularly having panic attacks and shutdowns. Because her response to demands is to 'freeze' or 'flop', things had to get fairly extreme before anyone really noticed and stopped saying she was 'fine in school'. She will curl up in a ball on the floor and be unable to speak, but others may have a 'fight' or 'flight' reaction.

Aged 9, she had what I can only describe as a mental health breakdown. She couldn't speak, move, or tolerate touch, and she barely ate. Three years later, there has been a very, very slow journey to recovery. At the time, my husband worked away from home, I worked full-time, and the pressure was intense. I couldn't leave the house as my daughter was so unwell; I couldn't go to the shops to buy milk.

> God has taught us to rely on him: we didn't know how to ask for help; we didn't know what we needed. It would have been very easy to have disappeared and never gone to church again, as life was just so hard. I asked for prayers. Friends from church offered to be a safe person in the house so I could go for a walk, brought food, prayed. One dear friend from church came away with us for a week so my husband and I could spend some time together. Our church provided one-to-one support so we could go to our church weekend away.
>
> What I think is hard is that this isn't temporary. Our daughter finds noise overwhelming and busy places terrifying, which makes going to church very difficult. Our church has been very supportive, in providing a safe quiet space for our daughter. We are now praying that God will show a way of how to integrate her back into the church community so she can participate and have friends.

It is characteristic of PDA that avoidance strategies may be social by nature. For example, their initial response to demands may include actively distracting someone with conversation, negotiating, or making elaborate excuses for not being able to do something. They may pretend to be an animal or pretend to be a teacher; in this way they avoid demands by role-playing a role others will not make demands of or a role of someone in a position of authority. Externally, they can appear sociable, often mimicking other people's social interactions, but they are likely to struggle to understand or recognise social hierarchies (such as their group leader being 'in charge').

Like autism, the presentations of PDA can vary greatly. One way PDA can affect individuals is by making their anxiety about interacting with others so great that they 'shut down' and become incapacitated in some way. They may become unable to speak, walk, or even see, unexplainable by any medical causes. PDA can be a cause of 'selective' or 'situational' mutism.

Many typical approaches to supporting those with autism do not apply to individuals with PDA. For example, a visual timetable can be perceived as a demand, making it anxiety-inducing rather than relieving. For adults with PDA, there can be an overwhelming desire to avoid the demands of everyday life, seeming to thrive on novelty and change. Mood swings can be a big part of living with PDA. For children with PDA, a collaborative approach and an invitation to participate, rather than an instruction, can often offer better chances of inclusion and engagement. An individualised approach is always the best when thinking about how to include and best serve somebody with PDA. For more specific information on PDA, the PDA Society has some excellent resources.[8]

SPECIFIC SKILLS AND SERVING

Many autistic people have a 'special interest'. This is an area of interest on which the autistic person can hyper-fixate, and provides refreshment and fulfilment to the individual. If you have ever had an autistic person monologue about their area of interest, you may have realised that special interests can easily (and often) become specialisms and areas of a huge amount of knowledge. For some autistic Christians, this can directly correlate to an area of serving in church. Musicians, AV teams, youth and children's work – if it's an area of interest for an autistic person, the likelihood is they will serve excellently, passionately, and with enthusiasm in that area.

TRIONA'S STORY

Triona, one of the authors of this book, is autistic. She shares her experience of three weekends away over three years, giving us an insight into her experiences and what has helped her.

Weekend 1
Arriving at my first church weekend away, a few months after graduating and beginning my new life in London, I began to feel the uncertainty and anxiety rise within me. I could hear noises from down the corridor, the lights were bright, and it was cold. I spotted a familiar face at the check-in table, the church administrator, and cautiously headed towards her. Thoughts were racing through my mind. *What am I supposed to do now? What do I do after I have checked in? Am I late for dinner? Is all that noise coming from the restaurant? What will the food be like? What if I don't like it? Is there anyone I know well here yet?*

I put on a smile and said my greetings. I was given my room card, and shown on a map where my room was, but my mind was fuzzy with the stress of a long day and all this new information hurtling towards my brain, jamming it and waiting to be processed. I was looking at the map but I couldn't see it. I set off in the direction I was pointed, looking for room 114. All the corridors seemed endless and confusing, and my brain just wasn't working properly. I felt on the verge of tears, and simultaneously really silly for getting myself worked up. I was an adult and a professional! Surely I could find a hotel room by myself.

Inside my room, I had no idea what to do next. I scoured the weekend's programme, but all it had was a vague 'Dinner 7–8.30'. Did that mean dinner started at 7 and I needed to rush as I was late? Or were you to arrive between 7 and 8.30? I texted some friends to see if they had arrived yet, and set off to find them, working my way back around the maze of corridors, clutching my programme and hoping things would become clearer soon.

In the dining hall cutlery rattled and scraped and clanged, and what felt like thousands of voices filled the air, competing with one another to take up the most space in my head. I couldn't take in the food options properly and just accepted whatever was offered. I found a seat, and sat, looking around the room, not feeling at all like eating due to the huge knot inside of me. A friend came to join me. 'You look like a startled meerkat!' he said, laughing. I gave a small, half-hearted laugh, slightly delayed because it took a while to turn the sounds he was making into words. 'Are you okay?' he asked, looking more closely at me. 'It's loud,' I replied.

I ate my food quickly and practically ran back to my room for some quiet. Lois came to find me, and as she sat on my bed I burst into tears, and could not stop. 'I just don't know what I'm doing, and I don't know why I can't just be normal. I should be able to be on a weekend away, but it's horrible,' I sobbed.

I was down to sing in the band, and the last thing I wanted to do was go back out into the chaos again. But I pushed my emotions and overwhelm down, and headed out to try to find somebody who could tell me where rehearsal was. I came across our vicar, a wonderfully optimistic and kind person. 'Hello Triona!', he greeted me warmly. 'Are you enjoying the start of the weekend?'

'No.' I replied bluntly. Somewhere deep inside my brain, I felt a voice saying, *That's rude! You shouldn't have said that! Say something else!*, but my words were all tangled together in an uncomfortable knot in my chest, and nothing more was coming out of my mouth.

'Oh,' said our vicar. 'Anything in particular?'

I searched for the words to communicate with him, but it felt like walking through thick, wet sand in heavy boots. 'I don't know what I'm doing or where I'm supposed to be,' I managed, still clinging to my programme as if it could help me. I could feel that tears were not far away.

'Have you been here before? This is your first weekend away with us, isn't it?' he asked kindly. 'How about I show you around, so you can see the rooms we will be based in for this weekend?'

I nodded gratefully, blinking back the tears, and followed closely as he talked me through the space and the programme. I could feel the tension beginning to dispel as the world of the conference centre began to make sense, and I was able to predict what the rest of the weekend would be like. The vicar dropped me off at the main meeting room, the last stop on the tour, and where the band rehearsal was beginning. Although I was still struggling to speak more than the bare minimum, once we began rehearsing I was able to sing, and the rhythm of the music began to soothe me, helping me relax.

For the rest of the weekend, I was able to engage with the sessions and find my way around, but during the social parts of the weekend I would again feel overwhelmed. I retreated to my room instead of joining afternoon activities, pleased for the refuge, but sad that I didn't feel able to get to know my church family.

Weekend 2
My phone buzzed, and I looked down at the text that had come in:

> *I have the list of questions you had about the new CWA venue. I've got answers to all of them, so I'll message you tomorrow with that. Hope that's okay! Looking forward to seeing you and hanging out this weekend!*

The week before our church weekend away, the venue had contacted the church to say that they had double-booked, and we could no longer come! An absolute organisational nightmare for the staff team, and yet while also sourcing a new venue in record timing, they had thought to keep me in the loop about it! Two years after arriving at the church, I felt very settled and at home at church. I had made friends, was part of a home group I adored, and I loved being part of both the youth and kids and music teams. Church community was one of my favourite things about the church, and I was really excited for the weekend.

It also helped that in building friendships and relationships, people had begun to know and understand me. As a late-diagnosed autistic person, it wasn't always obvious that there were certain things that could really throw me, last-minute changes being one of them. One of my home group leaders was on the staff team and had alerted me early to the change in venue. She let me send a list of questions about the venue that she took on the visit, so that I could begin to understand what to expect ahead of arrival. I knew that my room would be near to a close friend, and because I had now been to two church weekends away ahead of this one, I knew roughly what to expect from the structure of the weekend. I was really looking forward to spending time with church family… and a swim in the pool!

Packing ready to go, I made sure I had my earplugs. I knew that some parts of the weekend would be loud, and I had discovered these earplugs that reduced the noise without fully blocking it out were helpful in giving me a greater tolerance for noisy environments, while still allowing me to join in conversation.

Upon arrival, I bounded up to the administrator with a smile on my face, happy to be part of the church weekend away.

Weekend 3
I travelled to the weekend away with a family from church, chatting and making owl noises to amuse their toddler. I arrived at the venue, dropped off my stuff in my room, grabbed my earplugs and headed to dinner. In the dining hall I spotted the visiting speaker and his family. They used to be part of our church before he went for training, so I knew him and his wife, but I hadn't seen their son since he was a few months old. I suddenly clocked that he would be in the kids group I was running for the weekend!

I went over and asked to introduce myself, so that he would know who I was before being dropped off in the morning. I was very much looking forward to spending four sessions with the 2–4-year-olds of our church. I had spent the weeks leading up to this weekend preparing a toddler-friendly Bible overview, and all the various songs, crafts, and themed free-play activities to go with it. I loved teaching some of the youngest of the church family, and having a job to do at a weekend away helped me feel grounded, confident, and calm.

'Triona, great to see you, how are you feeling about the weekend? Prepared?' asked the optimistic vicar who had seen me on the brink of tears in a similar setting four years previously.

'Yep. Everyone seems surprised that I feel prepared, but I know I am!', I replied. 'I'm really looking forward to it!'

He gave a small laugh and said, 'Well, maybe it's because it's a rare thing to be so well prepared at our church!'

I laughed and went to join a group of friends for a chat.

I was able to join the rest of the church family for the first evening session of the weekend. I felt the familiar nerves of deciding where to sit. I spotted somebody from my small group and sat with them. Now I had someone to sit with, I could relax into the evening. I stood to sing feeling content.

'And a good example of this is our new strapline, which is?' Without missing a beat I began loudly, 'Every life… following… Jesus…' I trailed off a little embarrassed, as I realised no one else was answering the question aloud. I sank down in my chair as people turned and smiled. Oops. I thought I was getting better at recognising rhetorical questions!

I thought back a number of weeks to an occasion on which I had enthusiastically called out a response in a sermon, misjudging the expectation. And then there was the time I had really thought I nailed it, sitting quietly, yet the rest of the congregation seemingly had some sort of ability to determine that this was the one time the speaker *did* want an audible response!

Oh well. I sat back up. I was sure that nobody thought any less of me for making these mistakes, and it was my pride that was making me feel embarrassed. Time to chill out and be thankful for grace!

The weekend was refreshing and encouraging. Many commented on how exhausted I must be after spending the weekend with so many small children, but I had loved every minute. I had also taken great joy in running a seminar with Lois and Claire on accessibility and our church. Accessibility, inclusion, and SEND is one of my deepest and greatest passions. And the chance to share some of God's heart on it with church family was fantastic! The energy I had gained through these things meant that I was able to socialise with confidence and really enjoy spending time with the members of our church.

Although I had missed the main teaching sessions, there were engaging conversations I was able to join throughout the weekend. Being involved in the weekend away in this capacity meant I had much more information ahead of time, and I was able to use my love of routine and structure to plan the 2–4-year-olds' sessions in a way that meant we were organised and prepared. I found refreshment in God's word in the preparation of the material, and while I know I was serving the church family, the weekend still served me massively.

TOP 10 FOR EVERYONE

① Do your best with language: autism is not an illness which can be 'caught' or 'cured', and many autistic people find 'high-' or 'low-functioning' labels misleading or offensive.

② Allow autistic people to drop their 'mask' where possible when you're around; don't try to force 'normal' behaviour on them, even if it makes you uncomfortable.

③ Challenging behaviour from a child or young person may be their way of communicating that they are struggling; react with compassion, not anger.

④ Communicate details in advance when arranging to meet an autistic friend from church.

⑤ Take time to have a conversation with a non-speaking member of your church.

⑥ Invite an autistic child to come and chat to you (or at you…) about their special interest: you will make their day.

⑦ Offer to babysit for a family with an autistic child to give them rest time.

⑧ Offer to help someone in your church or Christian community work through the forms and applications required to access support or assessment.

⑨ Offer to produce visuals (photographs or drawings) for your church website which might support an autistic person considering attending for the first time.

⑩ Check in on autistic members of your church family when routines change or in unusual events to see if you can support them.

10

Sensory processing disorder

TRIONA BRADING

Sensory processing is the way that our bodies receive and make sense of information. We may be aware of the five senses: sight, touch, taste, smell, and hearing. However, when we think about our sensory processing, we must also consider the lesser-known senses: proprioception (the awareness of our body in the space around it), interoception (an awareness of our internal body feelings, such as hunger, thirst, need for the toilet, and temperature), and vestibular processing (which helps with balance and movement).

We all use our senses every day to interact with the world around us, and we are all sensory beings. It is God's design to create a multisensory world that we can explore and enjoy. When we read through the creation account in Genesis, we can imagine this perfect, vibrant world filled with different colours, patterns, textures, sounds, tastes, and smells, which God declares very good. In the New Testament we are given sacraments, the Lord's supper and baptism – both highly sensory experiences – as a way to remember and proclaim what Jesus did for us at the cross and our commitment to following him.

Many church activities, such as midweek music, 'stay and play' groups aimed at toddlers, or Messy Church, already make use of the senses to engage children and adults in the message we are sharing. We have seen immersive drama used effectively in schools outreach at our local church. These sensory activities and experiences can be particularly engaging for those with sensory processing disorder.

Sensory processing disorder (SPD) affects the way the brain processes sensory inputs. It can show itself as either hyposensitivity (under-sensitivity) or hypersensitivity (heightened sensitivity) to sensory stimuli. This applies across all eight senses listed above. SPD is a trait commonly associated with diagnoses such as autism, ADHD, foetal alcohol spectrum disorder (FASD), and learning disabilities, as well as it being possible for an individual to have SPD without a co-occurring condition.

Many different combinations of senses and hyper/hyposensitivity are possible, so the way that any individual with SPD experiences it can be hugely varied. For example, an individual could be hypersensitive to tactile input, while hyposensitive to sounds. We may sometimes use the terms 'sensory seeking' and 'sensory avoidant' to describe an individual's engagement with different sensations. If somebody is hypersensitive to touch, for example, they may be averse to hugs, handshakes, and certain fabrics. Yet if they are hyposensitive, they may seek sensory input, either through bumping into walls or people. Perhaps they crave tactile input, like rolling on the floor or having deep pressure applied in a hug or from a weighted blanket. You can imagine how this could play out across the other senses, with individuals seeking or avoiding sensory input.

If someone is overwhelmed by sensory input, it can make it harder for them to manage emotions or communicate needs. This can lead to behaviour that could seem unrelated to the sensory situation, yet it is that sensory discomfort that has triggered the behaviour. Conversely, certain sensory input can be used to help regulate an individual with SPD and be a useful tool in managing emotion, stress, and anxiety. My experience has been that, as well as causing challenges, my sensory processing can also be positive. The uninhibited pure joy that I experience through positive sensory input can be contagious. When a certain texture, sight, light, or sensation inexplicably brings about an intense and all-encompassing feeling that your spirit is soaring, your heart is peaceful, you are somehow both inside and experiencing the sensation at the same time and you can't stop smiling. It can lead you to praise God and delight in him and be filled with thankfulness for this gift he has given you.

Because SPD overlaps with so many other diagnoses, it is important to consider any adaptations for an individual holistically, taking into account their other needs. The way that an individual can communicate sensory discomfort or needs may also vary. For example, an autistic adult with low social communication support needs may very well have sensory strategies in place that they can explain to you verbally. I will often use earplugs or my noise-cancelling headphones if a situation is too loud, and I can communicate clearly to others what I am doing and why. For someone who does not communicate verbally or has higher communication support needs, they may express what they need through what they do. A young girl we know will take my hands and wrap my arms around her in a hug, showing she needs some deep pressure to regulate.

One mother shared the challenges SPD gave her daughter at church.

JO'S STORY (CONTINUED)

My daughter is extremely sensitive to noise. She experiences unexpected noises and loud noises as pain. Some smells can be overwhelming, which can cause her to sound like she is choking. Similarly, she cannot tolerate unexpected or unwanted touch. She struggles with her interoception (awareness of what is happening in her body) and often doesn't know until the last minute that she needs the loo or is unaware that she is thirsty or hungry and can go all day without a drink unless prompted.

In a church environment, this is really difficult – the worship music is too loud, as are the talks – so it's close to impossible to get her into a service, and we often feel lonely and excluded. This can lead to sensory overload and shutdown. She likes to be under something to feel safe, a blanket or a table, in a quiet room. While this may help manage her senses, it also isolates her.

Here are some things to consider for those with sensory processing needs.

VISUAL INPUT

Is the space busy or cluttered? Is there a way to make it less visually stimulating, if that is overwhelming? For example, if the carpet in your home where you meet for your small group is patterned, is there another space that you could sit in for the time together? If the lighting is visually overwhelming, a zone of the church could be deliberately left clear or even a little blackout tent constructed to offer an escape. For those who seek visual input, can you use images or visuals to support points you are making? We might be used to this in children's work, but it can be helpful for adults, too.

SOUND/NOISE

Have an awareness of anyone who may be sound-sensitive in your church. Perhaps it would be helpful to them if you chose to take your tea or coffee into a quieter space for a chat after the service, rather than in a noisy, busy main meeting space. If you see someone using earplugs, headphones, or ear defenders, consider that this could be their way of managing a sensory need and participating in a church service or event. Most ear defenders do not block out all noise fully, so don't assume that the individual is trying to ignore the speaker. You may consider having ear defenders available for general use.

For those who seek auditory input, think about how you can make times of quiet and reflection more manageable (this is explored in chapter 11).

FOOD

Throughout the Bible, food and meals are very important, and we often have events and activities that involve eating and drinking. Therefore it is important to be aware that for some, food can be a difficult sensory issue. Some people are so sensitive to the textures and tastes of food that their diet is incredibly limited, and they may have a diagnosis of avoidant restrictive food intake disorder (ARFID). ARFID is an eating disorder that is characterised by restriction in intake not motivated by weight or appearance. While there can be other causes of ARFID (such as emetophobia, a fear of being sick), many people with ARFID have a sensory-based avoidance. Being aware of this means we can be understanding and accommodating if people prefer to bring their own food to events. It could also be that you choose to spend time with people without the involvement of food, if it is a cause of distress to an individual. This awareness is also helpful in understanding that someone may not be simply 'a fussy eater', but there could be a complex sensory reason behind their restricted diet.

MOVEMENT

Chapter 11 explores some ways we can pre-emptively build movement into our Sunday services, small groups, and children's activities to support those with a need for movement. Many people with sensory processing issues will seek movement input naturally through stimming, a repetitive action which provides regulating sensory input. Although it is possible to stim with any of the senses, such as making repeated noises, the most obvious stims are movement-based, such as hand flapping, pacing, rocking, or tiptoe walking. It is helpful to understand why someone may choose to stim. Sometimes a child's stim will be harmful to themselves or others, and it can be necessary to redirect them to a safer way of getting the same input.

TOUCH
(INCLUDING PROPRIOCEPTIVE INPUT)

Children who are hyposensitive to touch may crave extra tactile input in a way that seems inappropriate. For example, they may stroke random objects, bump against things, or always choose to eat food with their fingers. Adults may continue to bump into people or give people too little personal space. They may choose to keep a coat on indoors to give them a sense of being cocooned.

Balancing different needs, for example, physical safety or safeguarding considerations, may require us to think of other ways to provide tactile input. Playdough or fidgets could provide this input to the hands or a weighted blanket to the whole body. We can be understanding rather than judgemental and have a conversation with them about strategies which would help them, if it is causing distress to others.

On the other hand, others may be very sensitive to touch – whether it's handshakes or the feel of cotton wool. We can try to be aware of these and not force anything on them!

Some common sensory struggles with touch involve uniforms or items of clothing that have to be worn as part of a ministry. For example, some children's ministries have their leaders wear T-shirts to identify them. Sometimes at holiday clubs, conferences, or camps, the children or young people are given T-shirts they are expected to wear. If this is a barrier, there could be creative solutions, such as lanyards, badges, or stickers, to identify the individual. It may simply be a case of unpicking the neck label, so ask what would help. Many clothing brands have seam-free options, so if it is likely to be needed regularly, it may be worth customising one of these.

JOSHUA'S STORY

Joshua is nine and has recently been diagnosed with autism and ADHD, but his sensory challenges have always been the most obvious aspect of his neurotype. He craves tactile input, often seeking it in all the most inappropriate ways; he will roll around on the floor or sit on the lap of any available adult. When he was first in the midweek club for primary school children at the church, the group leaders tried to apply the same discipline system they were using for everyone else. While others were pretty quick to respond to a loss of privileges, Joshua continued to deliberately bump into things, sprawl across the floor, or chew on his clothing or colouring sheet. Punishing him didn't seem to make any difference, although he clearly wanted to please the leaders and get it right. His stress levels rose noticeably when there was a lot of background noise, particularly after church services when lots of people were talking. This often led to misbehaviour and getting into fights with other children.

As his parents, we've grown to understand Joshua's sensory needs more and we've become better at being ready with suggestions. A fidget in his pocket helps him get some of the movement he needs. He knows that a fidget is a tool not a toy, and should be put away if it becomes a distraction. As he's got older, it has felt increasingly problematic for him to sit on unknown adults' laps, even though he would still like to! The leaders have now given him a weighted blanket at Sunday club, and he can sit on the sofa with the blanket over him if he needs lots of tactile input. He has a chew necklace which he can use if needed. He's also getting better at learning when to use his ear defenders. He finds the pressure of the ear defenders around his head gives him extra tactile input, so they are doubly beneficial to him. As his needs have been met, and we have listened to what he feels would help him participate well, some (though not all!) of the behavioural challenges have improved. He hasn't become perfect overnight, and we wouldn't expect him to. But he knows that he can ask for support and that he will be heard.

This is how he describes his own experience of church: 'I find that when I hear a lot of loud noises, it really, *really* annoys me, which makes me frustrated and can cause some major accidents. I also find that the teachers help a lot by providing something for my hands. It distracts my brain a lot and stops me getting frustrated with the noise. I'm not getting to move around, so to have something for my hands to move about with helps when I'm just sitting still… the weighted blanket feels like it's just holding me down so I don't have to get up, which means I don't cause mayhem and mischief too much.'

As parents, it has often been hard to have the 'badly behaved child' – especially before he had any diagnosis and we were trying to work out whether we'd failed somewhere! It's sometimes easy to feel slightly excluded when your child hasn't built peer friendships in the same way as others and other families in church seem to have closer bonds as a result of their children's friendships. However, we have been blessed by the group leaders and other adults at church being consistently kind to Joshua, willing to hear him monologue about his interests or have him sit on their laps. When we've made suggestions for accommodations, they've been well received even when they mean a bit more preparation.

SMELL

People should be aware that aftershaves, perfumes, and air fresheners add to the sensory experience of the environment. I dislike the smell of air fresheners and found it very difficult to have conversations in a friend's car while distracted by the smell of their air freshener. Once I'd told them, we started moving it to the boot of the car for longer journeys together.

The best way to cater for somebody who has SPD, or sensory sensitivities, is to get to know their personal sensory profile and consider it while planning anything that involves them, from having them over to your house through to where you chat at church on a Sunday. Be somebody in their life from whom they are comfortable to ask for accommodations, and be open to other people's use of sensory aids. Don't assume that someone will not want to do something you think may cause sensory overload (such as attend a concert with you), but do ask if there is anything you can do to help make them comfortable.

TOP 3 FOR EVERYONE

① Seek to understand other people's sensory needs: ask what they find hard and what they love.

② Once you have understood someone's needs, try to meet them as far as it depends on you, whether that's avoiding physical contact or choosing quiet spots to meet to chat.

③ Be open to variety – even if you love loud music in church, embrace opportunities to have a quieter service with fewer instruments involved for the sake of others.

Attention deficit hyperactivity disorder (ADHD)

CLAIRE WOOD

WHAT IS ADHD?

While some of the conditions mentioned in this book are comparatively rare, ADHD affects 5–7% of children and adolescents,[1] and an increasing number of adults are now seeking diagnosis for the condition.[2] In the UK, it is possible to get a diagnosis through the NHS, but it can be a long process. This means that in addition to those with a formal ADHD diagnosis, we may encounter individuals who are undiagnosed but exhibit many of the traits we will explore in this chapter. This is particularly the case among women, as diagnostic criteria have only recently been improved to pick up the differences in the timing and features of ADHD in women. Many people with ADHD prefer the term 'ADHDer'. Unfortunately, this doesn't work very well grammatically, so we have chosen to use 'with/has ADHD'.

ADHD is much more complicated than simply having a short attention span. It can look different in different people, but has three core presentations: inattention, impulsivity, and hyperactivity. People are diagnosed with inattentive-type ADHD, hyperactive/impulsive-type ADHD, or a combination.

Inattentive-type ADHD might look like having a short attention span, being easily distracted and constantly changing from one activity to another. People with inattentive-type ADHD will often appear to be unable to listen to instructions or learn from mistakes, may appear forgetful, lose possessions, and struggle to organise their time.

Those with hyperactive/impulsive ADHD can often hyper-focus, meaning that they may become utterly absorbed in a particular activity and struggle to move on to a different one. Hyperactivity may manifest as difficulty in sitting still, struggling to be calm or quiet, excessive talking, fidgeting, a tendency to act or speak without thinking, take risks, and be constantly on the move. There can even be 'hyperactivity of thought' – a racing mind that can't manage to switch off and bounces from one chain of thought to another.

Scientists have noticed that the prefrontal cortex, the part of our brain responsible for concentration, emotional regulation, and decision-making, seems to develop later in people with ADHD. Chemicals in the brain responsible for generating motivation or reward and maintaining focus, like dopamine, seem to work less well or be reduced for people with ADHD. This explains their particular need for movement, as it triggers the production of more dopamine. Many of the drugs used to treat ADHD are stimulants, acting to increase dopamine levels. Some choose not to medicate with stimulants, as while they can improve some aspects of life for someone with ADHD, they may exacerbate other tendencies or simply have unwanted side effects.

A frequent challenge for those with ADHD is executive function. This is 'the cognitive process that organises thoughts and activities, prioritises tasks, manages time efficiently, and makes decisions'.[3] An individual with difficulties in this area may struggle to adjust their behaviour to unexpected changes. They will thrive in church gatherings that follow a similar pattern, for example, and may be unduly stressed by an attempt to 'mix things up' unexpectedly. They may struggle with working memory, which is the ability to hold key information in mind while using it: this may be particularly evident in a Bible study or a small group. Their ability to keep track of things (both possessions and remembering tasks) will also often be affected.

People with ADHD often experience emotional struggles. This may be due to hyper-focusing on an emotion, meaning that it becomes harder to move on or see the bigger picture. The reduced dopamine levels present in many with ADHD mean that some of the natural 'pleasure' feedback cycles of the brain are also reduced. An underdeveloped prefrontal cortex (that part of the brain making rational decisions) in young people may lead to increased decision-making from a different part of the brain (called the amygdala), which is linked to impulsivity and aggression. They may also experience increased stress as a result of trying to cover up certain behaviours to appear 'normal', which can in turn lead to mental health problems. ADHD can also make it very difficult to fall asleep at night, resulting in tiredness and the emotional challenges which accompany this. Psychologists have identified a heighted sensitivity to injustice and rejection as a common emotional response in children and adults with ADHD.[4]

People with ADHD will often struggle to meet our expectations of behaviour. Children with ADHD may be found trying to climb parts of your church building. For example, they may find it hard to stay quiet in a service well beyond the age when we would typically think they 'should' be able to manage this. Adults with ADHD may struggle to remember events in the church calendar or find it hard to arrive on time. They may be the ones constantly interrupting in Bible studies or fidgeting all the way through the service. Some of these differences can appear rude or badly behaved, and understanding the condition can help us move away from seeing them as behavioural problems towards seeing them as communication of needs.

This understanding does not undermine Christians' belief in the naturally sinful state of humanity, which we explored in chapter 1. We can believe that an action is wrong, yet also recognise that better support would have enabled the individual to act differently. Some actions may not even be wrong, but only culturally unexpected. In chapter 4, we saw that God looks at the heart. Instead of looking at the external behaviour, we can try to understand the motives and heart attitudes behind this behaviour and reflect on our own hearts, too.

We may hear people using their ADHD diagnosis as what seems like an excuse for laziness or unwillingness to make the effort to change. In the church, we point to the fruit of the Spirit, which include qualities such as faithfulness and self-control. Surely we should expect the work of the Spirit to counteract the natural tendencies of the brain? We can look again at our understanding of the 'now and not yet' of the Christian life, explored in chapter 4. As Christians, we can rejoice in our identity as children of God, confident of full transformation in the new creation. In the meantime, we expect to be on a gradual path of sanctification, becoming more like Christ: 'We instructed you how to live in order to please God, as in fact you are living. Now we ask you and urge you in the Lord Jesus to do this *more and more*' (1 Thessalonians 4:1, emphasis added). Those who experience different challenges should not look down on or judge those still working on these areas, and should be aware that not everyone faces the same struggles with sin.

One area which can be a struggle for people with ADHD is addiction. The dopamine-seeking ADHD brain means some people with ADHD are more likely to struggle with drug or alcohol abuse[5] or behavioural addictions, such as gambling or pornography.[6] The impulsivity and mood swings associated with ADHD can also make anger and violent behaviour more likely. If you can relate to this or are supporting someone with these struggles, knowing that ADHD may be part of the cause is helpful in working out how to break free from these behaviours.

Despite all these challenges, many of the characteristics of the typical ADHD brain may be seen as advantages in the wider Christian community. The ability to hyper-focus can lead to immense productivity – most of us simply do not have the capacity to see huge projects (whether practical ones for the local church or working through the whole Bible tracing a particular theme) through to completion. Curiosity and creativity is also common in people with ADHD, along with a quick wit able to come up with pertinent verbal quips at a moment's notice. The challenges they will have experienced often make them determined and willing to work hard to overcome difficulties, while their tendency towards risk-taking may enable them to take on projects which the rest of us are too scared to start. The challenge of experiencing everything all at once can enable them to see patterns in a way which others are less able to do. These skills are real gifts of God to Christians, and it is no surprise that many of our great preachers and church leaders have ADHD, along with many of our musicians, church planters, AV technicians, and youth workers.

ADHD AND ACCESSIBILITY IN CHURCH

Where might particular challenges lie within the church, and how can we all work together to ensure that people (whether adults or children) feel as though they belong in our churches? We will work through many of the typical aspects of ADHD presentation, thinking about where these might cause difficulties to members of our churches. Every church and every individual is different, so not everything here will be equally relevant in your context, but we hope that these give a flavour of the areas we should be considering.

CHILDREN AND YOUNG PEOPLE

We will focus first on adaptations which might need to be made in youth and children's ministries. This may be where ADHD is most obvious, as many adults with ADHD will already have built in coping mechanisms to help them operate in church. It is important to remember the delays in some areas of brain development which can lead to children behaving 'younger' than their age. In addition, the interaction of hormones with the ADHD brain can throw up some particular challenges for teens with ADHD.

NICK'S STORY

We recently heard the story of a neurodivergent boy, Nick, who grew up in a Christian family. He had a horrific time at school, where his teachers gave little support despite his diagnoses. At church, he was constantly challenging boundaries. For example, on one occasion his mother was leading the singing from the front, and he went up to join her, which was considered 'disrespectful' by many members of the church. The Sunday school volunteers would shout at him, and decided that it wasn't fair that they should give up their Sundays to look after a naughty child, so excluded him, at the age of four, from all junior-church activities – not just the Sunday school, but all meetings and gatherings. His siblings were welcome at everything, but not him. Living in a small village, where everyone knew everyone else, all his friends knew he had been officially excluded. He was not allowed to rejoin until he was 17, and only then because he could play the drums. To face this in church as well as at school was really hard for Nick. His mother described him to us as 'still hurting' as a result of his childhood experiences.

Thankfully, the church where this happened 25 years ago has changed, and now even has fidget toys available for use throughout the service. Nick's challenges also led his mother to train as an assessor for neurodevelopmental conditions. She was then able to use this training within a charity she set up to enable many more children to be diagnosed, as the area where they lived was notorious for long waiting lists within the NHS.

While we can understand that Nick's experience isn't the ideal we're aiming for, we can also sympathise with the junior-church leaders – they'd given up their time, they probably hadn't had a lot of training in the area, and challenging behaviour can be really exhausting! As we try to show God's love to children with additional needs, we'll need to bear with one another as we work towards getting this right. With support and understanding, we can work towards a different ending for children like Nick in our clubs, activities, and services. Chapter 12 has some additional strategies for managing behaviours that can leave us scratching our heads and wondering if inclusion is possible!

We will review some of the common features of ADHD in children to help us understand what needs children are communicating through their behaviour. Meeting those needs will often help resolve the behaviour. We will also consider some more 'reactive' behaviour management strategies at the end of this section.

Having a short attention span or being easily distracted

This might be a problem during a talk or long activity. If there are children in our groups who seem to be struggling to focus, we can think about splitting it up into smaller chunks; for example, could we deliver the talk as two short talks with a moving-around game in between? By providing opportunities to move around, we offer a natural stimulant to the brain, which will help with listening later on. If the space does not allow for a running-around game, we can still be imaginative with opportunities to move and exert energy – drawing big pictures on a whiteboard, pouring drinks from a heavy jug of water, or even having a sensory swing (if budget allows) can offer a similar kind of stimulation to running around.

If movement alone does not help, opportunities for active participation may – put children in pairs to discuss something before asking someone the answer to a question, so that everyone has a chance to talk about the answer and engage with the topic. Using a variety of inputs will help, too – pictures, drama, readings, videos, and objects related to the theme or Bible story.

Likewise, seeking a variety of outputs from the children will aid concentration – not only spoken or written answers, but also drawings, acting, or singing. If you are giving a talk to children or young people, many find a sheet with tasks helpful, such as drawing a picture, putting a tick in a box when you hear a particular word or phrase, filling in blanks.

Appearing to be unable to listen

Many children with ADHD may appear to be 'unable to listen' because they are moving around while you talk, not making eye contact, and not answering questions. However, this does not necessarily point to a failure to listen – the child may be using their movement to help them stay focused. I have observed a child who appeared distracted throughout the Bible teaching, at points even facing in the opposite direction or sitting under a table. However, when questioned at the end of the session, their recall of the story was spot on!

Finding it hard to stick to tasks that are time-consuming, or constantly changing activity

Inattentive ADHD may present as struggling to 'stick' at any activity for long. Sometimes this is because the number of steps involved in carrying out an activity is overwhelming. Examples of what you are trying to achieve (for example, a completed craft project) or stations which they can move to after completing each stage of the activity (which isolates each task) can help to separate the activity into manageable chunks and incorporate some movement.

Being unable to sit still, especially in quiet surroundings, fidgeting, 'excessive' movement

Churches are often places where a high value is placed on sitting still and being quiet. This may be an area where we need to balance the needs of different people – some will find it hard to concentrate on worship without this tranquil atmosphere, and silences (such as a time of contemplation before a confession or during Communion) can be a very important tool in enabling everyone present to come to worship in the right way. A child with ADHD may find the quiet surroundings reduce the level of stimulation their brain is receiving, and so will naturally compensate with even more movement, fidgeting, and maybe even trying to fill the silence by shouting out. Their impulsiveness may mean that there is no opportunity to see these outbursts coming, and very little their parents can do reactively to 'control' them. This presents us with a challenge, where the needs of some appear to be in conflict with the needs of others. Understanding and love on both sides will be needed – it can be extremely painful for a parent who is desperate for their child to be seen as 'well-behaved', and this pain will be exacerbated by comments about keeping children under control. On the other hand, this can easily swing the other way, and a parent, constantly aware of their own child's needs, becomes oblivious to their effect on others in the room.

In addition to love and understanding, we can also work out ways to balance everyone's needs. We may already have children's groups during the parts of the service where quiet is most desirable, so that the children are not put under undue pressure. If children are in the service, we can consider our physical space – are there parts of the church where it would be less disruptive to move around or call out? Assuming we are already using microphones and speakers, and possibly even live-streaming our services as well, it might be valuable for some families to have a separate room they can easily move into for parts of the service. This is the sort of provision that may be needed in the summer, when it is hard for churches to continue staffing their children's groups.

Even when children and young people are in groups, where typically movement and noise are more accepted, this can cause challenges. Understanding that a child finds it harder to sit still does not mean that you have to throw out all your boundaries and rules – in fact, quite the contrary! Most neurodivergent children find familiar, consistent rules reassuring and helpful. However, we should consider what our rules are. Suddenly deciding that it is not acceptable for a child to flap their arms in our children's group may come as a surprise (you probably didn't communicate this in advance), and when we think about it, is motivated more by our own comfort (it's distracting for us as the adult in the room) than safety or morality. Simple rules like 'we use kind hands' and 'we look after our things' can be used to remind a child that if they need to flap, they can find some space where they won't hurt another child, themselves, or the furniture. Positive, clear, simple rules can be repeated every week and represented visually.

We can also make sure that our groups offer lots of opportunity for movement. Here are some examples designed for a range of ages:

- A basket of 'fidgets' which children can easily access if they need something to keep their hands moving during a talk. This could be particularly helpful for older children and teenagers, who may be expected to sit through the service.

- Games which involve big movements – this can be harder in a small space, but think creatively about what you have. It is important to remember that teenagers with ADHD may still need this kind of movement.

- Get rid of chairs and sit on yoga balls or even on the floor (if choosing to do this, you may need to consider the physical needs of the rest of your group). Spinning desk chairs may be helpful for some but can easily become a distraction to the group as a whole.

- Swap partners for discussion activities to allow some movement around the room.

- Act out parts of a Bible story or application scenarios.

Talking all the time and struggling to wait for their turn

Children with ADHD may dominate group discussions, unable to wait for a space in the conversation to communicate something. It can be helpful to keep a stack of sticky notes to hand and ask them to draw or write something to remind them of what they wanted to say, so that you can come back to it later. You will have to keep your promise to do so, though! Clarity in when their turn will come will help them to wait. In younger groups, putting hands up and letting them know when you'll call on them may help, though this is likely to be seen as patronising in an older group. Understanding that this is a challenge for a child helps the adults responsible use the right language to remind them that someone else is still speaking, and while practice will help, we should not be surprised if this is something we have to keep working on.

Impulsive behaviour and decreased sense of danger

Impulsiveness often heightens the difficulties mentioned above, but it can be a particular challenge when linked to a decreased sense of danger common in children with ADHD. You may turn your back for a moment, and they are climbing a wall simply because it occurred to them in that moment. Young children with ADHD are often the ones we describe as 'escapers' or 'runners', due to their tendency to be found wandering down the street outside the church 20 seconds after their parent took their eyes off them last.

It is vital in any church that good safety procedures are put in place to prevent children getting out of the building unnoticed and to protect children from possible hazards. For example, are your biscuits right next to the coffee, which could lead an impulsive child to scald themselves while reaching for one? If you are serving hot drinks, are these brought into the same spaces where children are running around? If so, could lidded reusable cups help to prevent accidents? Is there a stack of chairs, AV equipment, or kneeler cushions sitting in the corner which would fall over if climbed on? Thorough and frequent risk assessments of your space and the way you use it will help to keep everyone safe.

Difficulty handling emotions, especially relating to a sense of justice

Having a strong sense of justice is a wonderful instinct, reflecting God's heart for the outsider. However, strong emotional reactions and an intense sense of justice can also lead to difficulties. Children may try to 'fix' the scenario through physical or verbal retaliation and need support to manage those emotions positively. They can also struggle with competition or feeling like they have 'lost' a game. Keeping a good mix of cooperative and competitive games helps to avoid too much upset in this area. Sometimes, a child or young person just needs a safe space and some tools to help them self-regulate. A calm corner (not used as a punishment but as a choice) with reminders of helpful breathing techniques and sensory equipment can be useful. Squeezy balls, toys like a Hoberman sphere (which can be used as physical reminders to take slow and deep breaths), or snow globes can all act as calming devices. These do not need to be expensive – many sensory tools can be easily made yourself or found among everyday objects which church members may have at home.

Consequences for ADHD children

Making accommodations does not mean that we neglect boundaries and consequences. Alongside understanding and meeting needs, we can continue to have clear and reasonable expectations of behaviour, and consequences when these expectations are not met. For those working with children in a Christian setting, whether that's a midweek club, a Sunday group, or a holiday club or camp, part of our role will be helping the children behave in a way which is respectful and safe, and enables everyone to learn. There are no neat, 'instant fix' solutions to this: unlike many modern secular parenting books, we know that children, like adults, are sinful by nature, as we saw in chapter 1.

In a children's group, we may make use of some rewards and sanctions alongside our teaching, but find that this isn't working well for our ADHD children. It is helpful to remember that the ADHD child's brain has an underdeveloped prefrontal cortex (responsible for rational decisions) and inhibited dopamine transmission. The typical brain is able to be motivated by relatively far-off benefits, and starts receiving dopamine *in advance* in anticipation of those rewards. Likewise, the typical brain has a built-in 'fear response' which prevents us doing things we know will lead to bad outcomes. The ADHD brain does not respond in the same way: the 'fear response' and the 'distant reward dopamine' are both far less effective.[7]

This means it is more effective to encourage expected behaviour with immediate praise (especially specific praise which focuses on exactly what they did well) or rewards. Neurodivergent children often respond well to rewards centred around a special interest; this might be five minutes of a carefully chosen video or even a reward chart where they can add a sticker to a chart or marble to a jar with their favourite superhero on it. Behaviour charts of this kind should not be displayed publicly, to avoid a sense of public humiliation for those who have not done well on this occasion. This type of extrinsic motivation will be helpful in the short term, though we are likely to need to find new strategies fairly frequently as the original excitement wears off.[8] These can be beneficial in keeping order in a children's group, but we should not neglect the deeper work of discipling the child's heart, where true change will happen by the Holy Spirit's work.

In addition to the strategies mentioned here, readers may find the PACE model, discussed in chapter 12, helpful for children with ADHD.

We have focused on aspects which might be seen as negatives, but it is worth pointing out that children and young people with ADHD are usually a joy to have in our churches. They are often witty, willing to chat to adults and children alike, and are committed in attendance. As they are likely to find more love and understanding within the church than outside it, they often develop a genuine love for their church family at a fairly young age. Their ability to hyper-focus can make them committed servers, willing to give time generously.

One family who have many positive stories of accommodations made shared their experiences with us:

ONE FAMILY'S STORY

My little family is very different. My son is a genius. He eats maths for breakfast, lunch, and dinner. My daughter is a ball of creative energy, and even though she's just as smart as her brother, she's pretty nonchalant about it. We have home-educated both children from the start, eat organic food, and home-make as much as possible. We love Jesus. We love our church family. We give generously and care deeply for those in need. If I stopped there, or perhaps you are lucky enough to meet us on our very best day, you may be inclined to believe this 'Instagram-filtered' account of our family and move right along. Eccentric and fun. All true.

What is also true is that my maths-eating son barely eats actual food, and was declared as 'failing to thrive' shortly after his fifth birthday, when he had a cardiac episode that changed our lives and lifestyle. My creative daughter struggles to speak, even though I can see the clever ideas behind her eyes. I have barely slept since 2016 owing to both children's chronically disordered sleep. Both children have such serious metabolic issues that they become chronically ill from the healthiest of 'typical British diets'. Neither can sit still: understatement!

Both struggle to concentrate. One hates noise; the other craves it. On our worst days, there are violent outbursts, dysregulation, social confusion, sensory struggles, fatigue, anxiety, and more stress than feels fair. What a list! In fact, caring for our very different children required me to leave my career and become a full-time carer as well as educator. My family is labelled as neurodiverse, and like many families with similar stories, we spent many years desperately seeking answers, reading libraries of books, filling out forms, and going through innumerable appointments; praying, advocating for our children's emerging needs and differences, and scuffing against social structures in our modern world that were not built to accommodate different children. Both children have now received diagnoses of autism, ADHD, SPD (sensory processing disorder), and PDA (pathological demand avoidance).

These diagnoses, as much as they have helped us and our children (who can now receive a strong foundation in their early years), are in a sense an abstract pathology. The real and deeply experienced differences have challenged every expectation we had for our family and have changed the future as we once saw it unfolding, and, yes, the spiritual impact is perhaps most deeply felt. The differences that cause our children to struggle in themselves and scuff against the world are very real and oftentimes play out in very public ways, never more so than at church.

I'm not sure if we are in the habit of thinking about church as a social structure, but one of our biggest historical struggles has been against inflexible church culture. From my son's early toddler years, it was clear there was a large and growing gap between the need we arrived with and what our church at that time a) expected in terms of parenting/behaviour and b) could (or would) physically offer to help meet that need. We have experienced everything from withering glances as we arrived late (and loudly) to the service, desperately tried to confine our hyperactive toddler to our row of chairs (resulting in some loud and obvious protestations mid-prayers), and managed meltdowns in Sunday school, all the way to accusations of poor parenting, being the topic of gossip at mothers' groups, and eventually exclusion from services altogether.

By the time we received diagnoses and were able to 'explain' why things had been so chaotic and hard, and that it genuinely was not due to poor parenting, we were already strangers in our congregation of more than 15 years. This sounds really shocking, but to be honest, I understood at least some of it. Our children's differences are obvious, loud, inconvenient, and distracting. They were very hard to include in children's work, already underserved and struggling for volunteers. The children found the rigid structure (and sensory overwhelm) needed to keep order in a tight space very hard to cope with, resulting in even more distressing behaviour. We had become an uncomfortable fit in our rather inflexible church, with children who were growing increasingly inflexible in their own ways owing to their neurology. We were stuck between a rock and a hard place, and we inevitably 'broke' and gave up.

After much prayer, God led us on a very straight path to our current church. From the moment I walked into this church, I saw 'inclusion' everywhere – from a basket of stim toys placed in a purposefully apparent and accessible place, to the sofas placed to the side of the regular chair rows for those who need more space or find sitting in the rigid rows uncomfortable. The welcome was warm as expected, but what was genuinely different was that nobody blinked, inhaled through teeth in that slow 'that's-not-going-to-work' way, or commiserated when I mentioned autism. In fact, I felt as if our arrival had been anticipated!

God had not been surprised by our children's differences, and neither were the staff and congregation at this church. There was room for us there, to come as we were. The presence of neurodiverse teens and adults validated this church as a 'safe place' for all. We felt 'at home', instantly loved and our children welcomed with deference to and accommodations for their needs.

The children's worker has been a constant encouragement in her dogged efforts to keep us engaged. When medical issues and serious demand-avoidant-anxiety meant that our children were unable to come into the service for some months, she offered to meet us in the empty church building on a weekday for 'Sunday school' instead. Kids' team helpers came to visit us at home. Meals were delivered. Help offered even when we didn't need it and hadn't asked. We were prayed for, over, and with. We were served in ways we never knew we needed by these amazing people who were the hands of God's providence to us at a time where we needed it most. Words cannot express our love and gratitude for our church and the compassionate culture of acceptance fostered there, where despite a smaller congregation and a smaller budget, culture made all the difference.

I have open and positive communication with the children's team, and I anticipate that this communication will continue as our children grow and their (and our family's) needs change. I also anticipate that there might need to be an ongoing push towards educating the wider church family as we grow with them, especially with peers who might feel confused as to why the rules apply differently to our children. Encouragingly, we *can* communicate about these things because church culture has made space for it.

Finally, the strain of parenting children with additional needs can be very taxing on a marriage, beyond the typical attrition of navigating life and typical parenting. It may be the case that one parent is also neurodivergent and may need additional pastoral care as they navigate parenting through their own limitations and differences, or perhaps process their own late-in-life diagnosis. We have been carefully and compassionately served in this way by pastoral staff at our church. We are the blessed and lucky few, and it is my prayer that every neurodiverse family could find this radical acceptance and generous welcoming at their own church.

ADULTS

These challenges continue into adulthood, though have usually become more manageable. This will partly be due to the brain's ongoing development, and partly due to the adult working out for themselves how to ask for accommodations and harness the positives of their neurotype. Research is increasingly shedding light on how the ADHD brain continues to cause challenges into adulthood, which can be helped by understanding and accommodation by others. As we get to know these individuals and their needs, we are also likely to discover some wonderful examples of service and skills used for the glory of God.

Inability to prioritise, continually starting new tasks before finishing old ones

Many busy adults will struggle with this to some extent! Our instant-media-driven lives and the relatively low value placed by our culture on self-discipline mean that for many of us, our brains become habituated to being easily distracted and trying to achieve too many things at once. For those with ADHD, this will often be a debilitating part of life, leading to difficulty maintaining the home or relationships. Understanding this can allow us to be more loving in our friendships – a friend with ADHD may need a follow-up to arrange to meet, for example. If someone with ADHD is being asked to host a small group in their home, their small group members can show love by making sure the washing up is done before they leave and by taking it in turns to provide snacks.

Forgetfulness and poor organisational skills

The ADHD brain may continue to find organisation hard into adulthood. While an individual with ADHD can make use of additional tools to help them stay organised, such as Post-it notes, reminders on phones, and to-do lists, there will be occasions, especially in stressful seasons of life, when these routines fail. This may be a good time for those around this individual to offer to help with one or two items which may be tipping them over the edge.

Restlessness

Adults with ADHD may benefit from fidgets to help them with restlessness. If they are struggling to stay focused on a sermon or in a small group setting, they may choose to bring a small fidget like a Rubik's cube or a necklace or bracelet which allows them to fidget in an unobtrusive manner. We can help by offering a space where they do not feel judgement for their use of such an aid. 'Body doubling' is a tool many people with ADHD have found helpful: someone calm, quiet, and undistracted can model a behaviour, which allows the person with ADHD to reflect these behaviours.[9] You could offer to come and work in the same room if someone is struggling to meet a deadline at work or set up a video call while you're both getting housework done.

Difficulty keeping quiet, often interrupting others

One tendency shared by many adults with ADHD is the impulsive need to say what they want to say immediately. This can be frustrating in conversation and small group time, when we want everyone to have a chance to say something. If you are a small group leader with individuals like this in your group, good group leadership can get the best of both worlds: techniques such as calling on individuals rather than asking a question generally to the whole room or asking people to discuss a question in pairs mean that everyone has a choice to voice their thoughts, and the 'interrupter' isn't shamed for their tendency. If you are the interrupter, and are still fighting this urge to speak, it can be helpful to set *yourself* some rough guidelines around how long you will wait to say something, focusing first on letting people finish what they are saying. Once again, love and understanding on both sides is important.

Mood swings, irritability, and a quick temper

Adults with ADHD may be much more likely to have a 'short fuse'. This is often exacerbated by additional stressors in their life, so good pastoral care or discipleship should include identifying these and suggesting or offering support.

Inability to deal with stress

ADHD can make it much harder to deal with additional worries and anxieties in life. This can make other tendencies, which someone may be managing at other times of their life, much more obvious. As with anyone facing worries, we can both pray and show practical love. It is helpful to be aware that something which seems small to one person may be very stressful to another, so minimising the concern may not give the intended relief. Instead, take time to hear their concern and pray for them, as well as pointing them to promises in the Bible. Those with ADHD may find themselves more prone to feeling stressed by stories of social injustice on the news, and they may need help to not become obsessed by them.

It's important to remember the many benefits and gifts God gives to this neurotype. To highlight an example of this, we will finish with a personal story from one man who God is using not in spite of his ADHD, but through it and because of it.

GRAHAM'S STORY

It's often assumed that children will grow out of ADHD by the time they are adults, but that's a myth. I was diagnosed at the age of 46. Trauma often exacerbates the way conditions like ASD and ADHD manifest themselves. It's not that I became 'more ADHD' at that age, it's just that I lost the energy to 'mask' because my teenage son had died.

I'd always been the chatterbox in my family at school. I'd blurt things out at the dinner table and my dad would urge me to 'connect mouth to brain before speaking', which left my brothers laughing at my expense. I had a lot of energy and would sometimes run from the back of the house to the front and back again repeatedly to 'get my zoom out'.

I get distracted easily. I give thanks there was no social media for me growing up as I would have been quickly addicted. Maps and calculators were early obsessions for me. I found that when I did what I was fascinated by, I could hyper-focus and achieve remarkable results. Thankfully, at the age of 8 I became fascinated with Bible reading and prayer after my mum died, and that has served me well. By the time I was in secondary school my special interests were maths, computers, and science. When the floating Operation Mobilisation bookshop came to Liverpool, I bought a 'teach yourself calculus' book instead of a book on world evangelism. Even this maths obsession helped a 'comprehensive kid' from Birkenhead to be the first family member to go to university.

People call ADHD a disorder – attention deficit hyperactivity disorder – but for me it's always been more of a blessing than a curse. I am able to deep dive into the subjects I'm fascinated by. My current interests are evangelism, missiology, mental health, intimacy with God, the works of Herman Bavinck, and the staff, ministry, and history of the London City Mission. I never get tired of these subjects and can work for hours on them. Try to get me excited about clothing or the different shades of paint available from Dulux and my brain literally switches off. I actually find it painful to go shopping for clothes or to try to read a detective novel. That's just the way I'm wired.

My type of ADHD also makes me a 'highly sensitive person'. I cry easily and 'over feel' the emotions of the people I meet. This leaves me exhausted, but it also gives me insight when I'm serving someone. I literally feel the Holy Spirit burning in my heart when I speak of the need to love the lost and bring them the good news of Jesus.

My ADHD does trip me up sometimes, but it is also my greatest strength. When I preach, I am almost overwhelmed by the message I proclaim. When I counsel, I feel someone's emotions as if they are mine. When I strategise, I can deep dive into every background detail relevant to the issues at hand and remember the relevant data points in my head. It might look like I'm making impulsive comments, but often I've been toying with the idea and researching it for weeks.

ADHD is not a behavioural thing. It's a genetic, neurodevelopmental thing which seems also to be impacted by the environment of our first years and even the difficulty of our birth. It's not an illness, but if it was, I would not want to be cured. I'd like to be able to concentrate more when my wife is talking about the family shopping, but I wouldn't want to change from being the passionate, Bible-believing, Jesus-proclaiming evangelist who is bowled over by the grace of God. I have 'time blindness', get distracted and addicted easily, and I make commitments impulsively. All of this can be adjusted for. I try to work alongside planners and activists who have strengths where I have weaknesses. I often have an extra person in important meetings who gently stops me from making impulsive promises and remembers the promises I have made.

I have to be open about my weaknesses, but I hope people will see me as more than a sum of my weakness. When we recognise our strengths and weaknesses and work in a team with a variety of gifts, we can thrive. When we try to create a group of identical clones with the same sought-after behaviours then we miss out on all kinds of blessings.

TOP 10 FOR EVERYONE

1. Remember people with ADHD are all different, especially if they have other co-occurring conditions.

2. Respond with love when you see a child 'misbehaving' in church, both to the child and to their parents!

3. Be patient with lots of movement from children who may have ADHD, even if you don't know their diagnosis.

4. Don't assume an adult using a fidget toy in church or a small group is being rude.

5. Avoid too much competition which allows a single 'winner', both in small groups and whole-church activities.

6. Adjust your expectations of 'polite' behaviour from a friend in church with ADHD – their interruptions or colouring book at the dinner table aren't intended to be rude.

7. If you see something potentially unsafe in your building, act on it as soon as possible. Fixing the environment will help the people.

8. Don't be surprised if a child or adult with ADHD has an emotional outburst. Give them time and space to regulate themselves.

9. Offer to act as a 'body double' to a friend with ADHD.

10. Offer to pray with a friend feeling stressed by their own life or world news.

Social, emotional, and mental health (SEMH) in children

TRIONA BRADING

In 2014 the term SEMH (social, emotional, and mental health) needs replaced BESD (behavioural, emotional, and social difficulties) and EBD (emotional and behavioural difficulties) in the SEND (special educational needs and disability) code of practice. It is a broad term used to describe a range of needs based on difficulty in regulating emotions and behaviour. The term SEMH was the first to drop 'behaviour' from the title, reflecting an understanding that behaviour is a means of communication rather than the root of the need.

Both adults and children can have SEMH needs or difficulties; however, it is a term more commonly used around supporting children, as adults will tend to come under mental health support, and may experience different challenges. For this chapter, I will be referring to children with SEMH needs; we have chosen not to address adult mental health needs directly in this book. Because of the way children may experience SEMH needs, they come under the SEND umbrella, despite SEMH not being a 'disability'.

SEMH needs can manifest as difficulties associated with one's mood: this may include challenges managing emotions, anxiety, depression, self-harm, and/or withdrawal. It can look like difficulties with conduct: disruptive or antisocial behaviour. For example, children with SEMH needs may exhibit frustration or uncooperative behaviour, crises and meltdowns, anger and verbal aggression. And yet, this is a list of behaviours; the outworking of the root problem. The underlying need may be difficulties in relationships and interaction or an attachment disorder. While the behaviours with SEMH needs are often obvious, the cause of the behaviours is where we find the need and where we can try to meet the child.

There is no one cause for SEMH needs; however, there are some known contributing factors. Adverse childhood experiences, attachment difficulties, and severe family adversity can all contribute to the likelihood of having SEMH needs. Children who have spent a significant amount of time in hospital or undergone a lot of medical procedures could experience similar difficulties. There are also some neurodivergent individuals or those with learning disabilities who may present as having SEMH needs co-occurring with their neurodevelopmental condition, particularly if other needs are not being recognised or met. Further to this, in a post-COVID world, all children have experienced a degree of trauma, stress, and anxiety during the pandemic.

Those who have experienced the care system, whether they are adopted or looked after (under local authority care), are more likely to have SEMH needs than their peers.[1] There is a common misconception that once children are adopted, the trauma they have been experiencing ends. Statistically, children who are adopted experience preferable outcomes to those who continue to live in care. However, the impact of the separation from their birth family, potentially multiple moves and placements, the huge change that comes with adoption, and a feeling that decisions about their life have been made without their consent will impact a child's development and well-being. It is also important to recognise that a child's trauma does not disappear through adoption. This means there is often a lifelong need for extra support.

As Christians we all have an example of adoption within scripture. God is described as 'A father to the fatherless, a defender of widows... God sets the lonely in families' (Psalm 68:5–6). God has a heart for the vulnerable, as we discussed in chapter 2, and adoption and fostering is one wonderful way that people may choose to live out their faith. This means that although we may not all be fosterers and adopters, as Christians, we should seek to be aware and ready to support those with SEMH needs and their carers within our context.

You may feel daunted, overwhelmed, or anxious considering how you can include a child who struggles to regulate their behaviour and conduct. It can be difficult to know how to manage situations well, particularly if you are concerned other children or adults are at risk. SEMH is an area of SEND that is lesser known and can feel intimidating to step into.

I have spent a large portion of my professional life working in SEMH provision in a primary school and can attest that it can be a challenging thing to support individuals with these needs. However, I can also say that I loved my work in SEMH, and I have learnt so much of God's love and how he cares for us through my work. The gospel is one of restoration and transformation through unconditional love. In a nutshell, supporting someone with SEMH needs is striving to do just this, and the fact that these strategies and approaches can and do make huge changes to individuals bears witness to this. Throughout my practice I found myself reflecting on my personal relationship with the Lord and his attitude and care towards me. As Christians who are recipients of this unending love, we are well placed to take that into the way we love those in our community who are struggling with SEMH needs. Throughout my time at the school, I was very aware of the verse 'We love because he first loved us' (1 John 4:19) and found it very relevant to the approach I was taking. I hope and pray that if you ever have the opportunity to love and include a child with SEMH needs in your context, that it will deepen and enrich your own faith in ways you could not have expected. This is the experience of one adoptive parent I met.

KIA, AN ADOPTED DAUGHTER

I adopted Kia, my bright and beautiful daughter, when she was two years old. Two years before I had told my pastor I wanted to see if God would open this path to me as a single person. We sat in his home as he prayed with me for the child God might have in his plan. For months my home group prayed for the child God might bring into our church family, that we might have the opportunity to point the child to him. He answered our prayer, giving us wonderful Kia. The investment the church made in prayer meant it felt like Kia was part of our church family before we even knew her name. Now when milestones are reached and challenges are overcome, everyone celebrates the child we once asked God to allow us to welcome!

Kia had multiple family members care for her as a baby, with care deemed so lacking and neglectful that she was removed from her birth parents and placed in foster care aged 7 months. Kia's foster care placement also failed to be a place for her to find safety and nurture, and so she was removed urgently and placed with me when she was 2 years old. Kia had significant developmental delay, including not being able to speak. Very quickly I learned that teaching a child to speak is the easy part. Teaching an abused child that they are safe and slowly unpicking the wound caused by being separated from a birth parent is a lifetime's work that's hard and all-encompassing for both of us, and it only seems possible to bear with the hope of Jesus.

Before Kia arrived, an elder in our church attended the adoption training provided by social care, fully investing in understanding how to support a child with these needs. This helps support Kia now. A few nights before she arrived, the ladies of my church sat in her soon-to-be bedroom and prayed. I've always welcomed people into my home, but when Kia arrived, what she needed was very different to that. Church members dropped food parcels in our porch, deliberately not disturbing us, allowing Kia time with me to settle. Members of the church gave us space when we first came to church, their eyes filling up with joy from a distance! I would point and say, 'That's Paul who painted your bedroom,' and, 'That's Bruce who filled in the pond in our garden so it would be safe for you.' What a witness their service is, even when a child cannot manage direct interaction. Friends in our church made the effort to engage her as she clung to me, and her playful side started to emerge. They followed my lead sensitively and didn't give up. Now she has such confidence in her interactions with them, giggling hysterically as they joke and play!

Everyone listened in the first year when I said I needed to be with her throughout kids' church, and they soon learned I couldn't be counted as 'one of the adults' as Kia couldn't manage another child crawling onto my lap. Children's church was an important place we could build and reinforce our attachment. They don't ask questions when there are times Kia feels wobbly. They don't cajole her into separating from me, which would without doubt scare and trigger her. In fact, there are many things I've had to teach people outside of our church family about what Kia needs, that I just haven't had to do with our church family. Our church family see Kia every week in the same place, which is a very consistent and helpful pattern for an attachment-disordered child. They have watched attentively, and they've wanted to see and learn what makes Kia feel safe. It's felt easy and transformational. We now have a support group in our church for those parenting neurodivergent children and praying together is a joy and great support. To support an attachment-disordered child, it is mostly about supporting their parent.

One couple from church have walked by my side from the very start and are her godparents. Her Godmummy is without doubt the most trusted adult in her world after me. When it comes to babysitting or emergencies, she's the only person I can call on, because she is the only other person Kia can allow to care for her. This is challenging practically. Her commitment and consistency in time and love is huge and sacrificial. She offered herself without hesitation not knowing what it would involve. Kia's unpredictable and dysregulated behaviour is not a problem to her. Kia is loved and accepted, trauma and all. This type of love and support is valuable beyond words.

I needed people in my church family who understood why Kia might be untrusting and abrupt, missing the usual manners adults expect from children. Despite how tall and how capable she is, her emotional development has gaping holes, so she can have tantrums fitting for a child half her age. You need people in your church family to see that your child's needs are different and to not just say, 'That's normal, that's just children.' Once a mum in church told me Kia was 'harder work than all of her four children put together'. I cried with relief because mostly you just think you're struggling because you're not getting it right.

Kia needs a lot of intense emotional support from me. Past trauma haunts her silently and her anxiety is strong. She is triggered by any negative feedback. The smallest thing can lead to nights of broken sleep for us. Keeping on top of cooking food and getting her to school can be hard. When there are church 'bring and share' occasions, I find myself overwhelmed by the spreadsheet where I should sign up to say I'm bringing a plate of something. I've always thought this is because practically I don't have the time to serve in this way. However, I've realised it is because I am emotionally overwhelmed and spent. When her Godmummy says, 'Don't worry. I've signed up to cook for both of us,' I suddenly feel like I can manage once more. Providing meals for a family with a new baby helps in the initial days. However, a family caring for a child with additional needs benefits from little-and-often support – a meal every now and then.

Receiving teaching from God's word feels like pure gold. The opportunities for me to spend time in his word are, however, limited, as Kia needs me all the time. Reading a Christian book is not really an option! It has to be bite-sized. You can feel like an outlier, but more dangerously you can fall away because you so lack this nourishment. Prayer is important.

Teaching Kia about God, a Father who is good, is more important than anything else she could learn, as she didn't experience this. Ensuring she is soaked in God's truths I pray will lead her to faith. Our church weekend away to a Bible festival feels an important part of that. Attending this felt scary, as I knew the implications of taking Kia away from our home and how hard she might find it to be in the kids' sessions without me in a new setting. The SENCo reached out to me in advance. She took time to hear about Kia and what I thought might help. When I said, please don't cajole or let her 'cry it out' if she needs me, she informed everyone of this plan, and I had full assurance that I'd be called immediately. More than that, she is a professional with specific expertise. She had knowledge and understanding of trauma, ideas and strategies to add to an individualised plan. She educated the other team members. As Kia loves dens, she brought a pop-up tent for Kia to use as a breakaway space with fidget toys there. We arrived early and met our one-to-one the day before. We were greeted by the same one-to-one at each session. She told us the colour of the T-shirt Kia's group would be wearing and sent a social story days before. Kia had an 'all about me' profile, which means adults can know what she likes and what will ease her anxiety.

All these things make a world of difference – she is now learning all about our wonderful God. Returning each year builds familiarity. Still, each time, Kia's anxiety is intense. I hand her over and as I'm walking away I feel the weight of the anxiety we've been managing together leading up to this. However, I know there's been so much care to understand this little individual that God has created.

Kia's attachment difficulties mean that she is often preoccupied with worry that I will die and she will be without me. We teach children in our church about death and salvation through Jesus, and the topic of death is probably much more frequently spoken about than to a child who isn't a Christian. It means that we talk about salvation and eternity together often. This is a good thing, but it is helpful to be mindful

> that it can lead to some anxiety and preoccupation for a child with an attachment disorder.
>
> Overall, it has been incredible. A little two-year-old arrived in my home and within days her hair started to thicken, teeth grew, language emerged, and it felt magical to witness. She seemed immediately convicted that I was Mummy and she would be okay. Our church family have invested and loved us with the sensitivity it needs. We feel so blessed.

ATTACHMENT DISORDER

Everyone has an attachment style that is formed during their early childhood. When a baby and their primary caregiver have a strong and healthy bond, a secure attachment is formed. If anything disrupts that attachment, such as ill health, mental ill health, neglect, pervasive stress (such as a low income), separation, or bereavement, then a child may develop an attachment disorder. There are patterns of behaviour that can be recognised in a child with an attachment disorder. These are often evident in relationships and communication. This could include unusual responses to adults and peers (being obsessive, overly familiar, passive, or even fearful). The NSPCC explores this in more detail.[2]

As with all SEMH needs, positive, consistent relationships form a vital role in supporting an individual with an attachment disorder. However, an awareness of attachment disorder can be helpful in our Christian communities as it is frequently a part of the picture for a child with SEMH needs.

RELATIONSHIPS

In SEMH, relationships are the foundation of all support. While this is applicable across all disabilities and differences, it is imperative in SEMH. It is only off the back of a positive relationship that a child will trust you and feel safe enough to take the risk of listening to you. The S in SEMH stands for 'social', which indicates that children with this profile struggle with social interaction, expectations, and building and maintaining relationships. Added to this, the child may have had multiple negative experiences of being perceived as 'naughty', 'difficult', or even 'scary'. This messaging can perpetuate the problem and lead to a distrust of people and a fear of their rejection. Children who have experienced this negative feedback are also likely to believe these things as their identity, that they are 'bad' and unlovable and should live up to others' negative expectations of them. Because of this thinking, children and young people may try to sabotage positive relationships in order that they may control the ending of it, rather than face rejection. This negative cycle can be difficult to break and needs loving adults to break in and show that a different pattern is possible. This will not happen quickly, as these beliefs and understanding of the world can be very deep-rooted.

It can be challenging and even painful when a child or young person in whom you have invested time and care pushes you away. If this is happening, it is good to remember the reason behind it is fear, anxiety and perhaps an attachment disorder. The best way that you can respond is to consistently show that you are still there and care for the individual.

To address the imbalance of negative interactions, you can look for ways to recognise the positives. Some children may not be able to cope with direct praise, so you may want to find alternative ways to do this. This could be telling another adult in the room how impressed you are with their kindness, colouring, and contributions, within hearing of the child. It could be a small thumbs-up or it could be praising them to their parents or carers.

This is not to say that you do not address inappropriate or unsafe behaviours: boundaries are a necessary way for children to recognise they are in a safe environment, in which the adults are in charge. It is also important that we teach children right from wrong, and encourage and disciple them in living like Jesus. However, for children with SEMH needs, we need to consider carefully how we do this. If you have a family over for lunch or perhaps you are chatting over tea and coffee after a service, and their child is acting in a way that is unexpected, you will need to follow the caregivers' lead on how that is managed.

A key part of building relationships is to do an activity or have a conversation with the child on a topic of their interest. It may be that your friend's child is struggling, and you don't know how to support the family. As well as being a listening ear and offering prayer support for your friend, if you begin to build a relationship with the child then you could end up with more opportunities to support your friend practically. If you are leading youth or children's work and you are struggling to manage the unexpected behaviours of a child with SEMH needs in your group, try to have one-to-one time with them in the session. This could be asking another adult to oversee the group craft while you spend some time doing the craft with the child, or perhaps you could do an activity of their choosing with them for ten minutes while the rest of the group is occupied.

Relationships with their parent or carer are also really important: how can we support and encourage them? Cheryl told us about her experience of fostering. She explained to us how her foster son's refusal to leave the house resulted in isolation for her as well, which had a negative impact on her mental health. She reflected on how few people understood the extent of the challenge of school attendance issues. Her story reminded us of the importance of supporting caregivers as well as the child in these circumstances. Their church families can surround them with love and care, ensuring that they are given a chance to be heard and practically supported.

DE-ESCALATION AND PACE

It is helpful to pre-empt challenges before they become a problem for the child and be proactive with solutions. However, this isn't always possible. In this case we will want to de-escalate the situation before it reaches a crisis point.

Consider your body language and voice. From the perspective of the child or young person, how will you be coming across? You can try to appear unthreatening by giving some space, standing side-on rather than squarely in front of a child and perhaps you could come down to the child's height. When speaking, are you speaking loudly or in a way that could be perceived as cross, intimidating, or scary? Try to use a gentle, calm, clear voice. It is also useful to remember that it is common for children who experience difficulties in social communication to find recognising facial expressions challenging. They may perceive a neutral expression as intimidating or angry. I have sometimes found it helpful to describe my emotion: for example, saying, 'Can you see that I am not frowning and my face is relaxed? That is because I am calm. I am not shouting, because I am not angry. Let's see if we can work together to make this better.'

Dan Hughes, a clinical psychologist, created the PACE model over 20 years ago. It is a trauma-informed approach that is particularly effective in supporting children and young people with a variety of SEMH needs. In our experience, a PACE approach helps all children and young people to feel safe and secure.[3] It can offer a helpful framework for interacting with children and young people, whatever their needs. PACE stands for:

- *Playfulness*: This is about having a light playfulness in the way that you interact with children. It is not about being funny and making jokes all the time, but instead helping children to experience positive connections. Playfulness may involve sharing a game or activity with a child or it could be used to diffuse a tense situation.

- *Acceptance*: Acceptance is about accepting how a child feels, their thoughts and perceptions of a situation. You do not have to accept behaviour that is harmful or dangerous to the individual or others, but you can recognise the motives behind it. This also does not mean that you never challenge the child's thinking.

- *Curiosity*: Being curious with a child is trying to understand them more. Trying to think about what their motives and perceptions are, and understand more of their experience. Wondering aloud with a child, 'I wonder what that could have been about?' is a different way to reflect on a situation than asking, 'Why did you do that?'

- *Empathy*: Different to sympathy, empathy is about understanding the child's emotions and letting them know you will go through it together, that you can see it is hard for them and you are not leaving them to manage it alone.

It can feel strange beginning to use the PACE approach in your interactions with children, whether that is as a children's leader or as a friend of the family. Common criticisms of the PACE approach are that it is 'too soft' or that it 'rewards bad behaviour'. However, when used as a way of interacting with children (alongside appropriate reflection and reparation for inappropriate behaviour), it does not leave wrongs unchallenged but treats children with care and dignity. For children who have SEMH needs and require a little extra thought and care in how we communicate with them, PACE can be an excellent model to use as one of your tools.

Further to this, reflecting on the PACE approach in light of Jesus' ministry, there are some parallels in how he interacts with people.

Jesus is *playful*. We see him being sociable, having joyful meals with his friends, and participating in weddings. We also see him using deliberately humorous images to make a point, like someone with a 'plank in their eye' or a 'camel going through the eye of a needle'.

Jesus *accepts* people's realities, without condoning sin. We see this in John 4 with the woman at the well:

> 'I have no husband,' she replied.
> Jesus said to her, 'You are right when you say you have no husband. The fact is, you have had five husbands, and the man you now have is not your husband. What you have just said is quite true.'
> JOHN 4:17–18

Jesus is *curious*, getting to know his disciples and encouraging them to reflect with questions, such as 'Who do you say I am?' (Mark 8:29).

And we know that God is the 'God of all comfort, who comforts us in all our troubles, so that we can comfort those in any trouble with the comfort we ourselves receive from God. For just as we share abundantly in the sufferings of Christ, so also our comfort abounds through Christ' (2 Corinthians 1:3–5). He shows us *empathy* in our sufferings and difficult times.

MANAGING DYSREGULATION

Sometimes, despite our best efforts at de-escalation and avoiding triggers, a child can still become dysregulated and struggle to manage their emotions in a safe and appropriate way. It can be challenging to know how to react if this is the case, and, depending on the context and your role in the situation, your response will be different.

The main thing to remember is that dysregulation is not bad behaviour. It is not a chosen, thought-through or rational reaction to a situation. It is a fear response in which the amygdala (the part of the brain responsible for fight/flight/freeze) has been triggered, and the individual cannot access the pre-frontal cortex (the part of the brain that helps us with decision-making and rational thinking). This understanding should help inform your next steps.

It may be that there is a dysregulated child in your service, weekend away, or midweek group, but you are not directly involved with them. Try to give them space and maintain their dignity. Ask the caregivers if there is anything they might need, but don't overcrowd or draw any further attention to the situation.

Maybe you are in a position where you are responsible for a child with SEMH needs. You may be leading their midweek club or Sunday group. Or perhaps you have offered to babysit so that their caregivers can have some quality time together. If this is the case, preparation ahead of time will be invaluable. Have a conversation with the parents or carers about the following:

- How does the individual appear when calm and content?
- Are there any signs I might notice that they are starting to become unsettled/agitated/anxious?
- Any known triggers to be avoided?
- What helps to calm/regulate them if they become dysregulated?
- At what point would you like to be contacted?

Together, you can work out a plan for how you can care for and support their child. I have often found that having the starting point of knowing to ask these questions has helped caregivers to feel supported, knowing that you are carefully considering how you can best meet the needs of their child while they are in your care. It can also give consistency and safety from the child's perspective, as if the adults around them are consistent, it can remove some of the anxiety and unpredictability that comes with a transferral of care.

Some practical advice to support regulation would be:

- *Try your best to appear calm.* This will help the child and any other children nearby to feel safe, knowing that as the adult you have things in hand.

- *Remove the audience.* If there are others around, try to find somewhere else they can go to preserve the dysregulated child's dignity and space to regulate. Moving a group could also be part of a dynamic risk assessment if you feel that anybody is at risk of being hurt (e.g. if a dysregulated child is throwing objects). This can require a level of flexibility that we may not find easy. If you are in a Sunday school session that you have worked hard on, and you need to take the group out of the room to support a child's regulation, this could be practically difficult (finding an alternative space) as well as feeling frustrating (you are having to stop what you have prepared, and try to improvise with your group). If this is a likely scenario, it could be worth thinking ahead to what your plan would be. It is also important that should this happen, the child is reintegrated with the group as soon as is safely possible, and the situation is explained in an age-appropriate way to the other children, e.g. 'Lily is feeling very upset and angry at the moment and needs some help calming down. We can be good friends by giving her space, so we are going to spend some time in the garden. When Lily is feeling better, she will come and join us again.' Removing the audience is a regulation strategy and should never be used as a punishment.

- *Change of face.* It may be that having a different adult come into the situation can help the child regulate. This is not because you were 'unable to manage', but sometimes a fresh face and voice can help reset the situation.

- *Deep pressure.* This can help soothe a child's nervous system. This could be provided with a weighted blanket or toy, rolling a peanut ball over the child, or even just gently but firmly pressing on their shoulders or arms. You can encourage a child to hug themselves, or squeeze along their own arms, or where appropriate a firm hug may be helpful.

- *Offer a drink or snack.* Crunchy snacks are particularly good at supporting regulation.

- *Redirection.* Have pillows, soft-play equipment, or beanbags that a child can safely hit, kick, or punch. You can redirect physical behaviour towards this safe alternative.

- *Other calming techniques.* Ripping paper, breathing exercises, listening to calm music, or distraction with a toy, book, or preferred activity can all be helpful.

- *Leave a way out.* Always leave an escape exit for the child – physically and metaphorically. Offer the child a way out of the situation that helps them 'save face'. This could be something like, 'I wonder if I close my eyes whether this mess will be tidied up and George will be back with the group ready to continue,' or, 'If you need to run around, you can run outside and I will come with you to make sure that you are safe out there.'

Which strategies will be most effective will vary from one individual to the next, and sometimes day to day.

When a child is dysregulated, it is important that we first calm them, then connect (via a conversation or activity) before going on to reflection and reparation. This is because the child will not be able to reflect or repair the situation while they are dysregulated. They need support in order to return to a place in which they can access their thinking brain.

REFLECTION AND REPARATION

For a child with SEMH needs, discipline can look quite different. As Christians, we know that repentance and feeling sorry for what we have done wrong is a healthy reaction that we can take to God. However, for a child with SEMH needs, there can be a susceptibility to getting stuck in shame. As Christians we want to move from shame to repentance and to live in the freedom and joy of forgiveness. Spiritually, we want to teach our children how to repent and leave their sin and shame at the cross. This can be particularly difficult for children with SEMH needs. The framework of reflecting on and repairing a situation can be helpful in working through how we manage this. When it comes to reparation and consequences, it is imperative that it is discussed with parents and carers to make sure we are accommodating any attachment or trauma-based needs the child may have. It can be useful to think over the situation together, perhaps wondering aloud to explore what happened. Some children may not be able to cope with reflecting directly on a situation and it may be more helpful to think together about a similar situation involving a toy or a character.

Once reflection has happened (whatever it looks like), reparations can be made. Again, these reparations need to be appropriate for the individual's emotional rather than chronological age. If a verbal apology is something a child finds particularly challenging, you could encourage them to make a sorry card or picture. Another form of reparation may be doing something kind for the person who has been upset or hurt. Once in my work I was thrilled to see a child initiate reparation with me following a difficult incident. They did not say sorry, give me a card, or any of the usual things we tried to encourage the children to do. They came over to me and told me they were going to play an imaginary game, and that I had a castle and a Ferrari in it. These were the things which they most wanted and dreamed of, so by offering them to me through play, they were holding out an olive branch. Times of reparation can also be a great opportunity to pray with the child and model repentance.

Once the apologies have been made, it is necessary to move on from the incident and demonstrate forgiveness and a fresh start in a very clear way. This can sometimes feel like a challenge if you are faced with recurring situations and you may not feel the individual is showing they are sorry by repeating their behaviours. As well as praying for the Lord to work and bring about change in the child's heart, pray that he will give you the patience and resilience to persevere, as your own demonstration of love and forgiveness will not be insignificant in showing God's love and attitude towards each of us.

FAMILY SUPPORT

As with all additional needs, family support is very important for those with a child with SEMH needs in their family. An invisible need, SEMH is often perceived as bad behaviour or poor parenting, which can take a toll on those caring for individuals with this profile. As well as this, it can be even more difficult to find clubs and groups that include these children, increasing the isolation of the child and their family. This can be difficult for family life and is an area in which Christian communities can really serve those affected. Walking alongside families with this experience can help to decrease loneliness and isolation, perhaps meeting at their house for a catch-up and check-in, if going out and about is a challenge. Offering a non-judgemental and supportive friendship that is flexible to the needs of the family can be an invaluable lifeline for the whole household. If you have children in your life who are peers to a child with SEMH needs, supporting and facilitating friendship is a great way to show love to a family who are used to being excluded or on the edge of social experiences. One charity which seeks to support families through the local church is Safe Families; they offer resources and training to churches seeking to do this well.[4]

HOW WE SPEAK ABOUT SEMH

When you are involved in the lives of those with SEMH needs, you can find yourself experiencing new situations that are unusual. These experiences can be sensationalised or make interesting anecdotes, where we come off as having experienced something dramatic either as a victim or a hero.

Imagine that you are volunteering at a holiday club that your church is running, and your job is to set up the juice and biscuits. While your back is turned, a child with SEMH needs comes and eats several of the biscuits. You ask them kindly not to do that as there needs to be enough for everybody, and you pride yourself on not making a big deal of it. The child then becomes highly dysregulated and starts throwing the drinks and snacks at you, and even flips a table. The other leaders, recognising the child is dysregulated and needs space, take the other children outside and start a game. You support the child's group leader in regulating the child and successfully use the PACE model to engage them, playfully splashing in the puddles of juice until the child is calm enough to help you clean everything up – which they do.

You may be tempted to retell this story to others with the emphasis on the shock factor of what happened or to tell of your de-escalation skills and excellent management of the situation. While sharing information of what appears to work or any reflections on the situation can be appropriate and helpful, it is important to make sure we are not gossiping and that we are preserving the dignity of both the child and their family. While this situation may be unusual for you to face, for the family of a child with SEMH needs it may be a common occurrence and a historical barrier to their belonging.

Let us use this fictional example to think of how we can speak about a challenging situation both to other children and to adults.

TO CHILDREN

We may need to reassure children that they are safe and that the adults are there to help them if they are feeling anxious or unsettled about a situation. It is important to be able to balance the needs of the child with SEMH needs with the needs of the wider group. We want to encourage a culture that accepts that we all make mistakes and we all struggle and that forgiveness is available.

You could say something like the following:

> I know that might have felt a little bit shocking, scary, or even funny when that happened. They were finding it hard to know what to do with some big feelings and they made some unexpected choices. We can all find it hard to manage our big feelings at times, can't we? Sometimes some children can find it really tricky and might need some space and

time and a bit of help from the grown-ups to feel okay again. Remember that the grown-ups are around to help you and to help them, so if you have any worries you can always talk to one of us about it. We will make sure that everyone is safe and looked after well at holiday club.

If the children continue to talk about it:

We've moved on from that now, and they have put it right by tidying up and saying sorry. We don't need to keep talking about it. We can move forward with a fresh start, the same way that God gives us all a fresh start.

TO ADULTS

When thinking about discussing an incident like this with adults, it is definitely worth considering who you are talking to and what the purpose of the discussion is. Those involved may benefit from a group discussion to reflect and process the experience, their own perceptions and feelings around it, things that may have been learnt from it that could be useful moving forward, and things that went well. This sort of conversation is important in ensuring those involved are well supported and able to manage any of their own emotions that could have come up during the incident, as well as thinking forward to further ways we can support the child involved.

We also need to communicate with the family what has happened in a way that demonstrates your commitment to include the child and care for them well. The caregivers could be used to many awkward and difficult conversations about the behaviours their child exhibits, and we want to be people who talk with grace, love, and respect about their child. This is where it is helpful to remember the language of 'dysregulation' and show that you are aware that the behaviour, though needing to be managed, was communicating something and that you want to work towards supporting the child in feeling calm and safe in your context.

The importance of relationships in this process is highlighted by one of the stories we received while writing this chapter:

ONE ADOPTIVE/FOSTER PARENT'S STORY

As a foster carer and adopter, I've cared for a number of children over the past twelve years or so, most of whom have experienced trauma and loss, and many of whom also have attachment difficulties, SEMH needs, and additional needs. It's often a combination of confusing, complex histories, and undiagnosed needs that makes my role as a therapeutic parent both a privilege and a challenge. My children are all beautiful, unique individuals who bring us so much joy – but I know that when I open my home to them, I also welcome in all the mess. When we go to church, all this mess goes with us – and this can present in lots of different, sometimes embarrassing, ways.

Having said that, I have found our church family to be living out what it means to be 'family' in sacrificial, embracing, and love-filled ways. They know us, they know our children, they spend time talking to them, they know what makes them scared or overwhelmed. We have a brilliant relationship with our church youth leader – who messages me about changes to the youth work provision so that my children are prepared, gives our middle child (who is autistic) a one-to-one, draws out visual timetables, and generally just checks in with us.

When we first started attending our current church, the pastor took time out to show our children around the building. My middle child is particularly fascinated/worried about alarms, noises, and electrical equipment, so our pastor gently pointed out and explained about everything. My child also loves very fast, very expensive cars and one day, a church member (who happened to own a Porsche) parked it at the front of church and took him on a surprise trip out in it. Little (big) things like this make our children feel noticed and special.

Some things are easier to resolve (getting told about the alarm system, for example) – but the ongoing complexity of having lived with significant trauma and broken relationships leaves hidden scars. My eldest can find church almost offensive. The notion of a father who loves us unconditionally, who will never go 'missing in action' as my child describes his earthly father, is just beyond belief. He is going through a lot of turmoil, and has many unanswered questions (that may never be fully resolved).

We have found previous churches to lack understanding of childhood trauma and therefore use language and approaches that alienate, upset, and isolate our children. Our current church, though, is making every effort, and this is predominantly done through relationship building. It takes time for our children to learn to trust adults. There are some guys in our church that have taken time to invest in our children, to the extent that on Father's Day last year, my eldest child reeled off the names of two men in our church who he had come to see as being a dad to him.

The importance is in seeing that the whole church can help care for children with trauma, SEMH, and other additional needs. If you know about alarm systems, happen to own a super car, can provide one-to-one for a child in their Sunday school class, or just simply are very good at being a listening ear, every action or effort matters. It might not always work or resolve some of those complex, lifelong challenges that our children often have, but it's noticed and appreciated.

And I wonder whether seeing us rock up at church every Sunday morning, looking slightly dishevelled and exhausted, is good for the church, too? After all, we're all messed up, imperfect people who need the grace of God. We offer up the little we have, and God uses it for his glory to benefit his church. Our experience of being foster carers and adopters means we can welcome and wrap around other foster and adoptive families. We live out the reality of brokenness so that other people don't feel that they have to have 'sorted' lives to be accepted by the church.

Our children have this natural affinity to draw alongside other children who feel different or excluded. Our eldest helps at youth groups, he plays with children on their own. My middle child quietly observes and if someone is hurt, he checks if they are okay. My little one dances and waves her hands during worship and shows everyone what it's like to wildly let go, to be yourself, to be free.

Every member of God's family is important. Everyone has their place around the table. And church would be poorer without them.

TOP 10 FOR EVERYONE

1. Get to know the child with SEMH needs and/or their family.

2. Remember that behaviour is communicating something. Don't be too upset/surprised by unexpected or disruptive behaviours.

3. In the event of disruptive behaviour, stay calm and keep treating the child with love and respect.

4. Ask the carers of a child with SEMH needs questions about what helps them feel regulated and how to tell when they're starting to become dysregulated.

5. Remember that for all of us, but especially for those with past experiences of rejection, reflection and reparation for mistakes should be spoken about in the context of forgiveness and relationship with God and his people.

6. Don't judge/compare other children's situations with that of a child who has faced trauma.

7. Offer to support families practically with meals, babysitting, or running errands.

8. Support the mental and spiritual health of the family as well as the child. Offer prayer and ask how they're doing.

9. Speak lovingly and without gossip, sensationalising, or malice in how you talk about a child with SEMH needs and their behaviour.

10. Look out for what God is doing in the child's life. Encourage their family with positive stories when you can.

Conclusion

One of the images the Bible uses a lot is a banquet. Eating together becomes a picture of God's people gathered in community, under the Lord of the banquet, Jesus.

- We see it in the Passover meal, which Israelites celebrate to remember God's rescue, and in which even foreigners can take part if they are willing to commit to full membership of God's people (Exodus 12:43–51).

- We see hints of it in Ruth, where the abundance of grain and the wedding with which the book ends signal God's blessing, and especially in the inclusion of the outsider by the guardian-redeemer (Ruth 4).

- Isaiah looks forward to a heavenly banquet, a 'feast of rich food for all peoples' when 'the Sovereign Lord will wipe away the tears from all faces; he will remove his people's disgrace from all the earth' (Isaiah 25:6, 8). Isaiah is clearly looking beyond his people's return from exile at this point, as at this feast, God will 'swallow up death forever'.

- Nehemiah and Ezra look forward to this banquet when (despite the people's sorrow for their sin, revealed by reading the law) Nehemiah tells them: 'Go and enjoy choice food and sweet drinks, and send some to those who have nothing prepared. This day is holy to our Lord. Do not grieve, for the joy of the Lord is your strength' (Nehemiah 8:10).

- Throughout Jesus' ministry, he eats with different groups of people, notably tax collectors and 'sinners', earning him the criticism of the religious elite (e.g. Luke 5:29–30).

- Eating together as a church is a way Jesus commands us to remember his death, as he institutes a new Passover meal, the Lord's supper. This is intended both to proclaim Jesus' death and express our unity in Christ (1 Corinthians 11:17–34).

Again and again, we see pictures of God's people, remembering God's rescue in the past, looking forward to his ultimate rescue in the future, making sure that every member of the covenant community is included and welcomed.

This image of the whole body of Christ, the universal church, being part of a giant party, where everyone is welcomed and given a 'seat at the table', should fill us with joy, especially as we look forward to its ultimate fulfilment. As we close, let's focus on two beautiful examples of this image being used, showing us once again God's heart for those on the outside, those excluded or suffering as a result of disabilities, and how we can work together to allow every member of God's people to experience the true belonging which is theirs in Christ.

MEPHIBOSHETH AT THE KING'S TABLE

In 2 Samuel, we are introduced to a character called Mephibosheth. He is first mentioned in passing in 2 Samuel 4, which describes the end of the house of Saul, the previous king. In this chapter, we learn that aged 5, after the news of his father Jonathan's death, he was dropped by his nurse in her panic and became disabled (2 Samuel 4:4). In other words, he's gone from being the son of the crown prince to a disabled member of a defeated royal family. A few chapters later, the new king, David, wants to fulfil his vow of friendship to Jonathan. We are repeatedly reminded of how Mephibosheth would be seen by those around him: 'He is lame in both feet' (2 Samuel 9:3, 13); he sees himself as 'a dead dog' (v. 8); he is of 'the house of Saul' (v. 3), David's enemy, and part of the regime God has deposed in favour of David's house. Not only this, but it would seem that the exclusion of those with disabilities from the presence of the king had become almost proverbial, as a result of the Jebusites' taunts against David. Sandwiched between chapters 4 and 9, where Mephibosheth is mentioned, we are told: 'That is why they say, "The 'blind and lame' will not enter the palace"' (2 Samuel 5:8). No wonder Mephibosheth was hiding out in a place called Lo Debar, which means something like 'no thing' – we might say 'the middle of nowhere'. All in all, he was a person most people wouldn't have gone out of their way to associate with, who felt his own weakness and exclusion keenly.

What does David, the king who is an Old Testament precursor to Jesus, do for this man? Does he throw that proverb in his face? Pension him off where no one can see him, so that he's kept his promise to Jonathan to be kind to his family? Instead, David restores his grandfather Saul's land to Mephibosheth (providing him with security and an income) and says, 'You will always eat at my table' (2 Samuel 9:7). Mephibosheth isn't given a place at the bottom of the table like an unwanted guest, but 'ate at David's table like one of the king's sons' (v. 11). In case the full significance of this act of generous inclusion and invitation to belong hasn't sunk in, the author repeats it in the final verse of the chapter: 'And Mephibosheth lived in Jerusalem, because he always ate at the king's table; he was lame in both feet' (v. 13).[1]

Like Mephibosheth, we are by nature 'dead dogs' – unable to contribute anything to our own salvation – and yet offered a seat at the king's table. We are not just welcomed, but given a place of honour. The story of Mephibosheth does not simply provide us with a metaphor applicable to every Christian. It also gives us a glimpse of the sort of family God wants us to be: one where every member, whatever their differences, is welcomed, included and given a place of belonging.

THE WEDDING OF THE LAMB

At the end of the Bible, we see where all these images have been pointing: to another, greater feast, the 'wedding supper of the Lamb'. All the threads we can see running through these biblical feasts come together in this one, true feast. First, we see the thread of celebrating God's rescue. The multitude in Revelation 19 shout, 'Hallelujah! Salvation and glory and power belong to our God, for true and just are his judgments' (Revelation 19:1–2). We see a great crowd, rejoicing that God has rescued them. Their worthiness to stand before the throne has been given to them. The church, the bride of Christ, is made ready: 'Fine linen, bright and clean, was given her to wear' (v. 8). In case we weren't sure, John tells us that 'fine linen stands for the righteous acts of God's holy people'. If we've ever been to a wedding, we can picture the scene – the bride arriving in her beautiful white dress, having carefully prepared herself for this important moment. On this occasion, however, the bride hasn't been responsible for finding her own dress – it has been given to her. The glory does not go to the bride, beautiful though she is, but to the Lord God Almighty: 'Let us rejoice and be glad and give him glory!' say the crowd (v. 7). In fact, they don't say this – they shout it, louder than the loudest rock concert you can imagine: 'like the roar of rushing waters and like loud peals of thunder' (v. 6).

We also see the thread of joyful inclusion of all God's people. There are no second-class citizens at this banquet. The angel speaking to John says, 'Write this: Blessed are those who are invited to the wedding supper of the Lamb!' (v. 9). We see 24 elders bowing down to God, representing both the twelve tribes of Israel and the twelve apostles of the New Testament church, symbolising a glorious unity of all God's people. Elsewhere, we also get more detail about the 'great multitude': they are 'from every nation, tribe, people, and language' (Revelation 7:9). Even at the wedding feast, we do not see uniformity, but unity. They are not united because they are all the same, but because they have all had their robes washed by the blood of the Lamb (Revelation 7:14) and they are all utterly focused on God, on his throne, at the centre. Both Revelation 7 and 21 repeat Isaiah's words, that the coming of the wedding feast of the Lamb will herald an end to sorrow and suffering: 'God will wipe every tear from their eyes' (Revelation 7:17; 21:4).

It will sometimes be hard, now, to ensure that everyone's needs are met and that those who are 'different' do not feel excluded. However, we look forward to a day when the unity which is ours now in Christ will be fully realised as we all join together praising him.

APPENDIX ①

Glossary

ACE: adverse childhood experience. There are ten recognised ACEs: physical abuse; sexual abuse; emotional abuse; physical neglect; emotional neglect; mental illness in a family member; divorce; substance abuse in the environment; violence against your mother; and having a relative who has been sent to prison. The higher an ACE score an individual has, the greater the risk they will develop health and social issues.

ADHD: attention deficit hyperactivity disorder. See chapter 11.

ASD: autism spectrum disorder. The autistic community currently prefers 'autism'. See chapter 9.

Attachment disorder/insecure attachment: impairment to one's ability to form and develop healthy emotional attachments. See chapter 12.

Attendance allowance: a UK benefit paid to those of state pension age or older whose disability requires others to help look after them.

DLA: disability living allowance. In the UK, DLA can be claimed to help with the extra costs of a child under 16 who needs significant extra care.

Dysregulation: when an individual is outside of their 'window of tolerance', they are 'dysregulated'. We may see this in particular behaviours, but these are communicating that the individual is unable to control their emotional response. Everyone can become dysregulated but not everyone has the same window of tolerance.

EHCP: education, health, and care plan. A legal document agreed with a local authority outlining the support the local authority is putting in place to help a child. *(Note: At the time of printing, the UK government and the Children's Commissioner for England are considering significant changes to the SEND system, including EHCPs.)*

IEP: individual educational plan. A document drawn up by a school describing the child's goals for the school year and how the school is helping them meet these goals. This is often done before applying for an EHCP or instead of one, if the school can meet the child's needs themselves.

Masking: adopting 'typical' behaviours in order to blend in with those around, usually at a high emotional/energy cost. See chapter 9.

Meltdown: an autistic person's response to extreme overload and stress, to a point where the feelings cannot be contained. See chapter 9.

Neurodivergent: having atypical patterns of thought or behaviour. This adjective is used to describe a range of different neurological types.

Neurodiverse: an adjective describing a diversity of brain types. An individual is not 'neurodiverse', but a group of people can be.

Neurotypical: having typical patterns of thought or behaviour, describing a brain which has developed in a typical way.

PIP: Personal Independence Payment (in England and Wales) has replaced DLA for adults. Adult disability payment is the equivalent in Scotland.

Regulation/regulate: emotional regulation is a way of describing strategies and methods individuals use to manage and respond to their emotions. It includes strategies which amplify, maintain, or decrease one's emotional responses.

SEMH: social, emotional, and mental health. See chapter 12.

SENCo: special educational needs coordinator. Someone coordinating care given to anyone with special educational needs and disabilities, usually in a school or large organisation.

Shutdown: harder to spot than a meltdown, but also an autistic person's response to extreme overload. See chapter 9.

SpLD: specific learning difficulty. See chapter 8.

Stim: self-stimulatory behaviours are often called 'stims'. These are frequently physical movements, but can stimulate other senses (for example, an oral stim can be chewing or sucking, and a vocal stim can be making repetitive noises). They are often involuntary and help calm the individual by increasing sensory input in a desired area.

Window of tolerance: a metaphor used to describe the optimal state of emotional arousal, in which an individual is able to operate optimally, neither feeling detached nor overwhelmed by their emotions.

APPENDIX

Accessibility audits

There are several good sets of questions you can use to work through how accessible your church is before putting together proposals for change.

Through the Roof provides a free, thorough audit questionnaire to all those who sign up to be 'Roofbreakers' or church disability champions at: **throughtheroof.org/forchurches/roofbreakers**

Denominational audits will help with questions specific to your church's governance structure, for example:

- Church of England. **london.anglican.org/church-and-parish-support/diversity-and-inclusion/disability-ministry/the-360-accessibility-audit**
- The Methodist Church. **methodist.org.uk/for-churches/property/practical-and-technical-guidance/making-buildings-accessible**
- Baptist Union. **baptist.org.uk/Articles/368694/Guideline_Leaflet_L12.aspx**

APPENDIX ③

Other organisations offering help in this area

Additional Needs Alliance
Helping churches to include, support, create places of belonging for, and spiritually grow children, young people, and young adults with additional needs or disabilities. A collection of individuals and organisations offering services and resources.

Anna Chaplaincy
A community-based ministry for people of strong, little, or no faith; it involves visiting older people wherever they may be living, whether in residential and nursing homes, sheltered housing, retirement complexes, or other private homes.

The Church of England: Disability Advice
Podcasts and resources to equip the church in becoming more inclusive.

Church is for All
A network of UK Christian disability-engaged organisations (formerly known as Churches for All).

Count Everyone In
Offers workshops, resources, and a support scheme for churches working with people with learning disabilities. This includes Makaton training, Bible study notes, and teaching resources, which may be helpful if you are running a group for adults with learning disabilities or simply wanting to make church more accessible.

Faith in Later Life
Faith in Later Life is sponsored by four Christian charities to help churches and individual Christians to engage with older people. They work to enable churches to 'reach, serve, and empower older people' in local communities and to encourage older people in their faith.

Go! Sign
A charity focused on making Deaf disciples of Jesus Christ.

Growing Hope
A charity providing free therapy through services based at churches.

Safe Families
Previously Safe Families and Home for Good. Supporting adoptive and foster families and children, primarily through churches.

Shaftesbury
Previously Livability, Shaftesbury provides a wide range of care, education, vocation, and rehabilitation services. It works both within and outside the church.

Through the Roof
Our partner on this book, Through the Roof is a must for any church seriously wanting to improve their accessibility. Anyone can sign up to be a 'Roofbreaker' disability champion in their own local church, or offer their services more widely. Support and resources are given as needed, and everyone involved is invited to join Roofbreaker Network events and receive two hours of free Disability Awareness training for their church.

Torch Trust
Help and support for Christians living with sight loss or supporting those who are.

Urban Saints
Offers additional needs training for working with children and young people, as well as a consultancy service.

Bibliography

PAPERS

Michael A. Akeroyd and Kevin J. Munro, 'Population estimates of the number of adults in the UK with a hearing loss updated using 2021 and 2022 census data', *International Journal of Audiology*, 63.9, pp. 659–60. doi.org/10.1080/14992027.2024.2341956

Matthew Bisset et al., 'Practitioner review: It's time to bridge the gap – understanding the unmet needs of consumers with attention deficit/ hyperactivity disorder – a systematic review and recommendations', *Journal of Child Psychology and Psychiatry*, 64.6 (2023), pp. 848–58. doi.org/10.1111/jcpp.13752

Rebecca Bondü and Günter Esser, 'Justice and rejection sensitivity in children and adolescents with ADHD symptoms', *European Child & Adolescent Psychiatry*, 24.2 (2014), pp. 185–98. doi.org/10.1007/s00787-014-0560-9

Claire M. Brown et al., 'Updated systematic review of suicide in autism: 2018–2024', *Current Developmental Disorders Reports*, 11 (2024), pp. 225–56. doi.org/10.1007/s40474-024-00308-9

T. Brugha et al., 'Estimating the prevalence of autism spectrum conditions in adults: extending the 2007 adult psychiatric morbidity survey', The Health and Social Care Information Centre, Community and Mental Health Team, 2012. files.digital.nhs.uk/17/DF543A/esti-prev-auti-ext-07-psyc-morb-surv-rep.pdf

Fabienne Cazalis et al., 'Evidence that nine autistic women out of ten have been victims of sexual violence', *Frontiers in Behavioral Neuroscience*, 16 (2022). doi.org/10.3389/fnbeh.2022.852203

Ken Eames, *Statistics for Mission 2022* (Church of England Data Services, 2023).

Joni Eareckson Tada and Jack S. Oppenhuizen, 'Hidden and forgotten people', *Lausanne Occasional Paper*, Lausanne Committee for World Evangelization, 2005. lausanne.org/wp-content/uploads/2007/06/LOP35B_IG6B.pdf

Thomas Frodl, 'Comorbidity of ADHD and substance use disorder (SUD): a neuroimaging perspective', *Journal of Attention Disorders*, 14.2 (2010), pp. 109–20. **doi.org/10.1177/1087054710365054**

Camille Hours, Christophe Recasens, and Jean-Marc Baleyte, 'ASD and ADHD comorbidity: what are we talking about?', *Frontiers in Psychiatry*, 13 (2022). **doi.org/10.3389/fpsyt.2022.837424**

Laura Hull et al., '"Putting on my best normal": social camouflaging in adults with autism spectrum conditions', *Journal of Autism and Developmental Disorders*, 47.8 (2017), pp. 2519–34. **doi.org/10.1007/s10803-017-3166-5**

International Classification of Diseases, Eleventh Revision (ICD-11), World Health Organization (WHO) 2019/2021. **icd.who.int/en**

Servet Karaca et al., 'Comorbidity between behavioral addictions and attention deficit/hyperactivity disorder: a systematic review', *International Journal of Mental Health and Addiction*, 15, pp. 701–24 (2017). **doi.org/10.1007/s11469-016-9660-8**

Edgar Kellenberger, 'Children and adults with intellectual disability in antiquity and modernity: toward a biblical and sociological model', *CrossCurrents*, 63.4 (2013), pp. 449–72. **jstor.org/stable/24462315**

Michael Oliver, 'Theories of disability in health practice and research', *BMJ: British Medical Journal*, 317 (21 November 1998), pp. 1446–49.

Mike Oliver and Colin Barnes, 'Disability studies, disabled people and the struggle for inclusion', *British Journal of Sociology of Education*, 31.5 (2010), pp. 547–60. **doi.org/10.1080/01425692.2010.500088**

James Phillips et al., 'The six most essential questions in psychiatric diagnosis: a pluralogue part 1: conceptual and definitional issues in psychiatric diagnosis', *Philosophy, Ethics, and Humanities in Medicine*, 7.3 (2012). **doi.org/10.1186/1747-5341-7-3**

Matthew Puffer, 'Human dignity after Augustine's "Imago Dei": on the sources and uses of two ethical terms', *Journal of the Society of Christian Ethics*, 37.1 (2017), pp. 65–82. **jstor.org/stable/44504864**

Jacqui Rodgers and A. Ofield, 'Understanding, recognising and treating co-occurring anxiety in autism', *Current Developmental Disorders Reports*, 5.1 (2018), pp. 58–64. **doi.org/10.1007/s40474-018-0132-7**

Justin Taylor, 'The gate of the temple called "the Beautiful" (Acts 3:2,10)', *Revue Biblique*, 106.4 (1999), pp. 549–62. **jstor.org/stable/44089460**

Jan Tøssebro, 'Book Reviews : C. Barnes and G. Mercer (eds): *Exploring the Divide. Illness and Disability*. Leeds: The Disability Press, 1996. L. Barton (ed.): *Disability and Society: Emerging Issues and Insights*. London: Longman, 1996. L.J. Davis: *Enforcing Normalcy: Disability, Deafness and the Body*. New York: Verso, 1995. G. Hales (ed.): *Beyond Disability*. London: Sage, 1996. J. Harris: *The Cultural Meaning of Deafness*. Aldershot: Avebury, 1995. M. Oliver: *Understanding Disability. From Theory to Practice*. London: Macmillan, 1996', *Acta Sociologica*, 40.4 (1997), pp. 409–13.

Saskia van der Oord and Gail Tripp, 'How to improve behavioral parent and teacher training for children with ADHD: integrating empirical research on learning and motivation into treatment', *Clinical Child and Family Psychology Review*, 23.4 (2020), pp. 577–604. **doi.org/10.1007/s10567-020-00327-z**

Andrew Whitehouse, 'Commentary: a spectrum for all? A response to Green et al. (2023), neurodiversity, autism and health care', *Child and Adolescent Mental Health*, 28.3 (2023), pp. 443–45. **doi.org/10.1111/camh.12666**

BOOKS

Herman Bavinck, *The Wonderful Works of God*, trans. R. Carlton Wynne (Westminster Seminary Press, 2020).

Brian R. Brock and John Swinton (eds), *Disability in the Christian Tradition: A reader* (Wm. B. Eerdmans Publishing, 2012).

Michael S. Beates, *Disability and the Gospel: How God uses our brokenness to display his grace* (Crossway, 2012).

Terry DeYoung et al., *Everybody Belongs, Serving Together: Inclusive church ministry with people with disabilities* (Faithward, 2021).

Nancy L. Eiesland, *The Disabled God: Toward a liberatory theology of disability* (Abingdon Press, 1994).

Debby Elley and Tori Houghton, *The Ice-Cream Sundae Guide to Autism* (Jessica Kingsley, 2020).

Michael R. Emlet, *Saints, Sufferers and Sinners: Loving others as God loves us* (New Growth Press, 2021).

Ross W. Greene, *The Explosive Child: A new approach for understanding and parenting easily frustrated, chronically inflexible children* (Harper Paperbacks, 2014).

Kerri-Ann Hayes, *The Accessible Church: Making the church a welcoming place for children with special needs and from traumatic backgrounds* (self-published, 2022).

David Howe, *Attachment across the Lifecourse: A brief introduction* (Palgrave Macmillan, 2011).
Amy Kenny, *My Body is Not a Prayer Request: Disability justice in the church* (Brazos, 2022).
Myra Kersner and Jannet Wright (eds), *Speech and Language Therapy: The decision-making process when working with children* (Routledge, 2012).
Sarah Naish, *The A–Z of Therapeutic Parenting: Strategies and solutions* (Jessica Kingsley, 2018).
Sarah Naish and Sarah Dillon, *The Quick Guide to Therapeutic Parenting: A visual introduction* (Jessica Kingsley, 2020).
Tony Phelps-Jones, *Making Church Accessible to All: Including disabled people in church life* (BRF Ministries, 2013).
Vaughan Roberts, *God's Big Picture: Tracing the storyline of the Bible* (IVP, 2003).
Daniel J. Siegel and Tina Payne Bryson, *The Whole-Brain Child: 12 proven strategies to nurture your child's developing mind* (Robinson, 2012).
Andrew and Rachel Wilson, *The Life You Never Expected: Thriving while parenting special needs children* (IVP, 2015).
Amos Yong, *The Bible, Disability, and the Church: A new vision of the people of God* (Wm. B. Eerdmans Publishing, 2011).

WEBSITES
CHAPTERS 1–4

Brandon Bathauer, 'Image-bearers: be fruitful and multiply', Discipleship.org, 25 February 2023. **discipleship.org/blog/image-bearers-be-fruitful-and-multiply**
Ros Bayes, 'A biblical view of disability', 17 February 2015. **bethinking.org/human-life/a-biblical-view-of-disability**
Rich Blake-Lobb, 'What is the face of the UK church to adults with disabilities? (A critical investigation)', dissertation, 2020. **cte.org.uk/app/uploads/2021/06/what-is-the-face-of-the-uk-church-to-adults-with-disabilities-a-critical-investigation.pdf**
Chris Corbin, 'On the catechism', Theodramatist, 25 May 2022. **theodramatist.com/posts/on-the-catechism**
The Church of England, 'Everyone counts 2014: diversity audit key findings', 2014. **churchofengland.org/sites/default/files/2017-11/everyone-counts-diversity-audit-key-findings-2014.pdf**
John Davies, 'The disabled God, living into the resurrection', Notes from a

Small Vicar, 18 April 2021. **johndavies.typepad.com/blog/the-disabled-god-living-into-the-resurrection.html**

Disability Rights UK, 'Nearly half of everyone in poverty is either a disabled person or lives with a disabled person', 6 February 2020. **disabilityrightsuk.org/news/2020/february/nearly-half-everyone-poverty-either-disabled-person-or-lives-disabled-person**

Journeymanpreacher, 'Are people with disabilities shut out?', 6 March 2012. **journeymanpreacher.wordpress.com/2012/03/06/are-people-with-disabilities-shut-out**

Esme Kirk-Wade, Sonja Stiebahl, and Helen Wong, 'UK disability statistics: prevalence and life experiences', 2024. **researchbriefings.files.parliament.uk/documents/CBP-9602/CBP-9602.pdf**

Lifeway Research, 'Being theologically intentional: the importance of the Sunday morning gathering', 5 November 2016. **research.lifeway.com/2016/11/05/being-theologically-intentional-the-importance-of-the-sunday-morning-gathering**

John MacArthur, 'What does it mean that Christ "emptied himself" in Phil. 2:6-7', n.d. **learn.ligonier.org/qas/what-does-it-mean-that-christ-emptied-himself-in-phil-2-6-7**

John Meunier, 'Leviticus, defects, and disability', 20 July 2013. **johnmeunier.wordpress.com/2013/07/20/leviticus-defects-and-disability**

National Autistic Society, 'Asperger syndrome (Asperger's)', June 2023. **autism.org.uk/advice-and-guidance/what-is-autism/the-history-of-autism/asperger-syndrome**

Office for National Statistics, 'Disability, England and Wales: Census 2021', 2022. **ons.gov.uk/peoplepopulationandcommunity/healthandsocialcare/healthandwellbeing/bulletins/disabilityenglandandwales/census2021**

John Piper, 'Did Jesus diminish his divine power to become human?', Desiring God, 18 December 2017. **desiringgod.org/interviews/did-jesus-diminish-his-divine-power-to-become-human**

Scope. **scope.org.uk**

Shades of Noir, 'Evolution of disability models', 1 April 2023. **shadesofnoir.org.uk/content/evolution-of-disability-models**

UK Government, 'Special educational needs in England', Explore Education Statistics. **explore-education-statistics.service.gov.uk/find-statistics/special-educational-needs-in-england**

Paul Woolley, 'The basics: bodily resurrection of Christ', Evangelical Alliance, 1 September 2008. **eauk.org/idea/bodily-resurrection-of-christ.cfm**

5 PHYSICAL DISABILITIES

Back Up, 'Common terms in spinal cord injury', 14 March 2022. backuptrust.org.uk/spinal-cord-injury/common-terms-spinal-cord-injury

Viktor Berg, 'Types of physical disabilities', Care Home, 21 October 2025. carehome.co.uk/advice/types-of-physical-disabilities

Bill Braviner et al., 'Equal access to church buildings', Cathedrals Fabric Commission for England, 2021. churchofengland.org/sites/default/files/2021-10/Equal_Access_to_Church_Buildings.pdf

British Deaf Association, 'What is Deaf culture?', 7 September 2015. bda.org.uk/what-is-deaf-culture

British Standards BS 8300-2:2018 (Approved Document M) and The Workplace (Health, Safety, and Welfare) Regulations 1992. **assets.publishing.service.gov.uk/media/66f6c5eec71e42688b65ee11/ADM__V2_with_2024_amendments.pdf**

Churches for All. churchesforall.org.uk

Cleveland Clinic, 'Quadriplegia', 1 May 2024. my.clevelandclinic.org/health/symptoms/23974-quadriplegia-tetraplegia

Colostomy UK, 'Guide to stoma friendly accessible toilets', 2023. colostomyuk.org/wp-content/uploads/2023/02/Colostomy-UK-Stoma-Friendly-Accessible-toilets-2.pdf

Harvard Medical School Department of Ophthalmology, 'Brain "rewires" itself to enhance other senses in blind people', 22 March 2017. eye.hms.harvard.edu/news/brain-rewires-itself-enhance-other-senses-blind-people

Headway, 'Communication problems after brain injury', 2017. headway.org.uk/media/12039/communication-problems-after-brain-injury-publication.pdf

Historic England, 'Easy access to historic buildings', 2015. historicengland.org.uk/images-books/publications/easy-access-to-historic-buildings/heag010-easy-access-to-historic-buildings

Rosie Jones, 'What do blind people see?', 26 July 2023. medicalnewstoday.com/articles/what-do-blind-people-see

NHS, 'Myalgic encephalomyelitis or chronic fatigue syndrome (ME/CFS)', 6 June 2024. nhs.uk/conditions/chronic-fatigue-syndrome-cfs

NHS, 'Paralysis', 28 November 2024. nhs.uk/conditions/paralysis

NHS Digital, 'Data quality of protected characteristics and other vulnerable groups – Disability', 6 June 2024. digital.nhs.uk/data-and-information/data-collections-and-data-sets/data-sets/mental-health-services-

data-set/submit-data/data-quality-of-protected-characteristics-and-other-vulnerable-groups/disability
Neil Robinson, 'How I was ordained a deacon', The Limping Chicken, 22 September 2016. limpingchicken.com/2016/09/22/neil-robinson-what-led-me-to-become-an-ordained-deacon
Royal National Institute of Blind People. rnib.org.uk
Sense, 'Deafness and hearing loss', October 2022. sense.org.uk/information-and-advice/conditions/deafness-and-hearing-loss
Visually Speaking, 'Deaf-mute, what?', 23 May 2023. visuallyspeaking.info/deaf-mute-what

6 AGE-RELATED DISABILITIES AND IMPAIRMENTS

Alzheimer's Society. alzheimers.org.uk
Greensleeves Care, 'Why dementia should be viewed as disability', 13 April 2021. greensleeves.org.uk/why-dementia-should-be-viewed-as-disability
Office for National Statistics, 'Disability by age, sex, and deprivation, England and Wales: Census 2021'. ons.gov.uk/peoplepopulationandcommunity/healthandsocialcare/disability/articles/disabilitybyagesexanddeprivationenglandandwales/census2021#disability-by-age-and-sex-in-england-and-wales-2021
Royal National Institute of Blind People, 'Key statistics about sight loss', 2021. media.rnib.org.uk/documents/Key_stats_about_sight_loss_2021.pdf
Shaftesbury Group, 'Dementia inclusive church guide: travelling together', 2024. shaftesburygroup.org/download/travelling-together
Kate Swaffer, 'The significance of dementia as a disability', Dementia Justice (blog), 11 March 2022. dementiajustice.org/post/dementia-as-a-disability
World Health Organization, 'Dementia', 31 March 2025. who.int/news-room/fact-sheets/detail/dementia

7 LEARNING DISABILITIES

Count Everyone In, Team news, April 2024. counteveryonein.org.uk/wp-content/uploads/2024/04/CEI-Team-News-April-2024.pdf
Emily Perl Kingsley, 'Welcome to Holland'. emilyperlkingsley.com/welcome-to-holland
Mencap, 'Profound and multiple learning disabilities (PMLD)'. mencap.org.

uk/learning-disability-explained/learning-disability-and-conditions/
profound-and-multiple-learning-disabilities-pmld

NHS, 'Angelman syndrome', 13 April 2023. nhs.uk/conditions/angelman-syndrome

NHS, 'Overview: learning disabilities', 14 January 2022. nhs.uk/conditions/learning-disabilities

8 SPECIFIC LEARNING DIFFICULTIES

Aurora Betony, 'Writing for a dyslexic audience', 17 November 2016. inclusivecommunication.scot/writing-for-a-dyslexic-audience

British Dyslexia Association. bdadyslexia.org.uk

Julia Carroll and Helen Breadmore, 'Morphological processing in children with phonological difficulties: executive summary', Coventry University & University of Warwick, October 2017. nuffieldfoundation.org/wp-content/uploads/2017/10/Morphological-processing-in-children-with-phonological-difficulties-executive-summary.pdf

Cognassist, 'Dyspraxia in the workplace', 18 March 2024. cognassist.com/insights/dyspraxia-in-the-workplace

The Dyscalculia Network, 'What is dyscalculia?', 29 February 2024. dyscalculianetwork.com/what-is-dyscalculia

Dyslexia Gifted, 'The big picture'. dyslexiagifted.com/bigpicture.html

Dyslexia Reading Success, 'Dyslexia big picture genius – what is dyslexia?', 15 April 2024. dyslexiareadingsuccess.com/dyslexia-global-thinking

Dyslexia Support South, 'Strengths of dyslexia'. dyslexiasupportsouth.org.nz/parent-toolkit/emotional-impact/strengths-of-dyslexia

Arije-Aike de Haas, 'Dyslexia simulation', Dyslexia the Gift Blog. blog.dyslexia.com/dyslexia-simulation

Sarah Kesty, 'A speed bump, not a roadblock', Edutopia, 31 October 2018. edutopia.org/article/speed-bump-not-roadblock

Amanda Kirby, Anna Barnett, Elisabeth Hill, Dyslexia Assessment & Consultancy, and SASC, 'SASC guidance on the assessment and identification of developmental coordination disorder (DCD)/dyspraxia', March 2020. sasc.org.uk/media/m2snu21n/dcd-dyspraxia-sasc-guidance-march-2020.pdf

Made By Dyslexia, 'How to employ dyslexia'. madebydyslexia.org/wp-content/uploads/Employ-Dyslexia-WDA-A4-30-Aug.pdf

Movement Matters. movementmattersuk.org

NIDCD, 'Developmental language disorder', 8 May 2023. nidcd.nih.gov/health/developmental-language-disorder

Oxford Health NHS Foundation Trust, 'Children's Integrated
Therapies – developmental language disorder (DLD)', 15 October
2021. **oxfordhealth.nhs.uk/cit/resources/dld**
RADLD – Raising Awareness of Developmental Language Disorder.
radld.org
Speech and Language UK: Changing Young Lives, 'Developmental
language disorder (DLD)', 31 January 2024. **speechandlanguage.org.
uk/educators-and-professionals/resource-library-for-educators/
developmental-language-disorder-dld**
Ginny Stacey, 'Living confidently with specific learning difficulties (SpLD)',
Taylor & Francis Group, August 2021. **routledgetextbooks.com/
textbooks/stacey/series-and-books.php**
Stone Soup for Five. **stonesoupforfive.com**
Laurence Turner and Nell Andrew, 'Thinking differently at work: dyspraxia
in the workplace', GMB Union, 2018. **gmb.org.uk/thinking-differently-
at-work/dyspraxia-toolkit.pdf**

9 AUTISM

Autism Speaks, 'Autism diagnostic criteria: DSM-5'. **autismspeaks.org/
autism-diagnosis-criteria-dsm-5**
Autistica. **autistica.org.uk**
Communication Matters and ISAAC (UK), 'What is AAC? Introduction
to Augmentative and Alternative Communication', 2015.
**communicationmatters.org.uk/wp-content/uploads/2019/02/
Speaking-with-Someone.pdf**
Natalie Engelbrecht Jones, 'The AQ-10', Embrace Autism, 20 April
2020. **embrace-autism.com/aq-10**
Amanda Hartmann, '7 ways to include AAC users in conversation',
AssistiveWare, 18 October 2024. **assistiveware.com/learn-aac/7-ways-
to-include-aac-users-in-conversation**
Clare Jack, 'From autistic linear spectrum to pie chart spectrum',
Psychology Today, 16 August 2022. **psychologytoday.com/gb/blog/
women-autism-spectrum-disorder/202208/autistic-linear-spectrum-
pie-chart-spectrum**
Jeemin Moon, 'Christian identity: worldly identity vs. Christian identity',
Biblical Counseling Coalition, 5 April 2024. **biblicalcounselingcoalition.
org/2024/04/05/christian-identity-worldly-identity-vs-christian-
identity**
National Autistic Society. **autism.org.uk**

NHS, 'Autism'. **nhs.uk/conditions/autism**
PDA Society. **pdasociety.org.uk**
Tomlin Wilding, 'Pathological demand avoidance'. **tomlinwilding.com/neuropsychology/neurodiversity/pathological-demand-avoidance**

10 SENSORY PROCESSING DISORDER

Centre for Autism Middletown, 'What are the senses?' **sensory-processing.middletownautism.com/background/what-are-the-senses**

11 ATTENTION DEFICIT HYPERACTIVITY DISORDER (ADHD)

ADDitude, 'School & learning'. **additudemag.com/category/parenting-adhd-kids/school-learning**
ADHD and Women. **adhd-women.eu**
ADHD Foundation Training Services, 'Neurodiversity in the workplace'. **adhdfoundation.org.uk/wp-content/uploads/2022/03/Neurodiversity-in-the-workplace-Free-E-Booklet-and-Training-Guide-forBusiness-August-2023.pdf**
Attention Deficit Disorder Association, 'The ADHD body double: a unique tool for getting things done', 20 February 2025. **add.org/the-body-double**
Charlotte Bailey, 'Moving forward with ADHD (attention-deficit/hyperactivity disorder)', The Association for Child and Adolescent Mental Health, 2 October 2023. **acamh.org/blog/moving-forward-with-adhd**
Russell Barkley, 'What is executive function? 7 deficits tied to ADHD', ADDitude, 3 November 2025. **additudemag.com/7-executive-function-deficits-linked-to-adhd**
Camille Hours, Christophe Recasens, and Jean-Marc Baleyte, 'ASD and ADHD comorbidity: what are we talking about?' *Frontiers in Psychiatry*, 13 (2022). **doi.org/10.3389/fpsyt.2022.837424**
King's College London, 'Understanding ADHD: current research and practice', n.d. **kcl.ac.uk/short-courses/understanding-adhd-future-learn**
Noelle Matteson, 'ADHD and transitions: change is tough; how to deal with it', HealthyPlace, 24 July 2018. **healthyplace.com/blogs/livingwithadultadhd/2018/7/adhd-and-transitions-change-is-tough-how-to-deal-with-it**

National Institute for Health and Care Excellence, 'Attention deficit hyperactivity disorder: Prescribing information'. **cks.nice.org.uk/topics/attention-deficit-hyperactivity-disorder/prescribing-information**

Gloria Oladipo, 'What to know about ADHD and dopamine', PsychCentral, 16 July 2021. **psychcentral.com/adhd/what-to-know-about-adhd-and-dopamine#causes-and-risk-factors**

Pamela Snow, 'Behaviour as a form of communication: what's the issue?', The Snow Report, 3 June 2018. **pamelasnow.blogspot.com/2018/06/behaviour-as-form-of-communication.html**

UCL, 'Significant rise in ADHD diagnoses in the UK', UCL News, 17 July 2023. **ucl.ac.uk/news/2023/jul/significant-rise-adhd-diagnoses-uk**

12 SOCIAL, EMOTIONAL, AND MENTAL HEALTH (SEMH) IN CHILDREN

Adoption UK, 'Written evidence submitted by Adoption UK', 2024. **committees.parliament.uk/writtenevidence/127697/pdf**

Fife Council, 'PACE: Playfulness, Acceptance, Curiosity, Empathy – A trauma-informed approach to supporting children and young people', Fife Council Educational Psychology. **girfec.fife.scot/__data/assets/pdf_file/0032/187484/PACE-School.pdf**

Olivia Guy-Evans, 'Emotional regulation', Simply Psychology, 13 December 2023. **simplypsychology.org/emotional-regulation.html**

Manchester University NHS Foundation Trust, 'Adverse childhood experiences (ACEs) and attachment', 19 February 2021. **mft.nhs.uk/rmch/services/camhs/young-people/adverse-childhood-experiences-aces-and-attachment**

Mentally Healthy Schools, 'Attachment and child development'. **mentallyhealthyschools.org.uk/mental-health-needs/attachment-and-child-development**

Nasen, 'Department for Education: exclusion data released', 4 August 2021. **nasen.org.uk/news/exclusion-data-released**

NSPCC Learning, 'Attachment and child development', 10 August 2021. **learning.nspcc.org.uk/child-health-development/attachment-early-years#skip-to-content**

UK Government, 'Suspensions and permanent exclusions in England: academic year 2023/24', 10 July 2025. **explore-education-statistics.service.gov.uk/find-statistics/suspensions-and-permanent-exclusions-in-england**

CONCLUSION

Shawn Lazar, 'Eating at the King's table forever (2 Samuel 9)', Grace Evangelical Society , 11 March 2019. **faithalone.org/blog/eating-at-the-kings-table-forever-2-samuel-9**

Dwayne Milley, 'Mephibosheth at the table of the King', Disability and Faith, 18 April 2024. **disabilityandfaith.org/mephibosheth-at-the-table-of-the-king-guest-post**

PODCASTS AND VIDEO RESOURCES

Triona Brading, 'Supporting autistic individuals in our churches', Through the Roof, 28 November 2024. **youtu.be/wjWGNTeaFas**

Triona Brading, 'Understanding autistic meltdowns and shutdowns', Through the Roof, 10 May 2024. **youtu.be/aDD8-exFb-s**

E. Drew and A. Smith, 'Faith in Parents #106 | Parenting & disability: a conversation with Nick and Dorothy Jones – Faith in Kids – Premier Plus,' n.d. **premier.plus/podcasts/faith-in-kids/episodes/faith-in-parents-106-parenting-amp-disability-a-conversation-with-nick-and-dorothy-jones**

E. Drew and A. Smith, 'Faith in Parents #117 | Autism and the church', 28 June 2023. **open.spotify.com/episode/6nSdT1liAkTNxcVb8gMCMu**

Emily Kircher-Morris and Donna Henderson, 'Challenging what we know about autism and PDA', *The Neurodiversity Podcast*, episode 246, 17 October 2024. **neurodiversitypodcast.com/home/2024/10/17/episode-246-challenging-what-we-know-about-autism-and-pda**

Chris Packham, 'Inside our autistic minds', *Inside Our Minds*, BBC Two, series 1, episode 1, 14 February 2023. **bbc.co.uk/programmes/p0bbnjvx**

Jen Wilkin, J.T. English, and Kyle Worley, 'What is a person? (Doctrine of man)', *Training the Church*, 26 November 2024. **trainingthechurch.com/episodes/what-is-a-person-doctrine-of-man**

Notes

INTRODUCTION

1. The Church of England, 'Everyone counts 2014: diversity audit key findings', The Church of England, 2015. **churchofengland.org/sites/default/ files/2017-11/everyone-counts-diversity-audit-key-findings-2014.pdf**
2. Explore Education Statistics – GOV.UK, 'Special educational needs in England, academic year 2023/24', 20 June 2024. **explore-education-statistics.service.gov.uk/find-statistics/special-educational-needs-in-england/2023-24**
3. Esme Kirk-Wade, Sonja Stiebahl, and Helen Wong, 'UK disability statistics: Prevalence and life experiences', 2024, **researchbriefings.files.parliament. uk/documents/CBP-9602/CBP-9602.pdf**
4. Office for National Statistics, 'Disability, England and Wales: Census 2021', 2022. **ons.gov.uk/peoplepopulationandcommunity/healthandsocialcare/ healthandwellbeing/bulletins/disabilityenglandandwales/census2021**

1 THE BASIS FOR LOVE: IMAGE-BEARING

1. We are aware that many Deaf people in particular reject the term 'disabled', though we hope that this example gives a sense of how we are using this terminology and will not be construed as offensive.
2. An image used by both Augustine and Martin Luther to describe sin.

3 IT SEEMS TOO HARD: SACRIFICE

1. A literal translation of the Hebrew in Judges 3:15 is that Ehud was 'restricted in his right hand'. Ehud may have been physically disabled, not simply 'left-handed'. See also Timothy Keller, *Judges for You* (The Good Book Company, 2013), p. 47: 'Judges 3:15 literally says "he was unable to use his right hand".'
2. Joni Eareckson Tada and Jack S. Oppenhuizen, 'Hidden and forgotten people', *Lausanne Occasional Paper*, Lausanne Committee for World Evangelization, 2005, p. 9. **lausanne.org/wp-content/uploads/2007/06/ LOP35B_IG6B.pdf**
3. **scope.org.uk/media/disability-facts-figures**

4 THE FUTURE OF DISABILITY: THE NEW CREATION

1. Mike Emlet, *Saints, Sufferers and Sinners: Loving others as God loves us* (New Growth Press, 2021).
2. Paul Woolley, 'The basics: bodily resurrection of Christ', Evangelical Alliance, 1 September 2008. **eauk.org/idea/bodily-resurrection-of-christ.cfm**

INTRODUCTION TO PART II

1. National Autistic Society, 'Asperger syndrome (Asperger's)', June 2023. **autism.org.uk/advice-and-guidance/what-is-autism/the-history-of-autism/asperger-syndrome**
2. James Phillips et al., 'The six most essential questions in psychiatric diagnosis: a pluralogue part 1: conceptual and definitional issues in psychiatric diagnosis', *Philosophy, Ethics, and Humanities in Medicine*, 7.3 (2012). **doi.org/10.1186/1747-5341-7-3**

5 PHYSICAL DISABILITIES

1. See Appendix 2 for accessibility audits suggested by various denominations and disability groups.
2. Currently (in the UK) within the Equality Act 2010, British Standard BS 8300-2:2018 (Approved Document M) and The Workplace (Health, Safety and Welfare) Regulations 1992.
3. Through the Roof keeps an up-to-date list of grant-making bodies who will award money for making disability-related improvements: 'Obtaining funding to make disability related improvements', Through the Roof, May 2024. **throughtheroof.org/forchurches/obtaining-funding-to-make-disability-related-improvements**
4. Bill Braviner et al., 'Equal access to church buildings', Cathedrals Fabric Commission for England, 2021. **churchofengland.org/sites/default/files/2021-10/Equal_Access_to_Church_Buildings.pdf**; Historic England, 'Easy access to historic buildings', 2015. **historicengland.org.uk/images-books/publications/easy-access-to-historic-buildings/heag010-easy-access-to-historic-buildings**
5. Harvard Medical School Department of Ophthalmology, 'Brain "rewires" itself to enhance other senses in blind people', 22 March 2017. **eye.hms.harvard.edu/news/brain-rewires-itself-enhance-other-senses-blind-people**
6. torchtrust.org
7. signsofgod.org.uk; gosign.org.uk

6 AGE-RELATED DISABILITIES AND IMPAIRMENTS

1. Ken Eames, *Statistics for Mission 2022* (Church of England Data Services, 2023), p. 7.
2. Michael A. Akeroyd and Kevin J. Munro, 'Population estimates of the number of adults in the UK with a hearing loss updated using 2021 and 2022 census data', *International Journal of Audiology*, 63.9, pp. 659–60. **doi.org/10.1080/1 4992027.2024.2341956**
3. World Health Organization, 'Dementia', 31 March 2025. **who.int/news-room/ fact-sheets/detail/dementia**
4. More detailed information can be found in Shaftesbury Group, 'Dementia inclusive church guide: travelling together', 2024. **shaftesburygroup.org/ download/travelling-together**

7 LEARNING DISABILITIES

1. Mencap, 'What is a learning disability?' **mencap.org.uk/learning-disability-explained/what-learning-disability**
2. Makaton, 'Know and grow: making the Christian faith accessible through Makaton signs and symbols'. **makaton.org/TMC/TMC/Learn_Makaton/ Other_workshops/Know_and_Grow.aspx**
3. The UK government and the Children's Commissioner for England are considering significant changes to the SEND system, including EHCPs.
4. Although the causes may be different, these strategies overlap with the de-escalation strategies mentioned in chapter 12.
5. Mencap, 'Learning disability helpline'. **mencap.org.uk/advice-and-support/ learning-disability-helpline**
6. **challengingbehaviour.org.uk**
7. Messy Church resources aim to bring the gospel to life in a multisensory way and are designed to be inclusive to people of all ages and cognitive abilities. **messychurch.brf.org.uk**
8. **counteveryonein.org.uk/events**
9. Count Everyone In, 'Prayer and power', April 2024. **counteveryonein.org.uk/ wp-content/uploads/2024/04/CEI-Team-News-April-2024.pdf**

8 SPECIFIC LEARNING DIFFICULTIES

1. The ESV has a full Dyslexia Friendly Edition, which even comes with different coloured overlays to reduce visual stress. The NIrV has shorter sentences while retaining much of the same wording as the NIV. The GNB also has individual books of the Bible in a dyslexia-friendly edition. Resources in this area are rapidly growing, with more options available every year.

2   For example, the YouVersion Bible App.
3   **Freebibleimages.org** is one good source of such images: these could be shared in advance through a news bulletin, or projected during a Bible reading or talk.
4   For example, Vaughan Roberts, *God's Big Picture: Tracing the storyline of the Bible* (IVP, 2003).
5   Aurora Betony, 'Dyslexia-friendly churches – A guide to help churches include dyslexic adults', Inclusive Communication, 2019. inclusivecommunication.scot/wp-content/uploads/2019/12/Dyslexia-friendly-churches-guidev24-Copy.pdf

9 AUTISM

1   Claire M. Brown et al., 'Updated systematic review of suicide in autism: 2018–2024', *Current Developmental Disorders Reports*, 11 (2024), pp. 225–56. **doi.org/10.1007/s40474-024-00308-9**
2   Laura Hull et al., '"Putting on my best normal": social camouflaging in adults with autism spectrum conditions', *Journal of Autism and Developmental Disorders*, 47.8 (2017), pp. 2519–34. **doi.org/10.1007/s10803-017-3166-5**
3   Fabienne Cazalis et al., 'Evidence that nine autistic women out of ten have been victims of sexual violence', *Frontiers in Behavioral Neuroscience*, 16 (2022). **doi.org/10.3389/fnbeh.2022.852203**
4   Some good books include Steve Midgley, *Understanding Trauma: A biblical introduction for church care* (Good Book Company, 2025); Helen Thorne-Allenson and Steve Midgley, *Mental Health and Your Church: A handbook for biblical care* (Good Book Company, 2023), and Graham Beynon, *Emotions: Living life in colour* (IVP, 2012). We also highly recommend the Biblical Counselling UK courses, which include both short courses which can be done within a church and a longer, more in-depth course for those seeking further training in this area.
5   Chris Packham, 'Inside our autistic minds', *Inside Our Minds*, BBC Two, series 1, episode 1, 14 February 2023. **bbc.co.uk/programmes/p0bbnjvx**
6   Mark's blog and resources for supporting autistic children in churches can be found at **theadditionalneedsblogfather.com**
7   PDA does not currently feature in diagnostic manuals, but the report a clinician produces following assessment for autism can include terminology such as 'ASD with a demand avoidant profile' (**pdasociety.org.uk/resources/evidence-for-use-of-pda-terminology**)
8   **pdasociety.org.uk/resources-menu**

11 ATTENTION DEFICIT HYPERACTIVITY DISORDER (ADHD)

1. Matthew Bisset et al., 'Practitioner review: It's time to bridge the gap – understanding the unmet needs of consumers with attention deficit/hyperactivity disorder – a systematic review and recommendations', *Journal of Child Psychology and Psychiatry*, 64.6 (2023), pp. 848–58. doi.org/10.1111/jcpp.13752
2. UCL, 'Significant rise in ADHD diagnoses in the UK', UCL News, 17 July 2023. ucl.ac.uk/news/2023/jul/significant-rise-adhd-diagnoses-uk
3. Russell Barkley, 'What is executive function? 7 deficits tied to ADHD', ADDitude, 3 November 2025. additudemag.com/7-executive-function-deficits-linked-to-adhd
4. Rebecca Bondü and Günter Esser, 'Justice and rejection sensitivity in children and adolescents with ADHD symptoms', *European Child & Adolescent Psychiatry*, 24.2 (2014), pp. 185–98. doi.org/10.1007/s00787-014-0560-9
5. Thomas Frodl, 'Comorbidity of ADHD and substance use disorder (SUD): a neuroimaging perspective', *Journal of Attention Disorders*, 14.2 (2010), pp. 109–20. doi.org/10.1177/1087054710365054
6. Servet Karaca et al., 'Comorbidity between behavioral addictions and attention deficit/hyperactivity disorder: a systematic review', *International Journal of Mental Health and Addiction*, 15, pp. 701–24 (2017). doi.org/10.1007/s11469-016-9660-8
7. Saskia van der Oord and Gail Tripp, 'How to improve behavioral parent and teacher training for children with ADHD: integrating empirical research on learning and motivation into treatment', *Clinical Child and Family Psychology Review*, 23.4 (2020), pp. 577–604. doi.org/10.1007/s10567-020-00327-z
8. Elaine Taylor-Klaus uses the acronym 'PINCH' for motivators which work for the ADHD brain: Play, Interest, Novelty, Connection and 'Hurry up' (urgency). impactparents.com/blog/adhd/five-motivators-to-get-anything-done
9. Attention Deficit Disorder Association, 'The ADHD body double: a unique tool for getting things done', 20 February 2025. add.org/the-body-double

12 SOCIAL, EMOTIONAL, AND MENTAL HEALTH (SEMH) IN CHILDREN

1. Adoption UK, 'Written evidence submitted by Adoption UK', 2024. committees.parliament.uk/writtenevidence/127697/pdf
2. NSPCC Learning, 'Attachment and child development', 10 August 2021. learning.nspcc.org.uk/child-health-development/attachment-early-years#skip-to-content

3   Fife Council, 'PACE: Playfulness, Acceptance, Curiosity, Empathy – A trauma-informed approach to supporting children and young people', Fife Council Educational Psychology. **girfec.fife.scot/__data/assets/pdf_file/0024/48903/PACE-School.pdf**
4   Safe Families is a charity that works with more than 35 local authorities around the UK. Safe Families 'offer hope, belonging, and support to children, families, and care leavers'. They do this 'primarily, but not exclusively, with and through local churches'. **safefamilies.uk/about-us**

CONCLUSION

1   Mephibosheth appears twice more in 2 Samuel, where he is first accused of betraying the king during Absalom's rebellion (2 Samuel 16), but later, in a last twist to the tale, turns out to have been betrayed by Ziba, the steward; the truth of his words is implied by his lack of self-care 'from the day the king left until the day he returned safely' (2 Samuel 19:24) and his lack of concern about getting his property back (v. 30).

About the authors

Triona Brading has worked with both adults with learning disabilities and primary-age children with social, emotional, and mental health needs. She leads the SEND provision at Revive Bible festival and is currently training in church ministry.

Lois Bunyan works in the disability arts sector and has experience facilitating workshops for adults with learning disabilities, people living with dementia, and those with brain and stroke injuries. She also serves in various ministries alongside her husband, a vicar in the Church of England.

Claire Wood is a secondary school teacher and parent of a child with special educational needs. She serves her local church through youth and children's ministry, as a PCC member and formerly as church warden.

Dementia is one of today's most feared health conditions, and Christians with the condition may also worry about losing their connection to God. However, there is still hope: those living with dementia can still find meaning in their life and their faith. Written by two practitioners in this field, *Dementia, God and the Church* aims to show how person-centred approaches to dementia can provide hope. Wendy Gleadle examines the difficulties of maintaining religious beliefs as cognition declines, while Frances Attwood asks how churches can better support those living with dementia. Throughout, space is given to stories of those with dementia, those working with them, and those caring for them.

Dementia, God and the Church
Journeying with hope
Wendy Gleadle and Frances Attwood
978 1 80039 433 9 £12.99

brf.org.uk

Why do more and more people advocate the idea that the generations should explore faith together, and what does the Bible have to say about this? How does this fit with our inherited model of age-related groups for learning and discipleship? And is it really practical to have an experience of church where the youngest to the oldest share the same meeting space, service theme, and time to worship? *Messy Togetherness* discusses Messy Church as an intergenerational expression of church, exploring current thinking about faith development and offering a biblical rationale for an all-age approach along with practical advice.

Messy Togetherness
Being intergenerational in Messy Church
Martyn Payne and Chris Barnett, edited by Aike Kennett-Brown
978 1 80039 002 7   £9.99

brf.org.uk

In *Messy Hospitality*, Lucy Moore, founder of Messy Church, demonstrates how hospitality can be practised in different church contexts to promote mission and faith formation, addressing the theology of hospitality and how it can be expressed at the welcome table, the activity table, the Lord's Table, the meal table, and in the home. Also included are insights from the secular hospitality industry, how to train Messy Church teams in hospitality, audit-style questions for the reader to apply in their own context, and five complete session outlines for Messy Churches.

Messy Hospitality
Changing communities through fun, food, friendship and faith
Lucy Moore
978 1 80039 454 4 £9.99 (available only as a PDF ebook)

brf.org.uk

God's Belongers should transform our thinking about what it means to belong to church. Uniquely, David Walker replaces the old and worn division between 'members' and 'non-members' with a fourfold model of belonging: through relationship, through place, through events, and through activities. From his extensive practical research, the author shows how 'belonging' can encompass a far wider group of people than those who attend weekly services. This opens up creative opportunities for mission in today's world.

God's Belongers
How people engage with God today and how the church can help
David Walker
978 0 85746 467 5   £8.99

brf.org.uk

Inspiring people of all ages to grow in Christian faith

BRF Ministries is the home of Anna Chaplaincy, BRF Resources, Messy Church and Parenting for Faith

As a charity, our work would not be possible without fundraising and gifts in wills.
To find out more and to donate, visit brf.org.uk/give or call +44 (0)1865 319700